THE
50 Most Influential Black Films

THE
50 Most

CITADEL PRESS

Influential Black Films

A CELEBRATION OF AFRICAN-AMERICAN TALENT, DETERMINATION, AND CREATIVITY

S. Torriano Berry and Venise T. Berry

KENSINGTON PUBLISHING CORP.
www.kensingtonbooks.com

CITADEL PRESS books are published by

Kensington Publishing Corp.
850 Third Avenue
New York, NY 10022

All Kensington titles, imprints, and distributed lines are available at special quantity discounts for bulk purchases for sales promotions, premiums, fund-raising, educational, or institutional use. Special book excerpts or customized printings can also be created to fit specific needs. For details, write or phone the office of the Kensington special sales manager: Kensington Publishing Corp., 850 Third Avenue, New York, NY 10022, attn: Special Sales Department, phone 1-800-221-2647.

First printing April 2001

10 9 8 7 6 5 4 3 2 1

Printed in the United States of America

Cataloging data for this title may be obtained from the Library of Congress.

ISBN 0-8065-2133-3

Contents

Acknowledgments

Many people helped to make this book a reality. Our measure of gratitude goes to God and our guardian angel, Toni Berry; to our family, Averi Bryant, Jean and Virgil Berry; to Torriano's wonderful pre-editor, Henri Johnson; to Doreen Mitchum, for assistance with the proposal. Our thanks go also to our early readers and friends Ayo Dayo, Vanessa Shelton, Stephana Colbert, Sharon Mack; to our research assistants, Rebecca Roundtree Harris, Joni Bradley, Sharon Carrington, Erin Barnes, Nancy Maturi, Jesse Wells, Janice Carter, Brian Shiloh, and Misook Baek; to our interviewees, and everyone who helped to make the interviews happen. And, finally, our thankfulness extends to Howard University, School of Communications, Department of Radio, Television and Film; the School of Journalism and Mass Communications at the University of Iowa; to Monica Harris, Andrew Richter, Susan Hayes, Margaret Wolf, Sara Blackburn, Donald J. Davidson, and Bruce Bender at Citadel Press; and to Kensington Publishing Corp. for coming through.

THE
50 Most Influential Black Films

Introduction

"Light . . . slashes through darkness, to splash upon
the screen . . . still dark."

—S. Torriano Berry

Once celluloid impressions of dancing coons, shuffling bucks, and
watermelon-munching pickaninnies paraded aimlessly within the
flickering of the projector's magic lamp. During its infancy (1894
through the turn of the century), these were the first and only
images of African Americans captured on film. Later, white actors
with "burnt cork" covering their faces would perfect this despicable
charade, and these filmic distortions would run rampant in the films
that followed.

In 1910, William Foster, a press agent for black comedy shows,
founded the Foster Photoplay Company in Chicago. He produced
The Railroad Porter in 1912, and made a series of short comedies
featuring all-black casts. Foster's productions laid the groundwork
for black films to come, and he became the first Negro to produce
and control his own image on the screen.

By the 1920s, there were over one hundred companies that produced all-black-cast pictures. Now most of these early "race
movies," as they were called at the time, no longer exist. The
nitrate-based stock in use then was highly unstable, extremely flam-
mable, and, over time, would disintegrate inside the film can. And
according to one film archivist that we spoke with, many Hollywood studios once stored their excess film prints "rent free" at the
bottom of the Pacific Ocean. As a result, only a few of these films
survived to represent early black cinematic history, while far too
many other sepia-tone gems will never be screened again.

The Fifty Most Influential Black Films is intended to be a
resource book that examines how these films have shaped and
reflected the times, what their impact has been on society, and how
they have influenced our culture. It is not intended to be a "Best
of," "Most liked," or "Greatest" black-films book. Our selections were

not based on great reviews, slick production values, popular demand, or high box office grosses, and they are not intended to reflect the opinion of the entire black community. Many films will not be included that are surely influential in other contexts; this is simply *our* list, and we will make the reasons for the selections as clear as possible.

We define a "black film" as having a majority black cast or a predominantly black-related theme or subject matter. Whether or not the film had a black producer, director, or script writer was considered, but was not a necessity for its inclusion. In wading through the cinematic cache of prospective films, we tried to cast a wide enough net to include a multitude of factors and resources, and chose to limit our search to theatrical feature films.

Crucial to our analysis was a film's changing of images, values, focus, or perspectives when addressing important issues in the black community. We looked at the societal impact of the films as well as the overall attitude, response, and discussion generated by their release. We considered whether or not it was a "milestone" or a "first" or was produced in a unique way, with a distinctly defined influential purpose. Several of the films selected have created industry shifts in the types or numbers of black films produced, thus increasing opportunities for blacks in the industry. We also considered the film's historical context and the social significance of its subject matter. Key to our exploration was the examination of film reviews, newspaper and magazine articles, feature stories, critiques, and other relevant materials. And, for a more personal touch, we've conducted interviews with relevant players from many of the films to provide a more intimate and insightful perspective.

Based on the films that have been saved, documented, and researched, from the earliest "sepia flicks" to the most recent independent releases and Hollywood blockbusters, this book is an examination of the fifty black films we have determined to be the most influential to the history of the motion picture industry, African-American culture, and our society in general.

1

Society Profile: 1900–1928

"The Silent Era"

In the early 1900s, just after the birth of film, the Census Bureau reported that 11.6 percent of the United States population was black and approximately 8.8 million Negroes lived primarily in the South. Despite the fact that President Lincoln's Emancipation Proclamation had been in effect for almost forty years, it was a confusing period of struggle and accomplishments for blacks.

With slavery abolished, a major black exodus out of the South had begun. This "Great Migration" was an escape from the new system of involuntary servitude founded upon tricky legal codes that often returned freedmen to the control of their former slave masters. Blacks were required to be employed by whites or they could be arrested for vagrancy and given excessive jail time. Often they were forced to serve this jail time in an illegal labor trade, working right back on the plantations.

Regardless of segregation, Jim Crow laws, lynchings, random violence, and race riots, many blacks fought back, persevered, and went on against the odds to accomplish great things.

Inventors like Elijah McCoy received a patent for his engine lubrication system, jazz music evolved out of Storyville and Congo Square in New Orleans. James Weldon and J. Rosamond Johnson wrote "Lift Every Voice and Sing," the black national anthem, on February 12, 1900, for Abraham Lincoln's birthday. And many major black newspapers, including the *Kansas City Call*, the *St. Louis Argus*, and the *Chicago Defender* were founded.

While some blacks led the way in science, music, politics, and the arts, others rallied behind leaders. Booker T. Washington and W. E. B. Du Bois were two of the best known, but these great minds had very different philosophies about the future and direction of black culture in America. Washington focused on leading his people toward integration and developing work skills, where they could earn positions of respectability. With the publication of his book *The Souls of Black Folk* in 1903, Du Bois openly challenged Washington's views, arguing that work and money were not as important as developing the intellect and pursuing positions of power and influence. Both men founded civil rights organizations that remain active today. Washington established the National Urban League, which focused on the social and economic issues in the black community, and Du Bois organized the Niagara Movement, which later was subsumed in the National Association for the Advancement of Colored People (NAACP).

In 1912 the first film produced by a black man emerged, and "race movies" were born. However, with the advent of sound motion pictures in 1926, most of the companies that produced all-black-cast films went out of business, because they could not afford the costly technology needed to produce "talkies."

One of the most important developments of the 1920s was the cultural phenomenon known as the Harlem Renaissance. Intellect and creativity abounded as black talent in poetry, fiction, music, art, and theater finally received the recognition it deserved. As films became more prominent, they not only entertained, but began to document events and address important issues.

By the end of this period there were more than ten million black people in America. Major cities like Chicago, Kansas City, St. Louis, Philadelphia, and New York experienced extensive growth as southern blacks found employment in factories and industrial plants. The stock market crash of 1929 set off the Great Depression, and the next decade would bring a slow halt to this crucial age of black creativity and advancement.

Film Fact . . . Before the Fiction

Johnson vs. Jeffries Fight Film
(1910)

George "Tex" Rickard, Fight Promoter

"Whoever controls the motion picture industry,
controls the most powerful medium of influence
over the people."
—Thomas A. Edison

In the early 1900s, the only film images of blacks were degrading to say the least: Racist films such as *The Masher* (1907), and the short comedy spoof, *The Wooing and Wedding of a Coon*, both featured white actors in blackface and reduced black entertainment value on film to the lowest common denominator. But on July 4, 1910, in 100-degree heat, film cameras rolled at an outdoor boxing ring near Reno, Nevada. The odds were 10 : 6 in favor of Jim Jeffries, who came out of retirement to become a reluctant Great White Hope, only to be pummeled and knocked halfway out of the ring by Jack Johnson, a black man.

The film shows the thousands of people who were in attendance, including over six hundred journalists from around the world. Before the bout begins, the master of ceremonies, Uncle Billy Jordan, invites some of the former champs into the ring for perfunctory applause and accolades. Famous fighters such as John Sullivan, James Corbett, Tommy Burns, Bob Fitzsimmons, and Tom Sharkey are among the attending pugilists. Then the referee, Tex Rickard, who is also the fight promoter, motions for the opening bell.

Jeffries instantly moves out of his corner and takes the fight to Johnson, as the black fighter shuffles about, cautiously avoiding his swings. For the first couple of rounds, Jeffries maintains a crouch-

Jack Johnson (right) takes the fight to Jim Jeffries in the fourteenth round of the official fight film. Public exhibition of the film was banned around the world after the black fighter won, and the U.S. Congress passed a law making it a federal offense to transport moving pictures of prize fights across a state line. (Library of Congress)

ing fighting stance and throws lots of straight lefts but with little effect. In round 3, Johnson catches his white opponent with a left jab that stands him straight up. The fight is on.

For the next twelve rounds, Johnson takes the fight to Jeffries. At the opening bell of round 7, Johnson bolts out of his corner and hits Jeffries with a right cross to the jaw, before the already battered fighter can get his hands up. For rounds 10 through 13, it seems Jeffries is tired and out of breath. He continues to fight and swing wildly but somehow keeps returning to the ring. Meanwhile, Johnson still looks strong as he constantly connects with both the left and the right. By round 14, Jeffries is beaten up pretty badly, he holds his arms low and moves slowly, looking tired and dazed. In the fifteenth and final round, Johnson knocks Jeffries across the ring and almost through the ropes. Spectators push the battered fighter back into the ring, and Johnson hits him again, with a pounding left to the head. Jeffries goes down but somehow staggers back to his feet for the final three blows. Again on the mat, he receives a ten count, and the referee raises Johnson's fist high into the air. The mighty black underdog has won.

As a result of Johnson's victory at least ten people lost their lives, and hundreds more were injured due to white retaliation, riots, and wild celebrations in the streets. For the first time in history there was, indisputably, a black heavyweight champion of the world. A black man had beaten a white man in the ring—and the feat had been recorded on film. But public screenings of the historical document aroused instantaneous protests. Atlanta, Baltimore, Capetown, London, and hundreds of other cities barred the film, claiming it was detrimental to public morals.

Although prizefight pictures, many of which showed a black man being beaten by a white fighter, had been exhibited publicly for years, the U.S. Congress passed a law that made it a federal offense to transport moving pictures of prize fights across a state line. Overnight, one of the most powerful and important portrayals of a black man ever captured on film was made virtually invisible by a set of specially concocted laws and regulations.

Sixty years later, producer Martin Ritt would take Howard Sackler's semibiographical, Broadway play about Jack Johnson to the big screen. The film version of *The Great White Hope* (1970) starred James Earl Jones, who, along with costar Jane Alexander, in her screen debut, received Academy Award nominations for Best Actor and Best Actress.

Note: The first fight film was of James J. Corbett vs. Peter Courtenay, 1894.

The Railroad Porter

William D. Foster, Foster Photoplay Company (1912)

"If you read [Langston] Hughes, you will see vivid,
and easy images. He says that 'a railway arch is a sad
song in the air,' and I ask you to look at that for
a moment. And again, that is what he can do, and
others can do things like it. That is what Negroes
have to give, and because they have something to
give, that is why there should be a black cinema."

—Robert Herring, "Black Shadows"
Close Up, August 1929

The Railroad Porter is a short comedy about a railroad porter who
leaves to go on his run one day. In his absence, his wife invites a
waiter from a colored café on State Street home for dinner. The
porter returns unexpectedly to find another man sitting at his table
and eating his food! Mad and insulted, the porter gets his pistol and
chases the man out of his house. The waiter goes and gets his gun,
comes back, and chases the porter. Fortunately, both are terrible
shots and no one gets hurt.

The film's style has often been compared to that of the Key-
stone Kops comedies of the same period; the cornerstone of that
popular series was the exciting and often farcical chase scenes.

William D. Foster, producer of *The Railroad Porter,* is known
to have incorporated various techniques from other films into his
productions, as well as successful comedy elements from the black
vaudeville stage. He was a multitalented man who intertwined many
careers in the course of his life. Foster, known also by the stage
name Juli Jones, was a press agent who booked talent for vaudeville shows and a sportswriter and circulation manager for the
Chicago Defender. He worked a short stint as a Hollywood publicist
and is best known for promoting the vaudeville comedy team of
Bert Williams and George Walker and their revues.

Moving pictures had barely crept out of the nickelodeon to dance upon the silver screen when Foster grasped the profit potential in this new and exciting medium. At the time, the portrayal of Negroes was nothing less than reprehensible. Even the titles of early films like *A Nigger in the Woodpile* and the degrading classic *The Watermelon Contest* demonstrated loathing and disrespect for the Negro, and did not try to hide their racist intent.

In 1910, Foster started Foster Photoplay Company in Chicago and set about taking control of the black image into his own hands. He had often booked vaudeville acts for the Robert Mott's Peking Theater Stock Company, and he turned to that pool of talent for his actors. Two years later, *The Railroad Porter* was in the can, and Foster would produce three more motion pictures in the year that followed.

In 1914, to help promote his previous success, Foster toured the South with a retrospective of the four Foster Photoplay short films. *The Railroad Porter, The Fall Guy* (1913) (another comedy), *The Butler* (1913) (a detective story), and *The Grafter and the Maid* (1913) (a melodrama). As part of the program, Lottie Grady, the company's leading lady, would sing and entertain between reel changes.

Review Summary: There is conflicting testimony among critics and film historians concerning the images of blacks in *The Railroad Porter.* Some felt the characters were a vast improvement over what had been seen before, while others believed they were just more of the same. According to Larry Richards, *The Railroad Porter* was not only the first race comedy, but also the beginning of the chase idea in film.

Mark Reid, in his article "Early Black Independent Filmmakers," explains that at the time of its premiere *The Railroad Porter* was applauded by The *New York Age*, a black weekly newspaper, for its positive representation of blacks. Reid includes the viewpoints of film historians Daniel Leab and Thomas Cripps, who contend that the film was simply an imitation of the work being produced by the larger film industry.

CREDITS: 2 Reel Short. B&W. Comedy. Silent.   CAST: Lottie Grady (*Wife*), Jerry Mills (*Porter*), Edgar Litterson (*Waiter*)

The Realization
of a Negro's Ambition
Lincoln Motion Picture Company (1916)

"The treatment of the Negro by the movie is inaccurate and unfair. It establishes associations, and drives deeper into the public mind, the stereotype conception of the Negro."

—Dr. Lawrence Reddick, *Journal of Negro Education*, Summer 1944

In *The Realization of a Negro's Ambition*, the main character, James Burton, a recent Tuskegee graduate with a degree in civil engineering, returns home to work on his father's farm. Unfulfilled by the daily agricultural grind, he strikes out on his own and heads west, leaving behind his father, the farm, and the woman he loves.

When he arrives in California, James finds that a major obstacle to getting the job he seeks is the color of his skin. Fate steps in when he risks his life to stop a runaway horse and buggy and in the process saves the life of the local oil magnate's daughter. James is appointed head of oil exploration for the father's company and decides to drill on his father's farm. He strikes the motherlode, and he and his father become very wealthy. His ambition realized, he stays on the farm, marries the sweetheart he left behind, and all live happily ever after.

In 1915, the Lincoln Motion Picture Company was funded in Los Angeles when two actors, Noble Johnson and Clarence Brooks, teamed with Dr. James T. Smith, a local druggist, and Harry Grant, a white camera operator from Universal Studios. As the second black-owned film company ever, their plan was to make positive family films, each structured around a black hero's struggle to accomplish some admirable ambition and succeeding. They opened a production office on Central Avenue and established a filming stage on Tennessee Avenue in West Los Angeles. Unlike the early

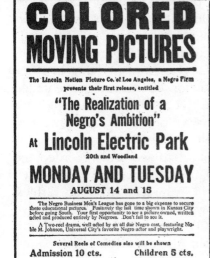

COLORED MOVING PICTURES

The Lincoln Motion Picture Co. of Los Angeles, a Negro Firm presents their first release, entitled

"The Realization of a Negro's Ambition"

At **Lincoln Electric Park**
20th and Woodland

MONDAY AND TUESDAY
AUGUST 14 and 15

The Negro Business Men's League has gone to a big expense to secure these educational pictures. Positively the last time shown in Kansas City before going South. Your first opportunity to see a picture owned, written, acted and produced entirely by Negroes. Don't fail to see it.

A Two-reel drama, well acted by an all star Negro cast, featuring Noble M. Johnson, Universal City's favorite Negro actor and playwright.

Several Reels of Comedies also will be shown
Admission 10 cts. **Children 5 cts.**

P. A. Franklin, Printer

black comedies that were meant merely to entertain (such as Biograph's *Natural Born Gambler* (1916), with Bert Williams performing his mimed card-playing routine, wearing blackface and white gloves) the Lincoln films had a dramatic story structure and stressed hard work, self-pride, and an individual's ability to reach his goals through persistence, decency, and integrity.

In the wake of the success of *The Realization of a Negro's Ambition*, Noble's brother, George P. Johnson, a mailman from Omaha, joined the company to oversee production on its second short film, *The Trooper of Company K* (1918). In an all-out attempt to provide an alternative to the stereotypical coon and Uncle Tom images of that time, the film tells a tale of change and redemption. A shiftless, good-for-nothing man joins the army and through the challenges he faces builds up his confidence, courage, and self-esteem. As a member of the historic all-black 10th Cavalry, he fights bravely in the battle against the Carramzista's soldiers at Carrizal, Mexico. He proves himself a man in battle, and returns home a hero, worthy of his sweetheart's love.

On September 3, 1919, Lincoln released *A Man's Duty*, their first feature-length film, which dramatized the black man's right to participate freely in American life. They followed it two years later with *By Right of Birth*, a black middle-class success story.

Company cofounder Noble Johnson played many of the leading roles. His light complexion enabled him to take on many nonwhite and ethnic parts in Hollywood films. He often portrayed Indians, Arabs, Mexicans, and Italians and was once a darkened, weather-beaten cowboy. Noble eventually left the company to work at Universal Studios.

CREDITS: 2 Reels. B&W. Silent.

CAST: Noble Johnson, Clarence Brooks, Webb King, G. H. Reed, A. Burns, A. Collins, Beulah Hall, Lottie Boles, Bessie Mathews, Bessie Baker, Gertrude Christmas.

George kept the reins as chief of production, head writer, booking agent, publicist, and distributor. He rented the films to exhibitors for $15 to $20 a day but had a hard time making a consistent profit. As a last resort, he approached the banks and lending institutions for a loan, but they saw no financial return in investing in black films. In the end, he halted all production efforts and concentrated on marketing the films already made. When an influenza epidemic closed many black movie houses, he was forced to close down Lincoln Motion Picture Company as well.

In the years that followed, George studied and recorded the progress of other production companies that were making black films. When he died on October 17, 1977, he left sixty years of files, clippings, photographs, scripts, correspondence, contracts, extensive notes, and his oral history to the UCLA Research Library. Unfortunately, only fragments of the Lincoln Motion Picture Company's films remain. George Johnson himself described his company's films as "the first successful Class A Negro motion pictures, minus all burlesque and humiliating comedy."

Another black film company worth noting is the Norman Film Manufacturing Company, founded by Richard C. Norman, a white man. His company produced several films with all-black casts, including *The Crimson Skull* (1920), with Anita Bush and Lawrence Chenault, *The Flying Ace* (1926), billed as the "Greatest Airplane Mystery Thriller ever produced," and *Black Gold* (1928), the story of the Oklahoma oil rush, filmed in the all-black town of Boley, Oklahoma.

Review Summary: Reviews of *The Realization of a Negro's Ambition* are generally quite positive. All of the reviewers commend the James Burton character, the film's main subject. In her plot summary in *Frame by Frame*, Phyllis Rauch Klotman describes Johnson's films as being done with "persistence, decency and integrity." Carry Richards, in *African-American Films Through 1959: A Comprehensive Illustrated Filmography*, agrees with the film's conclusive title by explaining how, after facing several difficulties, the main character of the movie does indeed arrive at the point of "ambition realized." In an article in The *Los Angeles Times* writer Carlton Moss describes the primary character as a man who is "fulfilling his ambition despite the prejudice around him." Moss goes on to say that the film was well received at the time of its release.

The Birth of a Race
(Lincoln's Dream)

Birth of a Race Photoplay Corp. (1918)

"Griffith's movie [*The Birth of a Nation*], apart from
its stature as a benchmark of the cinema art, and
synthesis of the rhetoric of the filmmaking
technique of its day, was calculatedly offered to its
audience as racial propaganda."

—Thomas Cripps, *The Making
of The Birth of a Race*

The Birth of a Race is a collage of biblical and historical milestones
that begins in the Garden of Eden and gradually moves forward in
time. Edited into two distinct parts, its cinematic tapestry includes
scenes of Pharaoh's Nubian army as it marches in pursuit of the flee-
ing children of Israel, a segment of Columbus's first voyage to the
new world, President Lincoln emancipating the slaves, stock shots of
soldiers marching into battle, and a sequence depicting a German
family divided by an encroaching war.

The second part of the movie is mostly a synthesis of the Gospels.
It portrays a white Jesus preaching to a multiracial crowd beset by
"doubt and prejudice." The only person of color given an identity is
Simon of Cyrene, a black man who helped Jesus bear the cross to
Calvary. The film then jumps to a montage of title cards displaying
positive messages like "Equality instead of slavery," and "Peace and
humanity." The story then cuts back to Columbus's voyage, moves
forward to Paul Revere's ride, and on to the Constitutional Convention in Philadelphia with a title card that reads: "At last, the
human family formed a government based upon equality." At one
point in the film, two farmers standing together in a field, one black
and one white, dissolve into uniformed soldiers. At the end, we see
President Lincoln on his deathbed, as he wishes for "peace."

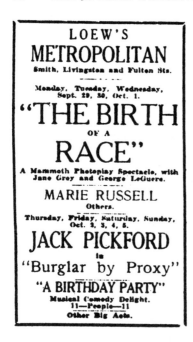

LOEW'S
METROPOLITAN
Smith, Livingston and Fulton Sts.

Monday, Tuesday, Wednesday,
Sept. 29, 30, Oct. 1.

"THE BIRTH
OF A
RACE"

A Mammoth Photoplay Spectacle, with
Jane Grey and George LeGuere.

MARIE RUSSELL
Others.

Thursday, Friday, Saturday, Sunday,
Oct. 2, 3, 4, 5.

JACK PICKFORD
in
"Burglar by Proxy"
"A BIRTHDAY PARTY"
Musical Comedy Delight.
11—People—11
Other Big Acts.

The film took over two years to make and cost over one million dollars. After researching the history of its production we hesitated to leave it on the list. By the end of production not only had the blacks involved been usurped of their power and creative integrity, but the story barely addressed the proposed struggles, aspirations, and accomplishments of the Negro race at all. However, after reading about the massive effort put forth by Emmett J. Scott, Booker T. Washington, W. E. B. Du Bois, the NAACP, and the countless others involved, we decided that their original vision and extensive efforts must not go unrecognized.

The film was conceptualized as a direct response to the racist propaganda of D. W. Griffith's *Birth of a Nation* and was further encouraged by the release of a film version of Edward Sheldon's stage play *The Nigger*. This racist one-two punch in the spring of 1915 jarred the NAACP into action, first, to protest and have these films banned from theaters, and, second, to seize the means of production and make their own rectifying filmic statement. They engaged writer Elaine Sterne, who conceived a story that would highlight black achievement and aspirations, which she called *Lincoln's Dream*.

At the same time, Booker T. Washington and his circle at the Tuskegee Institute began their quest to organize a motion picture based on his autobiography, *Up From Slavery*. Both groups approached Carl Leammle and his newly established Universal Pictures for financial backing. Leammle offered to provide the NAACP with his services provided they contribute $50,000 toward the film's $200,000 budget. However, because they were unable to raise their share of the funds, and because his southern business partners

---

CREDITS: Directors: William Selig, John W. Noble. Producers: Edwin Baker, Daniel Frohman. Writer: Emmett J. Scott. 12 reels/3 hours. B&W. Silent.

CAST: Marie Russell, Jane Gray, and George LeGuere.

showed mounting concern over the most positive portrayals of Negroes in the project, Leammle backed out of the deal.

For a while, the NAACP combined forces with the Tuskegee group, but Mary White Ovington, a member of the film committee, still could not rally enough financial support. Undaunted by the previous failed attempts, Emmett J. Scott, Booker T. Washington's private secretary, approached Amy Vorhaus, a writer with connections at Vitagraph, about a possible collaboration. Scott also tried to work a deal that would bring Tuskegee together with the Thomas Ince Studio. Both deals fell through, and the hope for a positive black cinematic counterweight to *The Nigger* and *The Birth of a Nation* fizzled out.

The Tuskegeeans decided to forge ahead. Their plan was to form their own company, produce their version of *Up From Slavery* right there at Tuskegee and, if need be, purchase portable projection equipment to screen the film in churches and meeting halls. They made a deal with Edwin L. Barker, of the Advance Motion Picture Company of Chicago, to do the production work, but Booker T. Washington died before they could sign the contracts. *Lincoln's Dream / Up From Slavery* was later reborn as *The Birth of a Race* and promised to be an inspirational black statement with a plea for mutual respect between the races. In September 1917, after several close starts, the production got under way in Tampa, Florida. By the next spring, however, their initial $140,000 investment had been spent. With the film but half finished, many of the investors and participants backed out, including William Selig, whose company had been brought in to do the production work.

Daniel Frohman, a vaudeville producer from New York, undertook to shoot the second half at his Tampa, Florida, studio. He also secured the budget, but with the loss of financial control, so went what Emmett J. Scott called "the colored man's point of view." With no thought for what was already in the can, the new producer shifted the story emphasis from black progress to a more universal progress. Much of the earlier black footage was left on the cutting-room floor.

In November 1918, *The Birth of a Race* premiered at the Blackstone Theater in Chicago. It was a disaster.

If Scott's initial vision had been realized, then perhaps *The Birth of a Race* would have become a "healing balm" instead of the "box office bomb" it turned out to be. However, this unfortunate setback did not deter Negro filmmakers. They surged ahead—fighting and struggling and occasionally achieving what they were never meant to achieve.

Review Summary: Contemporary reviews of *The Birth of a Race* are relatively critical. In *African-American Films Through 1959: A Comprehensive Illustrated Filmography*, Larry Richards essentially argues that the film just did not work, specifically as a response to D. W. Griffith's *Birth of a Nation*. Richards explains that the final product did not even concern blacks. *Variety* called it "the most grotesque cinema chimera in the history of the picture business." Thomas Cripps claimed it was a patchwork of two movies spliced into one and that it ignored its initial racial premises to the point that the spirit of the film was impeached. The picture introduced racial fighting in the portrayal of the Jews as victims of the pharaoh's black army, which countered the theme of racial harmony, and the majority of the Negro segments that remained were not at all presented in a positive light.

Two other reviews worth noting also appeared in *Variety*, but presented different views. The first article, from December 6, 1918, discusses the role that the war played in the making of the film and the subsequent changing of its theme, as well as its inaccuracies. The second, dated April 25, 1919, is in direct disagreement with the first, for it praises both the technical aspect of the film and some of the subject matter. Clearly, the reviews of *The Birth of a Race* demonstrate the historical complexity of this film; both then and now the diluted product received stinging criticism.

Body and Soul

Micheaux Film Corporation (1925)

"[Film] images have helped to define white society's
assessments and impressions of us, and at the same
time, have seriously hindered our own development
of a sense of pride and historical understanding of
ourselves and the role we have played in the
shaping of America and its culture."

> —Black Filmmaker's Foundation Brochure
> Introduction

At the dawn of independent filmmaking, one man, more than any
other, took it upon himself to put black stories and images up on
the screen. Oscar Micheaux, a virtual one-man dynamo, independently wrote, produced, directed, edited, and often self-distributed
more than thirty motion pictures in his thirty-year film career.

Much of Micheaux's work has been influential, from the way
he single-handedly got his films made, to his conscious choices of
controversial subject matters, but the main reason we chose *Body
and Soul* was that it marked the screen debut of Paul Robeson. In
researching the selection, we were amazed at how much early
material on Robeson negates this fact, as if he stepped directly off
the theatrical stage and onto the screen as the Emperor Jones.

Another important aspect of this film is that Robeson plays the
dual role of an escaped ex-con posing as a preacher and the heroine's good, upstanding fiancé. As the preacher, he's a worldly sinner
in a preacher's suit. He drinks heavily and openly associates with
crooks and gamblers, all the time exhalting the virtues of the "good
book" to his trusting congregation. While trapped in a storm with a
young woman in his congregation, he rapes her, steals her mother's
money, and ultimately ruins her life. At the film's end, the mother
wakes up to discover that it has all been a bad dream. Or was it?
The final dream sequence is said to have been added to appease
the film board censors who objected to the less-than-admirable portrayal of the minister.

An escaped convict, posing as a man of God, the Right Reverend Isaiah T. Jenkins, alias "Jeremiah, the Deliverer" (Paul Robeson), stresses the virtues of the Good Book to his unwitting congregation in Oscar Micheaux's *Body and Soul*. This was Robeson's first film role. (Museum of Modern Art)

Micheaux's work has been criticized for rough edges, poor production values, and stereotyping. Most of it can be explained very simply: Micheaux was a businessman out to make money. Lorenzo "the Black Valentino" Tucker, a lead actor in many of Micheaux's films, said in a spring 1988 *Black Film Review* interview, "Micheaux would laugh when he saw some of the money white producers were putting into black-cast films. He knew that the market wouldn't support the investment. The acting was sometimes bad [in his films] because he would only allow one take. He could have made better films, but he knew they wouldn't make any more money anyway."

CREDITS: Director: Oscar Micheaux. 75 minutes. B&W. Silent.

CAST: Paul Robeson (*The Reverend / The Fiancé*), Mercedes Gilbert (*The Girl*), Julia Theresa Russell (*The Mother*), Lawrence Chenault (*Former Jailmate*), Marshall Rogers (*Speakeasy Owner*), Lillian Johnson (*Pious Lady*), Madame Robinson (*Pious Lady*), Chester A. Alexander (*Church Elder*), Walter Cornick (*Church Elder*).

Micheaux's first film, *The Homesteader* (1918), was based on his novel about Jean Baptiste, a black farmer in the Dakotas who falls in love with Agnes, a Scotsman's daughter. Realizing the implausibility of an interracial marriage, he leaves and marries a girl of his own race. His new wife, Orleans, is a minister's daughter, but conflicts between Jean and his father-in-law eventually destroy their union. He returns to the Dakotas to find that the old Scotsman in his younger days had had an eye for women of a darker hue. Thus Agnes is actually of Negro blood, and therefore available.

The Homesteader was produced with $15,000 that Micheaux made by selling shares in his Western Book Supply Company. A shrewd businessman, he marketed his stable of dark film stars by giving them nicknames that associated them with other popular Hollywood stars. Bee Freeman became the Sepia Mae West, Ethel Moses: the Negro Harlow, and Slick Chester was the Colored Cagney. Micheaux would also reedit his films constantly; he would drop a Harlem cabaret scene of beautiful dancing girls in the middle of a serious melodrama strictly for its entertainment value.

To meet the challenge of talking pictures and the high cost of the new sound technology, Micheaux formed an alliance with Leo Brecher and Frank Schiffman, two white Harlem theater owners. The first film resulting from this merger was *The Exile* (1931), which expressed the emotional struggle of a young black man who must reject the woman he loves so that she can pass for white.

Of the thirty or more films produced by Micheaux only twelve survive. A 35-mm nitrate print of *Body and Soul* has been preserved and restored by the International Museum of Photography at George Eastman House in Rochester, N.Y., one of only three of his silent films known to still exist. More recently, 35-mm nitrate prints of *Within Our Gates* (1920) and *Symbol of the Unconquered* (1920) have been acquired from Filmotecha in Madrid and the Belgium National Film Archive in Brussels, respectively. The *Unconquered* print is now a part of the Museum of Modern Art Film Archives, in New York, and the *Gates* print is at the Library of Congress in Washington, D.C. Other known existing titles are *The House Behind the Cedars* (1925, adapted from Charles Chestnutt's novel), *Veiled Aristocrats* (1932, discovered in a barn by a private collector), a print of *Murder in Harlem* (1935, discovered as part of the Tyler, Texas, collection at Southern Methodist University's Southwest Film/Video Archives in Dallas), and film prints of *Ten Minutes to Kill* (1932) and *Lying Lips* (1939, in the UCLA Film Archives).

Review Summary: Published comments on *Body and Soul* address two subjects: Micheaux's manner of dealing with color variations among blacks, and the censorship the film encountered. Many comments are more concerned with the controversial filmmaker than anything else.

Firstly, Pearl Bowser and Louise Spence explain that Micheaux was often accused of casting according to color but that, in reality, his work challenged the color caste-system. This was evident in *Body and Soul* with the presentation of the same actor committing both good and bad acts, thus challenging the association of light with good, and dark with bad. However, a look at his body of work reveals that most of his leading ladies were in fact light-skinned.

As to the censoring of *Body and Soul,* according to film historian Donald Bogle, the New York Board of Censors was opposed to Micheaux's images of corrupt black ministers. Thus the film's ending was changed in order to soften the depiction.

The Scar of Shame

Colored Players Film Corporation of Philadelphia (1927)

"Only occasionally did a director or screenwriter
take it into his head to produce work in which a
Negro featured as a real character, and even when
this happened, he was always shown in an
unfavorable light and pictured inevitably with
one of two alternatives: hatred or contempt."

—Robert Herring, *The Negro in Silent Film*

The Scar of Shame firmly reveals the social and class divisions that
were once so prevalent within the black community and, to a lesser
extent, still are. The main story tells of the relationship between
Alvin, an aspiring black composer, and Louise, a lower-class woman
he takes as his wife. Ashamed of his new mate's lack of breeding,
Alvin keeps his marriage a secret, especially from his highly class
conscious mother.

Alvin weds Louise in an unselfish gesture to protect her from
Spike, her drunken, abusive father. Spike's good friend, Eddie, is a
dapper-dressing, cigar-smoking saloon owner who wants Louise to
sing at his club. Spike and Eddie conspire to coerce Louise into
singing with promises of fame and success, but first they must lure
her away from her protector. The duo send Alvin a fake telegram
saying that his mother is ill. Louise wants to go with him to meet
her new in-laws but learns that Alvin has not told his mother about
her and that he does not intend to. With the husband out of the
way, Spike and Eddie coax the rejected singer into performing at
the saloon.

When Alvin returns and learns what has happened, a fight
ensues. Guns are drawn, shots are fired, and Alvin accidentally
shoots Louise in the neck, thus marking her with a "scar of shame."
Alvin is taken to jail for the shooting but escapes to start a new life
as a piano teacher in a quiet upscale community. There he meets
and falls in love with Alice, an upper-class woman, who is more his

equal. Now happy and enmeshed in the life he's always wanted, Alvin runs into Louise again, and she threatens blackmail if he does not return to her. Regardless of the consequences, Alvin refuses to give up the new life he's made for himself. He rejects Louise outright, and she commits suicide. In a final note, Louise confesses that it was a bullet from Eddie's gun that had wounded her and Alvin is innocent of both the crime and the guilt. Now, with her out of the way, he is free to marry Alice, his sweetheart.

As a white-owned studio, the Colored Players Film Corporation of Philadelphia intended to bring black middle-class social values to a growing black urban audience. But, in doing so, it clearly took sides in regard to a divisive rift that had sprung up within the Negro community. *The Scar of Shame* asserted that the ideal Negro was reaching for the finer things, higher hopes, and loftier aims, and it directly played upon a serious social issue that had developed. During the great migration of southern blacks to the industrialized cities in the North, the wealthier and better-established blacks often looked down on the new arrivals. These uneducated Negroes were seen as a threat to their hard-earned social status. In response, these lower-classed southerners were compelled to exhibit contempt for what they considered the bourgeois emulation of white social values. *The Scar of Shame* not only exemplified these basic conflicts within the black community, but also blamed these southern newcomers for their own misfortune.

Sherman H. "Uncle Dud" Dudley, credited as producer, was a black vaudeville performer who had appeared in *The Simp* (1921), an early race movie produced by the Reol Film Company. He teamed with David Starkman, the white owner of a black theater in Philadelphia, to organize the Colored Players. Starkman ran the business and raised the production capital, while Uncle Dud used his vaudeville contacts to acquire talent. Al Liguori and Frank Perugini, two white journeymen, came on board to shoot and direct. Before making this film the Colored Players cut their eyeteeth on *A Prince of His Race* (1926), a social drama, and *Ten Nights in a Bar*

CREDITS: Director: Frank Perugini. Producer: Sherman H. Dudley. Writer: David Starkman. Photography: Al Liguori. 3 reels/90 minutes. B&W. Silent.

CAST: Harry Henderson (*Alvin*), Lucia Lynn Moses (*Louise*), Ann Kennedy (*The Landlady*), Norman Johnstone (*Louise's Father*), William E. Pettus (*Spike*), Pearl MacCormick (*Mrs. Hathaway*), Lawrence Chenault (*Mr. Hathaway*).

Tormented by an abusive father and neglected by her bourgeois husband,
Louise (Lucia Lynn Moses) ponders her fate in *The Scar of Shame*. (Museum
of Modern Art)

Room (1926), which starred the acclaimed actor Charles Gilpin, who
had originated the stage role of *The Emperor Jones* in 1920.

In 1969 a 35-mm original nitrate print of *Scar of Shame* was
found in a trash bin in the basement of an out-of-business Detroit
movie theater. It has since been restored and serves as a testimony
to the early, silent, all-black-cast efforts.

Review Summary: Reviews of *Scar of Shame* are generally positive,
despite some skepticism about the white director. However, Thomas
Cripps proposes that the film represents "a product of a white-
owned Philadelphia studio, shrewdly named the Colored Players,"
suggesting that such films presented black audiences with positive
messages in support of black unity, and were therefore in opposition to racism. Donald Bogle, in *Blacks in American Film and Television*, referred to *The Scar of Shame* as "Quite possibly the best
independent black film of the silent era." In his review, Bogle was
impressed by the variety of emotions inspired by the film. He also
pointed out that although it utilizes the Victorian formula for its
structure, a sense of newness was added by the black cast and plot.

2

Society Profile: 1929-1939

Early Sound Films

By the end of the 1920s Negroes in America accounted for less than 10 percent of the population. Black migration from the South continued, and almost 44 percent of all blacks now resided in the urban areas of the North. The common misery caused by the Great Depression brought about a sense of unity in some sectors of the country as farmers, construction workers, and war veterans worked together to secure food and shelter to sustain their families during the worst economic period in the nation's history. The Depression hit blacks extra hard, as they, too, rallied together to support each other. In some cities black unemployment reached over 70 percent because there simply were no jobs, and blacks usually found themselves the last hired and first fired.

It was in 1930 that the famed Billie Holiday, a.k.a. Eleanora Fagan, began her singing career at Pod's and Jerry's Speakeasy, in New York. She had changed her name to Billie in honor of her Hollywood idol, actress Billie Dove, and the motion picture that would later depict her tumultuous life story was *Lady Sings the Blues* (1972). That movie provided a major acting debut for former Supreme Diana Ross, who received an Academy Award nomination for her performance. Billie Holiday sold millions of records and received rave reviews at the Apollo Theater as well as Carnegie Hall.

In 1933, the New Deal, promoted by newly elected president Franklin D. Roosevelt, enabled blacks to believe again. Roosevelt and his wife, Eleanor, were concerned about the nation's poor, and many of those poor folks were black. Acting upon this concern, Roosevelt created a Civil Rights Division of the Department of Justice and brought in as black advisors Robert Weaver, Robert L. Vann, William Hastie, Eugene Kinckle, and, as director of the Negro Affairs Division of the National Youth Administration, Mary McLeod Bethune. Bethune, the founder of Bethune-Cookman College in Daytona Beach, Florida, would later organize the National Council of Negro Women (NCNC) to fight against racial and gender discrimination.

The New Deal also established the Works Project Administration (WPA) to help match people to jobs. Artists, musicians, actors, and playwrights were beneficiaries of this program as government funding created federal projects for black cultural research, ethnic stage productions, and all-black movie companies. The program was so successful that by 1935 the Department of Commerce could report that approximately five million black workers controlled an estimated buying power of $2 billion.

By the late 1930s, after catapulting performers such as Duke Ellington, Louis Armstrong, Eubie Blake, and Josephine Baker into the limelight, cultivating the intellectual debates of W. E. B. Du Bois and Booker T. Washington, and ushering a black contingent of writers to the forefront of American literature, the Harlem Renaissance had lost most of its steam. However, several movement alumni continued to produce. Zora Neale Hurston wrote her literary masterpieces *Mules and Men* (1937) and *Their Eyes Were Watching God* (1938). Singer and actress Etta Moten, who starred in *The Gold Diggers of 1933* and *Swing Low, Sweet Chariot*, became the first African-American actress to sing at the White House when she was invited to perform by President and Mrs. Franklin D. Roosevelt. Langston Hughes, who had, earlier in the movement, berated other black writers for imitating white writers instead of expressing themselves honestly, found success on Broadway with his play *Mulatto*. And Richard Wright's novel *Native Son* found huge crossover success by bringing a fresh perspective to the inner workings of the mind of a young and troubled black man. Wright himself would bring the character of Bigger Thomas to the screen in 1951. The film would be remade in 1986, from a script adaptation by Richard Wesley, who is better known for his film scripts for the Sidney Poitier, Bill Cosby buddy flicks *Uptown Saturday Night* (1974) and *Let's Do It Again* (1975).

By the end of the 1930s, three black female film stars would emerge. Former Cotton Club dancer Lena Horne began her Hollywood career in the black independent film *The Duke Is Tops* (1938). Hattie McDaniel became the first black actress to receive an Oscar from the Academy of Motion Picture Arts and Sciences for her role as Mammy in *Gone With the Wind* (1939), and former cabaret dancer Ethel Waters would find a notable career on the screen.

Hearts in Dixie

Fox (1929)

"Pappy, I ain't neva' gwine fo'get what'cha done fo'
me. I gwine study hard'n when I gets'ta be a big
doctor, I come back'n ya' won't neva' haf'ta wurry
no mo'!"

—Chinquapin to Nappus

In *Hearts in Dixie* Nappus, an aging tenant farmer, works his land
to provide for his daughter Chloe, his two grandchildren, and his
lazy, good-for-nothin' son-in-law, Gummy. Chloe becomes ill, and
despite the efforts of the local voodoo woman that her husband
sends for to treat her, she dies. With the loss of his only child,
Nappus decides that his eldest grandson, Chinquapin, should go to
study medicine in the North and someday return to the South and
help his people.

Despite the strict disapproval of Gummy, the boy's father,
Nappus makes the sacrifice. He sells his land and in the final, tear-
ful scene watches his grandson sail off on the riverboat *The Nellie
Bly*, knowing that the boy is going to "make him proud."

In *The Jazz Singer* (Fox, 1927), Al Jolson made film history
when he appeared in blackface for his musical number, "My
Mammy." It would be the first Hollywood feature-length sound film,
or "talkie," ever made.

Two years later, *Hearts in Dixie*, a musical drama set in the tradition of the Old South, was presented by producer William Fox as
Hollywood's first all-black, all-talking-and-singing musical! Set just
after the Civil War, *Hearts in Dixie* has been criticized for perpe-
trating happy-go-lucky darkies content with their sweat, toil, and
substandard lot in life with no thought of aspiring to anything
better. Scenes depict black plantation workers picking cotton in the
fields all day, singing and dancing all night, then up and ready to
hit the fields again the next day. There is actually just a skeleton of
a story line that's interspersed with the singing, dancing, cooning,
and an occasional minstrel shtick.

Rammey (Clifford Ingram) and Trallia (Mildred Washington) take a break from cotton picking in *Hearts in Dixie*, the first black sound film. (© 1929 Courtesy of 20th Century-Fox Film Corporation. All rights reserved.)

The picture was initially conceived as a short film that would showcase the minstrel-like shenanigans of black performers. Stepin Fetchit played a large part in the picture's expansion when the producers realized they had discovered a powerful, stereotypical, black character. Though Fetchit, a.k.a. Lincoln Perry, had already appeared in *The Ghost Talks* and a couple of silent films, *Hearts in Dixie* was the picture that launched his career.

Veteran actor Clarence Muse, who replaced popular stage actor Charles Gilpin for the lead role, is credited with some of the direct-

---

CREDITS: Director: Paul Sloane. Producer: William Fox. Screenplay: Walter Weems. Photography: Glen MacWilliams. Music: Howard Jackson. Choreography: Fanchon and Marco. 71 minutes. B&W. Musical.

CAST: Clarence Muse (*Nappus*), Stepin Fetchit (*Gummy*), Mildred Washington (*Trallia*), Eugen Jackson (*Chinquapin*), Vivian Smith (*Violet*), Zack Williams (*Deacon*), Dorothy Morrison (*Melia*), Bernice Pilot (*Chloe*), Gertrude Howard (*Emmy*), A. C. H. Billbrew (*Voodoo Woman*) Richard Carlysle (*White Doctor*), Clifford Ingram (*Rammey*), Robert Brooks, and the Billbrew Chorus.

ing. Composer Will Vodery was signed to the largest contract ever for a black musician at that time as supervisor of the film's soundtrack music. The A. C. H. Billbrew Choir provided most of the vocals and acted as background personnel and extras. The dance duo of Fanchon and Marco are credited with what is generally considered to be the film's stereotypical but supposedly "African based" dance choreography.

Review Summary: The most interesting reviews of *Hearts in Dixie* were written at the time of its release. The review by Robert Benchley in *Opportunity* magazine could easily be described as offensively positive. He suggested that because of their "natural ability" Negroes had ensured the future of sound film. Despite its thin story line, Benchley actually commended the film and expressed relief in the fact that the only interference of whites was in writing the script. Taking this even further, Benchley strongly implied that the white writers had "done well" in creating the comedy of the film because "Negro comedy tends to be childish."

Mordaunt Hall, of the *New York Times*, felt the movie took on a tone of romanticization. "The spirit of the Southern Negro of a year or so after the Civil War is cleverly captured in *Hearts in Dixie*." He applauded the gentle, entertaining, truthful, and funny nature of the film. He also pointed out that *Hearts in Dixie* did something that was rarely done on screen, in that it suggested Negro education. Sid, in a *Variety* review, liked Stepin Fetchit, along with the singing. However, he predicted that the film would not do well and referred to it as "slowly paced," and "simply a Southern Negro Study." A common thread in these reviews is the open acceptance of the stereotypical images of blacks as real and truthful, as if, presumably, they lacked exposure to anything else.

On the other hand, present-day write-ups for the most part are negative. Film critic Peter Noble acknowledges the film's historical role, but he also criticizes the film's perpetuation of stereotypes. The image of loyal plantation workers toiling and singing from sunup to sundown, and Stepin Fetchit's role as the "darkie," are just two examples of such negative portrayals.

An interesting current review comes from *The Motion Picture Guide*, where the film is rated rather well. It does mention the negative images of blacks in the film, then essentially dismisses it by stating that *Hearts in Dixie* is no worse than many other films that have come out of Hollywood.

Hallelujah

Metro-Goldwyn-Mayer (1929)

"You ain't never gonna stop sinning, gal. It's in your
blood!"

—Hot Shot to Chick

Hallelujah tells a simplistic story that contrasts right and wrong,
good and evil, redemption and salvation. Zeke, a black tenant
farmer, comes to town and sells his cotton crop for $100. Now a
rich man, he catches the eye of Chick, a seductive cabaret singer,
who lures him into a crap game with her fancily dressed, hoodlum
boyfriend named Hot Shot. In no time, Hot Shot wins all of the
gullible farmer's hard-earned cash with a set of crooked dice. Zeke
realizes the fix was in, and a fight ensues. In the struggle, he gets
hold of Hot Shot's gun, and as the gambler flees, Zeke shoots into
the crowd after him, killing his own innocent brother.

Devastated by the tragedy, Zeke becomes a preacher and ded-
icates his life to the Lord. After a series of beautifully photographed
outdoor revivals, at an old-time, down-by-the-river baptism, he con-
verts Chick to the church. Despite his newfound religion, Chick's
charms are still in full effect, and Zeke falls for her again. He even
leaves his sweetheart for her, until Hot Shot shows up and forcibly
tries to take Chick back. Zeke pursues them. During the chase,
Chick is killed, and Zeke chases Hot Shot into the swamp, where
he catches and kills him. Imprisoned for the murder, Zeke does a
stint on a chain gang. When he is released, he returns home to find
his forgiving ex-sweetheart, Missy Rose, patiently waiting to take
him back.

The music sequences ran the gamut from folk songs to spirituals, from baptismal wails to work songs, and even to the blues. As
for its characters, the film incorporated the typical stereotypes of
juke-jointers, crap-shooters, holy-rollers, happy plantation workers,
and Bible-toting Christian revivalists who pray and worship behind
a flatbed truck set up with a traveling gospel band.

Tenant farmer Zeke (Daniel L. Haynes), about to lose all of his money in a crooked crap game, smiles fondly at Chick (Nina Mae McKinney), his cabaret-singing unlucky charm in *Hallelujah*. (Metro-Goldwyn-Mayer)

Newcomer Nina Mae McKinney, as Chick, the loose, vivacious cabaret girl, would become known as the first "tragic mulatto" character in films. She came to Hollywood from the Broadway production of *Blackbirds* in 1928 and, at the age of sixteen, was billed as "the screen's first Black Love Goddess." She would go on to do the film *Sanders of the River* (1935) with Paul Robeson.

Ironically, the lead role of Zeke was originally intended for Robeson, who had commanded the screen in Oscar Micheaux's silent film *Body and Soul* (1925). But Daniel Haynes, a talented stage performer, was subsequently cast. Robeson would later comment on the picture, not so favorably, in *Film Weekly* (September 1, 1933): "The box office insistence that the Negro shall figure always as a clown has spoiled the two Negro films which have been made in Hollywood; *Hallelujah* and *Hearts in Dixie*. In *Hallelujah*, they took the Negro and his church services and made them funny. America may have found it amusing, but to English audiences, the burlesquing of religious matters appeared sheer blasphemy!"

As a maverick Hollywood director, King Vidor believed that the new sound technology being developed for motion pictures was a perfect way to explore the "Negro folk culture" that he had been privy to as a child growing up in Texas. However, uneasy about the director's lofty ideas on how he would portray his real, true-to-life Negro characters, Irving Thalberg, chief of production at MGM, gave the green light only after Vidor invested some of his own money in the project and agreed to work without salary. In *King Vidor on Filmmaking*, the director addressed several aspects of the film's production: "In the shooting of my first sound film, (*Hallelujah*, MGM, 1929) the studio had no portable sound equipment for use on location. Interestingly enough, this proved to be a distinct advantage. I concluded that for all location shooting we would have to put the sound in afterward. This left us free to use the camera, and the action of the people before it, in the same manner we would have in the silent days."

Synchronous sound editing equipment had not yet been developed, so matching the post-recorded sound tracks to the picture became quite a task. In the interim, a silent version of the film was also released.

Hallelujah enjoyed two separate and simultaneous New York premieres, one at the Lafayette Theater in Harlem and another downtown at the Embassy Theater. The Negro press denounced the dual screenings as racist, pointing out that whites didn't mind watching a screen full of darkies but did not want to sit next to one.

CREDITS: Producer-Director: King Vidor. Screenplay: Wanda Tuchock. Ransom Rideout. Based on a story by King Vidor. Photographed by Gordon Avil. Music: Irving Berlin. Editor: Hugh Wynn. Art Direction: Cedric Gibbons. 109 minutes. Sound. B&W.

CAST: Daniel L. Haynes (*Zeke*), Nina Mae McKinney (*Chick*), William Fountaine (*Hot Shot*), Harry Gray (*Parson*), Fannie Belle DeKnight (*Mammy*), Everett McGarrity (*Spunk*), Victoria Spivey (*Missy Rose*), Milton Dickerson, Robert Couch, Walter Tait (*the Johnson Kids*), The Dixie Jubilee Singers.

Review Summary: Early criticism of the film *Hallelujah* dealt with the stereotypical images of black people. In one of many protest letters to the *Herald-Tribune*, Cleveland Allen wrote, "It was a woeful misrepresentation of Negro life and does a grave injustice to the race."

White critics, not surprisingly, found the images less disturbing. They focused on the energetic music and splendid dancing. Jay Carr in the *Boston Globe* said, "Its musical numbers fly off the screen with immediacy." John Cocchi, in *McGill's Survey of Cinema*, wrote that the film "concentrates on a continuous flow of music to highlight each scene." Welford Beaton, in *Sound Magazine*, described the movie as "a gorgeous poem of the South, both dramatically and pictorially. Its all-Negro cast gives us some superb performances and Gordon Avil, with his camera, gives us a succession of views of surpassing beauty." A *Motion Picture Association Review* found the film to be "overly melodramatic with holy roller meetings, a wake, cabarets, and various scenes on the plantation," but it also says, "It is filled with humanity and a true understanding of the way it was back then."

The Emperor Jones
United Artists (1933)

"What I was then is one thing. What I is now, is another."

—Brutus Jones to Smithers

Unlike the stage play, which opens with Brutus Jones already on his ill-gotten throne, the film version of *The Emperor Jones* begins with the opening titles superimposed over what appears to be an African tribal dance.

The sounds and movements of this seemingly ancient ritual soon dissolve into a black church service with a similar praise chant, and nearly identical ritualistic dance steps as if it were all passed down from the motherland. In a back room of the church, Brutus Jones grins as he admires his statuesque form, freshly clad in his new Pullman porter's uniform. His gal, Dolly, watches. "Um . . . um, honey . . . you sure look wonderful in them clothes," she says, but his smug response tells us he already knows. Brutus says so long to Dolly and the well-wishing church congregation with a powerful praise hymn, then heads off on his first run for the railroad.

His pal, Jeff, shows Brutus the tricks of the trade, as well as the night life at the other end of the tracks. Brutus takes a liking to Jeff's girl, Undine, despite an early indication of his friend's intense jealousy. He sees her behind Jeff's back but dumps her when she laughs at him for having higher ambitions.

Later, at a crap game, Jeff comes in for some of the gambling action. He has a score to settle with Brutus, and a pair of fixed dice to help him do it, but he's caught cheating and a fight ensues. Jeff pulls out a knife and attacks Brutus but is killed with his own blade in the struggle. Brutus is sentenced to life in prison for Jeff's death and assigned to a chain gang working in a rock quarry. As his rich, baritone voice leads the work chants, he's all the time looking for a way out. One day, during an altercation, he kills a racist guard and makes his escape. Now on the run, Brutus finagles a job as a stoker on a steamship crossing the Caribbean. When he learns that they have "the wire" on the island of their destination and quite possibly information about his escape, Brutus inquires about a smaller island as the ship goes past. "Nobody bother go to that place. Ain't nothin' dere but trouble," a coworker with a West Indian accent informs him. "Trouble is my buddy," Brutus says, and jumps overboard.

Passed out on the beach, he is accosted by the local militia, labeled a troublemaker in court, and ordered to be thrown in the brig until Smithers, a white, unscrupulous trader, buys him from the island's ruler. Smithers senses that there's something different about this black man, but he underestimates Brutus's skills and ambitions, and ends up in business with him. Through a combined use of scams and trickery, they amass a small fortune, but Brutus has higher ambitions still. He tricks the superstitious natives into thinking he has a powerful charm against death and can only be killed by a silver bullet, and they all bow before the Emperor Jones.

Brutus rules the island with an iron fist for two and a half years until his hard line tactics trigger a revolt. Alone and isolated, he heads off through the jungle toward the coast and a supply ship that is set to sail, but Brutus never makes it out of the jungle. The dethroned Emperor Jones becomes lost and disoriented as the sound of a distant drum beats its haunting rhythm into his subconscious. Hungry, desperate, and fatigued, he slowly begins to go mad.

In a series of photographic special effects, he hallucinates his dark past and an even darker future. As the drumbeat continues steadily, the same superstitious beliefs that sustained his rise to power work to bring him down.

If ever an early film put a black man on the same level with a white man, *The Emperor Jones* did it. At times, Jones actually placed Smithers in the subordinate position by talking back to him, making him light his cigarettes, and standing toe-to-toe with the white man. However, as powerful as Brutus Jones may seem, he is still portrayed as a convicted murderer, an escaped convict, a womanizer,

---

CREDITS: Director: Dudley Murphy. Producers: John Krimsky, Gifford Cochran, William C. DeMille. Screenplay: DuBose Heyward. Photography: Ernest Haller. Music: Rosamond Johnson, Frank Tours. Art Design: Herman Rosse. 80 minutes. B&W. Drama. NR.

CAST: Paul Robeson (*Brutus Jones*), Dudley Digges (*Smithers*), Frank Wilson (*Jeff*), Fredi Washington (*Undine*), Ruby Elzy (*Dolly*), George Haymid Stamper (*Lem*), Jackie Mayble (*Marcella*), Blueboy O'Connor (*Treasurer*), Brandon Evans (*Carrington*).

Brutus Jones (Paul
Robeson) is an
escaped convict
turned island royalty
in *The Emperor
Jones*. (United Artists)

and an overall rogue. He also, in the end, pays for his obstinancy
with his life. Perhaps a warning to any would-be Emperor Joneses
in the audience.

Adapted from the Eugene O'Neill stage play, *The Emperor Jones*
was independently produced by a British company at Eastman Service Studios in New York. Although veteran actor Charles Gilpin
originated the character of Brutus Jones in 1920, when the play was
first staged in Greenwich Village, it was legendary singer and stage
performer Paul Robeson who played the character on screen. Perhaps his most forceful and memorable role in film, it made him an
international star. In the years that followed, Robeson starred in
Sanders of the River (1935), with Nina Mae McKinney; *Showboat*

(1936), *King Solomon's Mines* (1937), *Song of Freedom* (1938), *Dark Sands* (1938), *The Proud Valley* (1941), and *Tales of Manhattan* (1942), with Ethel Waters. Robeson's first role, however, was in Oscar Micheaux's 1925 silent film, *Body and Soul.* Robeson had many other opportunities to perform in film, but he was always leery of the stereotypical roles that were offered to him. When civil rights leaders picketed his film *Tales of Manhattan*, he joined them, and did not accept another role from Hollywood.

Fredi Washington, who portrayed Undine in the film, had to reshoot some of her more intimate scenes with Brutus Jones. During screenings of the daily rushes, studio executives came to fear that audiences might think Robeson was holding a white woman in his arms. Dark pancake makeup did the trick the second time around.

Review Summary: The critics agreed that *The Emperor Jones* was unquestionably Paul Robeson's film. Norman Kagan, in the *Negro History Bulletin* raved about Robeson's performance, "His immense talent and conviction is evident throughout the film, which he strides through like a colossus, occasionally raising his strong baritone voice in plaintive, sweet song, always dominating the screen by turns with emotional frenzy, diabolical humor, and hungry restlessness." Kathleen Karr, in *Magill's Survey of Cinema*, adds, "It is really a one-man show, however, and Robeson's bravura performance holds the film together and makes it ageless."

A few of the criticisms addressed the addition of the early scenes not found in the Broadway play. Robeson's scheming and manipulating progress as a Pullman porter, cheating on Dolly with his best friend's girl, the Harlem murder, and his bloodstained break from the chain gang all set him up as a strong but not so likable character. Also, since a sympathetic black character was rare in Hollywood during this period, critics complained that Robeson's positive role was unduly contradicted by primitive natives and his own ultimate transformation into a cruel tyrant.

As for the film's stance on race relations, Kagan suggested that Robeson's character was not even concerned with color. "Brutus Jones dies, but he does not die because he is black, but because he has a conscience, and is civilized. In fact, he deals with both whites and blacks as if color were pretty much irrelevant, trying always to simply get ahead."

Imitation of Life

Universal Pictures (1934)

"Let me through! It's my mother!"

—Peola at funeral

Imitation of Life brought the dilemma of being born of mixed-racial parentage in America to the attention of a wide and skeptical audience. Although it is mainly a subplot, this element of the story seems to rise far above the rest.

Beatrice Pullman, a young widow, hires a live-in Negro maid named Delilah. Both women have young daughters, Jessie and Peola, and they raise them together as a family. Impressed with

Delilah (Louise Beavers, left) and employer-friend Beatrice (Claudette Colbert) share a concerned moment in the original *Imitation of Life*. (Universal Pictures)

Delilah's delicious pancakes, Beatrice invests in the black woman's secret family recipe and opens a flapjack shop on the boardwalk. Soon "Aunt Delilah's" pancake flour is a national best-selling brand. As Bea becomes rich, she offers to give Delilah a 20 percent share in the company, but the Negro maid refuses, opting instead to remain in her menial position as keeper of the household.

Meanwhile, Peola, her light-skinned daughter, realizes early in life that people treat her differently whenever her darker-skinned mother is around. Ambitious and confused, she grows up and runs away. In an attempt to assimilate into white society, Peola abandons all contact with her mother, which breaks Delilah's heart. She returns home only after her mother has died in a too-late, and too-tearful, admission of who she really is.

The film's main story line revolves around Beatrice's rise to success and her eventual impending marriage to Stephen Archer, a suave and dapper longtime family friend. Just before the lavish wedding, Bea learns that Jessie, her now all-grown-up little girl, is also in love with Stephen. Rather than hurt her daughter, she cancels the wedding and sends Stephen away.

Imitation of Life was a tremendous box office success during the Depression era and left very few dry eyes at theater matinees. It was the only Hollywood film of its time to address or even suggest that there was a race problem in America. Early silent filmmakers appeared to have a deep concern for the mixed-race issue and realized the strong dramatic potential that exists within such a theme.

The Octoroon (1910) explored the tragic consequences of whites who have a few drops of Negro blood in their veins. *The Debt* (1912), ends tragically when a young couple in love discover that they are brother and sister, the girl being the result of a union

---

CREDITS: Director: John M. Stahl. Producer: Carl Laemmle Jr. Screenplay: William Hurlbut. Adapted from Fannie Hurst's novel. 106 minutes. B&W. NR.

CAST: Claudette Colbert (*Beatrice "Bea" Pullman*), Warren William (*Stephen Archer*), Ned Sparks (*Elmer*), Louise Beavers (*Aunt Delilah Johnson*), Rochelle Hudson (*Jessie, 18*), Fredi Washington (*Peola, 18*), Alan Hale (*Martin*), Clarence Hummel Wilson (*Landlord*), Baby Jane (*Jessie, 3*), Sebie Hendricks (*Peola, 4*), Marilyn Knowlden (*Jessie, 8*), Dorothy Black (*Peola, 9*), Henry Armetta (*Painter*), G. Huntly Jr. (*James*), Paul Porcasi (*Cafe Manager*), Paullyn Garner (*Mrs. Ramsey*), Wyndham Standing (*Butler*), Hazel Washington (*Maid*).

between the father and his octoroon mistress. *In Slavery Days* (1913), is the story of a slave's mulatto baby who is switched at birth with the master's white baby. The half-caste little girl grows up and sells the white girl into slavery, which was portrayed as a vicious and unforgivable act (though it would have been okay in reverse). Peter Noble, in *The Negro in Films*, stated: "In all the films made during this period (1910–1914), dealing with octoroons and mulattos, the apparent shame and degradation of being even in the smallest degree 'non-white' was exploited to the full, with obvious implication there was something practically sub-human in being black."

In 1959, *Imitation of Life* was remade by Universal. This new version was shot in vivid color and followed the same basic story line, with a few updated plot twists and name changes. Lora Meridith, who is portrayed by Lana Turner, is an aspiring actress, and Annie Johnson, played by Juanita Moore, is the black maid. Perhaps to appease a more socially conscious audience, Annie voluntarily moves into her position as housekeeper, more out of chance and circumstances than as a profession. Both have daughters, Susie and Sarah Jane, and the film's many contrasting ironies remain consistent with the earlier version. Lora is so into her career that she neglects her own daughter, Suzie. Annie takes up the slack and at the same time tries hard to provide love and nurturing to her own color-struck child Sarah Jane. Again, both mother-daughter relationships become tested and strained, and in the end are only resolved through pain, regret, and sacrifice.

Lightning struck twice for Universal when the remake became another huge hit. Juanita Moore and Susan Kohner (Sarah Jane) received Academy Award nominations for Best Supporting Actress.

Review Summary: Although the story changed significantly between the 1934 and 1959 versions, the critic's responses to *Imitation of Life* didn't change much at all. They referred to both films by using labels like "emotionally charged," "shameless tearjerker," and "classic weep-fodder."

A main source of concern for both films was the assignment of the mulatto role as a minor part. According to the *Literary Digest*, in the 1934 film, the role of the Negro daughter is the part that should have dominated the picture. Fredi Washington's portrayal is called "vital, straightforward, and splendidly in earnest."

Claudette Colbert and Louise Beavers, the lead actresses in the 1934 version, are complimented on fine performances by most critics, while in the 1959 version, Juanita Moore and, especially, Lana Turner are seen as somewhat unreal and elaborate.

In response to the film's social relevance, a *Variety* review by Land addressed its ability to "make some slight contribution to the cause of greater tolerance and humanity in the racial question." And Timothy Johnson, in *Magill's Survey of Cinema*, sums it up with "*Imitation of Life* has elements that are easy to criticize, but taken as a whole, it is a well-made film with many rewards for the viewer."

Harlem on the Prairie

A.K.A.: Bad Man of Harlem

Associated Features/Sack Amusement Enterprises (1938)

"With my rope, and my saddle, and my horse, and
my gun . . . I'm a happy cowboy."

> —Lyrics from *The Bronze Buckaroo*
> title song.

Ralph Cooper, acclaimed actor and founder of Million Dollar Productions, once stated that when we see black actors and actresses up on the screen it makes us feel as if we could be like that. And he was right. Films can make us believe we can achieve whatever status is up on the screen, and also help to open other people's minds to that possibility as well.

Imagine it's the 1930s. A group of little boys are about to play cowboys and Indians. The only black kid in the group is crying. He wants to be a cowboy, but his paleface little friends insist that he can't be because "there were no black cowboys." As the first black western ever made, *Harlem on the Prairie* reminded audiences that there were black cowboys and corrected a popular Hollywood image that up till that time had been consistently false, lopsided, and vastly exclusionary.

Filmed entirely on location at N. B. Murray's Black Dude Ranch near Victorville, California, *Harlem on the Prairie* tells the story of Doc Clayburn, an old-time medicine show performer and reformed criminal who returns after twenty years to recover a stash of stolen gold. While on the trail he's bushwhacked by outlaws and mortally wounded. As he dies, Doc reveals the hiding place of the gold to his daughter and her cowboy companion, Jeff Kincaid.

The film combines all the typical elements of a good old-fashioned western. Melodrama, comedy, romance, action, and suspense are woven together as the characters strive to complete the old man's last wish and search for the gold. Somewhere within all of the riding, shooting, and fighting bad guys Kincaid and his pistol-

Singing cowboy Jeff Kincaid (Herbert Jeffrey) discusses the reward on a Wanted poster with the town sheriff (Maceo B. Sheffield) in Sack Amusement's *Harlem on the Prairie*, the first black western. (Courtesy of the Academy of Motion Picture Arts and Sciences)

toting back-up group, the Four Tones, manage to sing both the title song, "Harlem on the Prairie," and the once popular hit "Romance in the Rain."

One of the most memorable scenes in *Harlem on the Prairie* presents a comedy routine by Flournoy Miller and Mantan Moreland, who were already a seasoned stage and vaudeville act when they signed on to do the production. Moreland portrays the hero's sidekick in the film, and Miller is credited with some of the writing. Spencer Williams, an accomplished actor and future movie producer and television star of *Amos 'n' Andy*, played the heavy. The film's hero, Herbert Jeffrey, who at the time was a popular singer with the

Earl Hines Band, initially conceived of making an all-black cowboy picture. He intended to distribute the film to the hundreds of black movie houses that had been set up across the South due to racial segregation. But fortunately, with the help of Gene Autry, another well-known screen cowboy, Jeffrey made a deal with Dallas-based Sack Amusement for national distribution. *Harlem on the Prairie* was so successful that company owner Richard C. Kahn approached Jeffrey about continuing the saga of the black cowboy. Since rights to the original character of Jeff Kincaid were tied up with the original producer, Jed Buell, they created the character of Bob Blake and introduced his trusty horse Stardusk.

The first film produced through this new partnership was *Two-Gun Man From Harlem* (1939). In it Bob Blake is a hard-working ranch hand who is falsely accused of murdering his boss. He escapes to Harlem. There he runs into the Deacon, a hot-tempered, former man-of-the-cloth gangster who happens to be his own spitting image (Jeffrey plays both parts). Blake assumes the identity and reputation of this crooked city slicker, including dress, dialect, and a pair of eyeglasses as a disguise, and returns to the Wild West to clear his good name.

In their second film, *Harlem Rides the Range* (1939), Blake is a wandering ranch hand out on the range. He and his trusty new sidekick, Dusty, mosey into Dog Valley looking for work. Thanks to an impromptu demonstration of Blake's lightning-fast, straight-shooting gun-handling abilities, they're offered jobs with a local rancher. While performing their duties, Blake and Dusty inadvertently stop a swindling crook from stealing a radium mine from a beautiful young heroine and her father.

The final film of the series, *The Bronze Buckaroo* (1939), has cowpoke Bob Blake and his Texas-based cowboys arriving in Arizona. Their mission is to help a wrangler friend named Joe, and his sister, save their gold-laden farm from a treacherous neighbor. The film is filled with fast riding, fistfights, a massive saloon shootout, and an action-packed rescue climax. In the end, true to tradi-

---

CREDITS: Director: Sam Newfield. Producer: Jed Buell. Screenplay: Fred Myton. Photography: William Hyer. Editor: Robert Jahns. 55 minutes. B&W. Western musical.

CAST: Herbert Jeffrey, Mantan Moreland, Flournoy E. Miller, Connie Harries, Spencer Williams, Maceo B. Sheffield, Nathan Curry, George Randall, Edward Branden, James Davis, The Four Tones (Lucius Brooks, Rudolph Hunter, Leon Buck, Ira Hardin).

tion, Blake rides off into the sunset with the girl. Dusty Brooks played his sidekick in the last two films.

Review Summary: On *Harlem on the Prairie* critics were split. *Motion Picture Guide* suggested the film was "just like a thousand 'B' westerns of the period." The *Motion Picture Association of America* review criticized poor acting and technical elements. However, Guy McCarthy, in his review in *Motion Picture Herald*, described the scenic backgrounds as well photographed and the picture as favorable when compared to similar white features. For *Time* magazine, a major concern was the lack of explanation for the large number of black people living out in the wide open spaces, and the reviewer suggested that such a film "shows how good a colored musical film might be, because the best parts of the picture are tunes." McCarthy concluded that "when considered as entertainment, it is a well constructed, modernly premised western."

HERB JEFFRIES

At his home, Encinitas, California
October 29, 1998

TOR: Could you give me your name, and spell it please? I've seen a couple of different versions.

JEFFRIES: My original name that was used on the series of western films was Herbert Jeffrey. Later on, when I went with Duke Ellington's band, I had a record that was relatively successful and somebody spelled my name wrong on it. They spelled it Jeffries . . . and abbreviated my first name to Herb. I thought it was more euphonious than Herbert Jeffery, and since I wasn't making motion pictures any longer, I decided to leave that name alone. Besides, there were six or seven hundred thousand records that had been sold, and we couldn't call 'em back, so I just said it doesn't matter. I continued to use Herb Jeffries and still use it today . . . never thinking that the western pictures would be historical.

TOR: There was a time when we heard all about Tom Mix, Rory Calhoun, and Roy Rogers, but who had ever heard of a black cowboy? How did it all come about?

JEFFRIES: I was traveling with Earl Hines's band in 1934. Traveling through the South, I noticed a thousand little tin-roofed theaters, created because of discrimination. Blacks couldn't go to white theaters, so they had their own makeshift theaters, and they were all playing white cowboy pictures. So it came to me that this was an opportunity to make something good out of something bad.

TOR: How much did you know about black cowboys then?

JEFFRIES: I had studied about black cowboys at my school in Detroit and knew that the black cowboy was very instrumental in pioneering our country. One out of every three cowboys who helped to set the state boundary lines during Westward-Ho were black. These black cowboys came about back during the slavery period. Some slaves escaped and were taken in by the Indian tribes. The Indians were great riders of horses. They also rode bareback, without saddles. When these blacks reentered the social structure after the Civil War, they had become great riders. In many instances, the ranchers who were transporting cattle back and forth from Kansas to California preferred the black cowboys, because they could powwow with the Indians and get the cattle through when many of the white drovers couldn't.

TOR: How did you go from being a band singer, to riding horses, shooting bad guys, and saving damsels in distress?

JEFFRIES: First, I had to raise the funds to do it. To make a cowboy picture in those days, and that went for Gene Autry, Roy Rogers, Ken Maynard, and all the rest, cost from $70,000 to $125,000— which was a lot of money. They were shot in five to seven days and called "quickies."

TOR: Where did you get the money?

JEFFRIES: I went back to Chicago, where I was working at the Grand Terrace for Earl Hines, and tried to get money from some of the policy barons back there. They were millionaires, and they paid that much money for a race horse—but they were not interested in going into the motion picture business. There were also two brothers who were black multimillionaires in the oil business living in Chicago at that time. I went to them trying to get some money, but they weren't interested either.

One day I read a news article on a man in California named Jed Buell, who had made a picture called *The Terror of Tiny Town*. He was a Caucasian, and he had made this picture with people who—for the sake of identification—were called midgets. He had made a cowboy picture with them, and it was very successful. I figured if he had made a western with little people, then he might be interested in doing a black cowboy picture. I came to California, and I talked to him, and we were able to put together the first all-black-cast cowboy picture ever made on Planet Earth, *Harlem on the Prairie.*

TOR: *Harlem on the Prairie* premiered in New York at the Rialto Theater on Broadway, but it wasn't initially meant to be a Hollywood picture, was it?

JEFFRIES: We thought it would only be distributed in the black theaters, but with the help of Gene Autry we found a distributor down in Dallas, Texas, called Saks Amusement, and we were able to get the film total distribution, not only in the black theaters, but in white theaters as well.

TOR: What was your character's name and what was he all about?

JEFFRIES: The original character in the first picture, *Harlem on the Prairie* was Jeff Kincaid. But Mr. Buell got so busy distributing a successful motion picture that he forgot to sign me for other pictures. Another man by the name of Richard Kahn got ahold of me. He was a director and had produced a few films, and he signed me for three pictures at one time. And with him we developed a character called Bob Blake. Also, in my contractual agreement, I was able to buy a horse instead of renting one, as we had for the first picture. So it was my horse, and he was called "Stardusk."

TOR: *Harlem on the Prairie, Two Gun Man From Harlem, Harlem Rides the Range . . .* why is *Harlem* in all of the titles?

JEFFRIES: Harlem was known all over the world as a black community, and when a picture had *Harlem* in the title, the distributors knew right away it had a black cast. After Bob Blake became established and successful, I decided that I didn't want to use *Harlem* any longer. So we came up with the title *The Bronze Buckeroo* for the fourth and final film.

TOR: Do you think they would have let you be a cowboy if you didn't sing?

JEFFRIES: [*Laughter*] That's a good question. I never thought about that. I don't know. I don't think I would have done so well if I had not been a singer, because at that time, the cowboys who were getting a lot of attention were Gene Autry and Roy Rogers, the singing cowboys. There were a lot of other cowboys making motion pictures who tried to sing and didn't do very well at it. [*Laughter*]

TOR: These "quickie westerns" were made with such small budgets. How much were the actors paid?

JEFFRIES: I couldn't tell you for sure what the extras or my costars were making. I could tell you what I made. For each picture, I probably came out with the great sum of about $5,000, a pittance today, but a lot of money back in 1936. If I did six, seven, or eight days of work and came out with $5,000 . . . I thought I was a millionaire.

TOR: You came up with the concept. Did you own any of it?

JEFFRIES: I never owned one piece of anything in any of the films, and I had no percentage deal. I was so happy to have the opportunity to do those pictures, and get the exposure that I felt young children needed in order to identify with some kind of hero, that I would have probably done it for nothing.

TOR: Can you tell us one of your best or funniest experiences on set?

JEFFRIES: One instance I recall was when I had a shoot-out with one of the bad guys. It was a quick-draw scene, and I had practiced and practiced because I really wanted to look quicker than he. And so when I got on the set, I said to myself, "I know what I'll do. I'll just cock the gun inside of the holster, and when I pull it out, I won't have to cock it back to shoot." Not realizing that if I hit the trigger when I reached in to grab the gun, it was going to go off right down my pants leg. Even though we used blanks, they had full loads in those days, and little pebbles of the burnt powder come out. It scatters down your leg and burns the side of your pants. I wound up picking powder burns out of my skin. Everybody got a big laugh out of that.

TOR: What were some of the difficulties you ran into as the first black film cowboy?

JEFFRIES: I am multiracial, of mixed parentage. It was always said that if a man had three drops of Afro-American blood in him, that made him a light-skinned Negro. Many light-skinned Negroes have passed for white. But when I saw the things I saw in the South, if there had been any possibility of me passing for white, I would have been ashamed to do it. There was no way I would want to be identified as anybody who would treat other human beings that way. But I also found it very difficult to identify myself as an Afro-American. We must be honest at this point of history and tell the truth about ourselves: we discriminate amongst ourselves too. There were people who said to me after I made the cowboy pictures, "What right have you got to call yourself a black man?"

TOR: So you weren't black enough to be a black cowboy?

JEFFRIES: I had the struggle sometimes of not being fish nor foul. And yet, it was still in my heart to see these things that were being done, undone. And if my reward was no more than to see a Denzel Washington, who doesn't have to play a specific type black man, because he plays any part he wants, then I'm satisfied.

TOR: What was the audience response to the films?

JEFFRIES: I'd take the Four Tones with me up on stage, and we'd do personal appearances at the screenings. I noticed that children, especially throughout Texas, were familiar with cowboys, but they had never seen a *movie* cowboy like the ones they had seen on the screen, hurdling a horse or doing tricks on a horse. When I walked down the street in my cowboy outfit, I was like the Pied Piper. Not only were black children following me around, but children of all nationalities.

TOR: On and off the stage and screen, women have considered you extremely good looking. With that kind of appeal, why didn't you do other film roles after *The Bronze Buckeroo*?

JEFFRIES: I went into the service in 1942. When I came out in 1946, I went back to my career in the record business. I went to France in 1949, opened my jazz club, and stayed there for ten years. It wasn't until I came back in the 1960s that I started doing television. I've done many *Hawaii 5-Os* as a character actor. I've done *The Name of the Game*. In *The Virginian*, I played a starring role in an episode called "The Stop Over," with James Drury. I also did a film with Jack Palance called *Hit Man*.

TOR: Conceiving of and making your own series of black westerns in the 1930s was an influential and historical accomplishment. You must be very proud of that.

JEFFRIES: Today I'm getting noticed for the black cowboy films more than I ever did, because they are winding up in museums. Some are in the Gene Autry Museum, and in the Smithsonian, and also in the Black Filmmakers Hall of Fame up in Oakland. So I'm starting to get some attention after all these years. At eighty-seven years of age, if the Father wants me to leave here whenever he desires, all I can say is thanks because I'm on hors d'oeuvres time. I'm very active. I play golf. I just finished three weeks of one-nighters, and my voice is probably better than it's ever been. I'm also writing my memoirs. The name of my book is *Skin Deep*. It will be interesting, and I'm going to nail them right up to the post! [*Laughter*]

3

Society Profile: 1940–1949

Race Flicks

For black Americans, the 1940s could be characterized as two steps forward and one step back. There was movement toward racial equality but, too often, progress was overshadowed by racism, Jim Crow laws, and negative attitudes toward Negroes.

In the arts, Frederick O'Neal and Abram Hill established the American Negro Theater of Harlem, which launched the careers of future film stars like Sidney Poitier, Ruby Dee, and Harry Belafonte. Yet the famed Cotton Club, which featured many of the premier black entertainers of the 1920s and 1930s, closed down.

Japan bombed Pearl Harbor on December 7, 1941, and the United States was precipitated into World War II. The "Black Eagles" of the 99th Squadron escorted Allied bombers into battle in the skies over North Africa and parts of Europe, and never lost a plane to an enemy fighter. These "Tuskegee Airmen," a nickname derived from the segregated military outpost in Alabama where they were trained, included Capt. Benjamin O. Davis, who later became the first black general in the U.S. Air Force. In 1995, based on a story by former Tuskegee Airman Robert W. Williams, an HBO original movie would be made to highlight the "Fighting 99th's" proud and heroic achievements.

While some U.S. troops were fighting in far-off lands, others were being dispatched to quell riots and racial unrest here at home. President Franklin D. Roosevelt opposed a march on Washington being scheduled by A. Philip Randolph, to demonstrate against discrimination in the defense industries. The intent of the march still had an effect, however, for Roosevelt later issued Executive Order 8802, which banned discrimination in American manufacturing plants holding national defense contracts.

In the mid-1940s, the United Negro College Fund was established with $760,000, by Frederick Douglas Patterson, president of Tuskegee Institute. This nonprofit organization has since provided much-needed financial assistance to black students, black colleges, and many other institutions of higher education.

In the sports arena, Jackie Robinson would leave the Negro American League's Kansas City Monarchs to join the Montreal Royals. He would eventually be moved to the Brooklyn Dodgers and become known as the first Negro to play major-league baseball.

On the airwaves, entertainer Nat "King" Cole's ground-breaking, "first of its kind" radio show would run for seventy-eight weeks on the NBC network. Elsewhere, the first black-owned radio station, WERD-AM, blasted across the airwaves from Atlanta. Publisher John H. Johnson added a second magazine, *Ebony*, to his already established *Negro Digest*. It quickly sold out at the newsstands and remains one of the most successful and widely circulated magazines in the world.

In December 1944, in the Battle of the Bulge, black and white soldiers fought side by side—a fact that did not make it into the 1965 Warner Brothers movie of that title. Still, as the 1940s came to a close, President Harry S. Truman did issue Executive Order 9981, which ended discrimination in the armed forces. And despite vicious protests from many whites Jackie Robinson became the most valuable player in the National Baseball League.

The Blood of Jesus

Sack Amusement Enterprises (1941)

"Raz, why don't you pray and try to get religion?
We could be so much happier if you would."
—Martha to her husband

The Blood of Jesus is a religious folk drama that revolves around the accidental shooting of a man's wife and his subsequent acceptance of Christ. The film opens on a typical church service with choral singing. Then, as a black farmer toils in his field, a voice-over relates the declining state of spirituality and warns of the signs of the times. Later, in a pilgrimage to the river to conduct baptisms, the congregation sings, "Everybody talkin' 'bout heaven ain't goin' there . . . heaven . . . heaven . . ." Once at the river, Martha Ann, the wife, receives the Lord and is rushed home by Sister Jenkins, her good friend, to dry off.

Raz Jackson, Martha's husband, has just returned from hunting rabbits. What's in his sack looks way too big to be a bunny, so he tells his wife there were wild hogs running loose in the woods. When Raz carelessly leans his hunting rifle against a chair, it accidentally falls and goes off, with disastrous results. As Martha lies dying, the church folk hold a vigil around her bedside. They sing spirituals and pray, but there is nothing more they can do, for her life is in the Lord's hands.

An angel appears to Martha and escorts her through an out-of-body experience. They journey into a cemetery as ghostly, wandering souls mourn their fate. "These were all good people," the angel tells Martha. "They came to teach the gospel, and were treated with scorn . . . they came to bring redemption, and were stoned and crucified . . . Oh, that the children of man should be so blind!"

The angel then takes Martha to a crossroads where she must choose. To the left lies the world of bright lights and good times; to the right, the spiritual world of peace and salvation. Meanwhile,

A church congregation makes the pilgrimage to the river to conduct baptisms in Spencer Williams's *The Blood of Jesus*. Williams, one of the most prolific independent film-makers of that time, produced, directed, and starred in the film. In the 1950s he would play Andy Brown in the television series *Amos 'n' Andy*. (Courtesy of James E. Wheeler © 1997, Museum of Modern Art)

observing from behind a tree, Satan (complete with devil suit) has an eye on Martha's eternal soul. He sends the handsome, smooth-talking Judas Green to tempt her with fancy clothes and the lures of the city. She takes the bait and enjoys a night of live entertainment at the swinging 400 Club.

Dancers and singers perform in the cabaret-like atmosphere while patrons clap, drink, laugh, and enjoy the show. Judas intro-duces Martha to local businessman Rufus Brown, who happens to run his own seedy juke joint. Rufus offers Martha a job at his place and she naively accepts, totally unaware of what is expected of her.

"God, have mercy on my soul," she cries when the realization sinks in, and she runs away. Meanwhile, one of the regular girls has stolen a customer's wallet and run away as well. Realizing what has happened, the irate patron and his pals run out after the girl but end up chasing the wrong woman. They catch Martha at the crossroads and are about to smash her head in with a big rock when the Lord's voice booms: "He that is without sin among you! Let him cast the first stone at her!" The men look up to find that the crossroads sign has become a huge cross, and apparently frightened by it and the voice, they all run away. Martha crawls to the foot of the cross, which dissolves into a crucifix holding the body of Christ, and as the Blood of Jesus drips down onto her face, she returns to her life.

Spencer Williams was a multitalented man, not only in front of the camera, but behind it. He was one of the most prolific independent film producers of the 1940s, making nine black theme films over a ten-year period. In association with Dallas-based Sack Amusement Enterprises, Williams was able to direct his own screenplays and enjoyed nearly autonomous control. Many of his early films were based on religious stories, and budgets were small, between $12,000 and $15,000. They included *Brother Martin: Servant of Jesus* (1942), *Marchin' On* (1943), *Go Down Death* (1944), and *Of One Blood* (1944). Later, his work would become more secular, as the titles indicate: *Dirty Gertie From Harlem, USA* (1945), *Beale Street Mama* (1945), *Girl From Room 20* (1945), and *Juke Joint* (1946). Williams moved from Louisiana to New York City at the age of twenty-three and studied acting and comedy with Bert Williams. After a stint in the army he pursued a singing career until he landed a job in film. He played the heavy in several black westerns that starred Herbert Jeffery, "The Bronze Buckeroo," and was cowriter on several black comedies with Octavius Cohen. When CBS brought the popular Amos and Andy radio series to television, Williams was cast in the lead role of Andy Brown. A few years later, protests from the NAACP resulted in the show's cancellation, and there has been little said about his career since.

CREDITS: Director: Spencer Williams. Producer: Alfred Sack. Screenplay: Spencer Williams. Photography: Jack Whitman. Sound: R. E. Byers. Music: Rev. R. L. Robertson and the Heavenly Choir. 68 minutes. B&W. Sound. NR.

CAST: Spencer Williams (*Raz Jackson*), Cathryn Caviness (*Martha Ann Jackson*), Juanita Riley (*Sister Jenkins*), Heather Hardeman (*Sister Ellerby*), Rogenia Goldthwaite (*The Angel*), James B. Jones (*Satan*), Frank H. McClennan (*Judas Green*), Eddie DeBuse (*Rufus Brown*), Alva Fuller (*Luke Willows*), R. L. Robertson and the Heavenly Choir.

Review Summary: Thomas Cripps suggests in *Black Film as Genre* that "religion speaks through myth, ritual, symbol, and in-group advocacy." In an extensive analysis, Cripps calls *The Blood of Jesus* exemplary: "Like a series of Sunday School posters, every image and symbol assumed literal and larger than life fundamentalist proportions in a cautionary tale, warning the faithful against the sinful life." Many critics seemed to be moved by the music. In the *Los Angeles Times* Kevin Thomas wrote that "giving the film its shape and impact is the magnificent heavenly choir whose hymns and spirituals are heard throughout the film." And when describing *The Blood of Jesus* in the *Afro-American Cinematic Experience*, Marshall Hyatt submits that "Although not superb in technical terms, the film gives insight into the serious nature of the theme tackled by many independent filmmakers, and it stands in marked contrast to the industry that continued to stereotype blacks and ignored realistic depictions."

Cabin in the Sky

Metro-Goldwyn-Mayer (1943)

"How am I gonna reform if I don't remember what a
mess I was in when I was dead?"

—Little Joe to the General

Cabin in the Sky was Hollywood's first all-black musical since *Hallelujah* (1929). It tells the story of Little Joe Jackson, a worldly man with an appointment with repentance. Despite his wife Petunia's best efforts to get him saved and into the church, he is constantly tempted by a life of sin. He consorts with gamblers and sporting folk and, no matter how hard he tries, just can't seem to break away. Little Joe loves his wife dearly and promises her he'll change his ways. But on the very day he is to join the church, he is shot down during a crap game by the high-rolling Domino Johnson.

With Little Joe on his deathbed, Lucifer Jr. and his boys are dispatched to retrieve his sinning soul. But some "terrific prayin'" by Petunia causes an emissary of the Lord to intervene. Through trick photography that seems to make these ethereal visitors appear and disappear, the General and his men arrive to keep Lucifer Jr. and his ragtag forces at bay, while heaven and hell contend for Little Joe's immortal soul. After much debate and posturing by both sides, the Lord rewards Petunia's prayers and grants Little Joe six more months on earth.

Little Joe returns to life and begins to walk the straight and narrow. But when it looks like he just might make the higher grade, Lucifer Jr. calls in his idea men for a think-tank session in Hades. This group of henchmen are an all-star cast of celebrities that includes Louis Armstrong, Mantan Moreland, and Willi Best. Together, they devise a sure-fire plan to get Little Joe back in hot water with the Lord. Enter Georgia Brown, a spicy temptress with a previous "hot" history with Joe. She is so hot that a bubble bath scene of her singing "Ain't It the Truth" was deleted from the film because it was considered too risqué by the film industry's Hays Office. Little Joe resists her charms and tries to stay true, but Lucifer Jr. sees to it that he wins the lottery. Now a rich man, Little Joe becomes brash and full of himself. He begins to live the high life with Georgia Brown, thus forsaking his wife and any previous commitments.

One night, while splurging at the local nightclub, Petunia comes in. She is dressed for the part and ready to enjoy a long-delayed night out on the town. Pistol-toting Domino Johnson is back in town as well, and he takes a liking to Petunia. When Domino won't take no for an answer, Little Joe comes to his former wife's rescue, with disastrous results for them both.

A few of the fabulous musical numbers in the film include Ethel Waters's moving renditions of "Happiness Is Just a Thing Called Joe" and "Taking a Chance on Love," Lena Horne and Rochester's engaging duet, "Life's Full of Consequences," and in a nightclub scene, Duke Ellington and his band playing "Going Up," one of his original tunes. The famed Hall Johnson Choir provided the heavenly spirituals, and there's a dynamic tap dance number by John "Bubbles" Sublet, who plays Domino Johnson, and ex-chorus girl Ethel Waters, playing Petunia, that includes an impressive, high-kicking jitterbug routine.

Cabin in the Sky was based on a book by Lynn Root, and originally turned into an extremely successful Broadway musical in 1940. Ethel Waters and Rex Ingram, who was Lucifer Jr., carried their stage roles from the theater to the big screen. Onstage, the part of Little Joe was performed by Dooley Wilson, but it went to Eddie "Rochester" Anderson in the film version.

Many of the outstanding cast members played dual roles. The General and his angels were also Petunia's real-life pastor and church folk, and Lucifer Jr. and his horned cohorts were actually Little Joe's crooked, real-life gambling cronies.

CREDITS: Director: Vincente Minnelli. Producer: Arthur Freed. Screenplay: Joseph Schrank. Based on a play by Lynn Root, John Latouche, and Vernon Duke. Photography: Sidney Wagner. Music: Roger Edens. Editor: Harold F. Kress. 100 minutes. Sound. B&W.

CAST: Ethel Waters (*Petunia Jackson*), Eddie "Rochester" Anderson (*Little Joe*), Lena Horne (*Georgia Brown*), Rex Ingram (*Lucius Lucifer Jr.*), Louis Armstrong (*The Trumpeter*), Kenneth Spencer (*Rev. Green, The General*), John "Bubbles" Sublett (*Domino*), Oscar Polk (*The Deacon, Flatfoot*), Mantan Moreland (*First Idea Man*), Willie Best (*Second Idea Man*), Fletcher Rivers (*Third Idea Man*), Leon James (*Fourth Idea Man, Poke*), Bill Bailey (*Bill*), Ford L. "Buck" Washington (*Messenger Boy*), Butterfly McQueen (*Lily*), Ruby Dandridge (*Mrs. Kelso*), Nicodemus (*Dude*), Ernest Whitman (*Jim Henry*), Duke Ellington and his Orchestra, The Hall Johnson Choir.

Little Joe (Eddie "Rochester" Anderson) is about to find out that "life's full of consequences" as he is tempted by the sultry Georgia Brown (Lena Horne) in the charming *Cabin in the Sky*. (Metro-Goldwyn-Mayer)

Review Summary: The talent in *Cabin in the Sky* is primarily seen as positive in the reviews. Manny Farber, writing in the *New Republic*, argues that "the one value of Negro films during this period is in giving Negro artists an outlet to showcase their talents."

Despite stereotypes abounding in the film, with blacks singing, dancing, shooting craps, and clowning throughout, Phillip Hartung in *Commonweal* commented that "Ethel Waters' acting ability and rich warm voice lend themselves beautifully to the role of Petunia and the good songs. And Eddie "Rochester" Anderson, as Little Joe, shows that he needn't confine his dramatics to being Jack Benny's stooge." In Rob Wagner's *Script*, Herb Sterne complains that Lena Horne was slighted by being given only one song, yet "she steals the show as sweet Georgia Brown."

Several critics mentioned that the film was not on the same level as the stage version. *Newsweek*'s reviewer explained: "While treatment and direction fail to take full advantage of the elbowroom the screen allows for fantasy, the cast more than makes up for an occasional pedestrian touch."

Stormy Weather

20th Century-Fox (1943)

"This cat ain't hip to the jive! Stop bustin' your chops!"

—Cab Calloway to Gabe, about Bill

Stormy Weather has been called the most important black musical of its time, and probably of all time. As a cavalcade of established black talent, the combined creative energy and artistry of this film has yet to be equaled.

Bill is a retired hoofer. He lives in his dream house, alone, without the woman he built it for. He spends his days sitting on his front porch, recounting his exciting days on the stage to the neighborhood kids. His story begins with a homecoming parade to celebrate the black soldiers returning from World War I, when he was a drummer with Jim Europe's 15th Infantry Band. Later that night, at a welcome-home party, he and friend Gabe meet Selina Rogers, the little sister of one of their wartime comrades. Bill is immediately smitten but remains the consummate gentleman. Selina is a well-known singer and has already heard stories about Bill's talented feet. Together they dance "The Cakewalk," a dazzling and beautifully choreographed number that could rival anything seen in the famed Ziegfield Follies. At the end of the evening, Selina hits the road to perform with show producer Chick Bailey, while Bill returns to his job as a riverboat deckhand.

Some time later, Bill becomes a waiter at Ada Brown's Beale Street Café, a jazz club in Memphis. One night, Ada hears that Chick Bailey and his entourage are in town; in anticipation of their arrival, she quickly gets her place in order; she has Bill slide several tables together and tells the best-looking band member to sit up front. When the celebrities arrive, Selina snubs Bill as just another waiter. The show begins and Ada sings the blues to the stirring music of Fats Waller and his band. Chick is impressed with the number and invites them to join his traveling show. When Selina finally realizes who Bill is, she talks Chick into hiring him, too.

Bill (Bill "Bojangles" Robinson, left) and Selina (Lena Horne) are estranged sweethearts being serenaded by band leader Cab (Cab Calloway) in the phenomenal musical showpiece *Stormy Weather*. (© 1943 Courtesy of 20th Century-Fox Film Corporation. All rights reserved.)

On the road, Bill is constantly at odds with Chick over his minimal role in the show. It all comes to a head when Bill outshines Chick on stage by dancing on top of the huge tom-tom drums used in one of the musical numbers. When Bill is confronted by Chick and fired after the show, he decks his former boss and quits. Fats Waller punctuates the event with a double take, and his famous line, "One never knows . . . do one?" Before he leaves, Bill asks Selina to come off the road and settle down with him, and shows

CREDITS: Director: Andrew L. Stone. Photography: Leon Shamroy. 77 minutes. Musical. NR.

CAST: Bill Robinson (*Bill*), Lena Horne (*Selina Rogers*), Cab Calloway (*Himself*), Emett "Babe" Wallace (*Chick Bailey*), Florence O'Brian, Dooley Wilson (*Gabe*), Ernest Whitman (*Jim Europe*), Thomas "Fats" Waller (*Fats*), Ada Brown (*Ada*), Zuttie Singleton (*Zuttie*), Flournoy E. Miller (*Miller*), The Tramp Band (*Themselves*), Mae E. Johnson (*Mae*), Robert Felder (*Cab Calloway Jr.*), Katherine Dunham Dance Troupe (*Themselves*), and The Nicholas Brothers (*Themselves*).

her his plans for their dream house. But singing is too much in Selina's blood. Sadly, they go their separate ways.

In time, Bill decides to put together a show of his own, but eventually he runs out of money. When his talent threatens to walk out on the opening night if they don't get paid, he runs into Gabe, his old army buddy, who's now shining shoes for a living. Bill relates his dilemma, and Gabe comes up with a clever scam to keep the show going. His plan eventually backfires, of course, but the show does go on.

The film's grand finale is a star-studded reunion performance, a tribute to the soldiers who are now about to be shipped off to World War II. The show features Bill, Selina, Cab Calloway and his Orchestra, the Katherine Dunham Dance Troupe, and a spectacular tap dance number by the world-famous Nicholas Brothers. When the show ends, Selina decides she's been on the road long enough, and is now ready to join Bill in their dream house.

Stormy Weather was Lena Horne's first starring role since her film debut in *The Duke Is Tops* (1937). She would later become the first black woman to sign a long-term contract with a major Hollywood studio, MGM. Bill "Bojangles" Robinson would continue to perform on film and on stage, and become better known through his multiple film performances with child star Shirley Temple.

The most notable performance in *Stormy Weather* was undoubtedly the Nicholas Brothers' in an amazing leapfrog into a tap splits routine, executed down a high staircase. Known as one of the best dance teams ever (personally, we'd say the Best), they had made their film debut in the all-black-cast musical short *Pie Pie Blackbird* (1932). They followed with the Hollywood feature *Kid Millions* (1934), with Eddy Cantor, and would do two more shorts and five additional features before culminating their film dancing careers with this awesome performance in *Stormy Weather.*

The original music director was William Grant Still, but when a white music supervisor criticized his music for sounding too good, saying, "Negro bands didn't play that well back then," Still resigned in protest.

All in all, *Stormy Weather* presents an exciting array of nonstop musical numbers, showcasing the unique talents of its stellar cast, all of whom were at their performing peaks.

Review Summary: Many critics found the script thin and the story line trite but suggested that the caliber of such artists as Lena Horne, Bill Robinson, Cab Calloway, and the Nicholas Brothers, and musical numbers such as "Ain't Misbehavin'," "I Can't Give You Anything but Love," and "Stormy Weather" more than made up for it. And according to Thomas Pryor in the *New York Times*, "The film's pacing moves smoothly, hooking the audience through the remarkably talented black entertainers."

A *Time* review indicated that even though a variety of types of Negro entertainment could be found in *Stormy Weather*, "some were good, and some were not so good." One dance number stood out for most of the reviewers. It was a flawless tap dance routine performed by the Nicholas Brothers. Donald Bogle, in *Blacks in American Films and Television*, notes that "Harold and Fayard perform a staircase/split number that is, in intricate technical terms, a marvel; stylized, yet spontaneous. It truly commands our respect and inspires awe."

FAYARD NICHOLAS

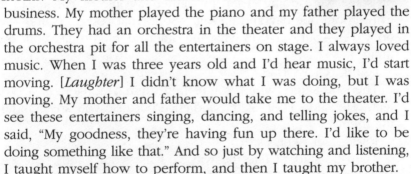

By telephone from his home in Woodland Hills, California
February 7, 1999

TOR: What got you interested in dancing?"
NICHOLAS: My mother and father were in show business. My mother played the piano and my father played the drums. They had an orchestra in the theater and they played in the orchestra pit for all the entertainers on stage. I always loved music. When I was three years old and I'd hear music, I'd start moving. [*Laughter*] I didn't know what I was doing, but I was moving. My mother and father would take me to the theater. I'd see these entertainers singing, dancing, and telling jokes, and I said, "My goodness, they're having fun up there. I'd like to be doing something like that." And so just by watching and listening, I taught myself how to perform, and then I taught my brother.
TOR: Did he come bugging you? Or did you just go grab him by the collar, and say, "Come here and learn this?"
NICHOLAS: Well, he would watch me. I'd do benefits and shows at school, and my brother would see me, so he got interested.
TOR: How old were you at that time?
NICHOLAS: Oh, gee, let me see. I think my brother was six years old, and I must have been around eleven.
TOR: When did the Nicholas Brothers start dancing professionally?

NICHOLAS: We started professionally in 1930. At that time they called us the Nicholas Kids, because we were just little boys.

TOR: When did you realize that you could dance for a living?

NICHOLAS: My brother and I got our little act together, and one evening when my parents came home from the theater, they saw that all the lights were on in the living room and asked us why we were still up. They said, "You should be in bed! You have to go to school tomorrow."

Then I said, "Sit down. We want to show you something."

So they sat down, and we started going through our different routines. After we finished, my parents looked at each other and said, "Hey, we've got something here." [*Laughter*]

Next day they took us to talk to the manager of the Standard Theater in Philadelphia, where they were playing. My father said, "I think my boys have a little talent. I'd like you to see them."

So we got up on the stage, and we started singing a song and dancing.

The manager said, "Oh, that's enough! You don't need to do any more . . . you're booked for next week."

TOR: As a choreographer, how did you come up with the dance steps? What was the process that you'd go through to make up a routine?

NICHOLAS: When I first started, I would do whatever the performers on stage were doing. Then my father saw me rehearsing in the living room one day and he said, "Son, what you do is fine—you do it well—but don't do what the other people do. Do your own thing."

I said, "Okay, Dad."

Then he said, "When you're performing, don't look at your feet." He said, "Look at the audience because you are entertaining them."

I said, "All right, Dad."

Then he said, "I like the way you use your hands." He said, "Do more of that."

I said, "Okay, Dad."

And I started using my hands more than ever. That's a trademark of the Nicholas Brothers, using the whole body. And using the hands with style, class, and grace.

TOR: When did you get that first big break?

NICHOLAS: The first big thing we did was the Cotton Club in New York City. We were playing at the Lafayette Theater in New York.

TOR: How did you get to the Lafayette from Philly?

NICHOLAS: The manager at the Lafayette Theater had heard about the Nicholas Brothers—since they were talking about us everywhere—Baltimore, Maryland, New York, New Jersey. So the manager at the Lafayette made a special trip to Philly. He came to see our show at the Pearl Theater. He came backstage afterward, and my father let him in to our dressing room. He said, "Your boys are good. I'd like to book them at the Lafayette Theater. I think they will be well received."

My father said, "Sure, we'd like to play the Lafayette Theater in NYC, if the price is right." [*Laughter*]

TOR: So you went to New York?

NICHOLAS: We opened at the Lafayette Theater, and we were sensational. Nobody wanted to follow us. We always closed the show. Didn't care who was headlining . . . they didn't want to follow us. [*Laughter*] So, the manager of the Cotton Club came by to see us and talked to my parents. He said, "I would like the Nicholas Brothers to open up the new show at the Cotton Club with Cab Calloway." He had us come to the Cotton Club while they were rehearsing this new show. Duke Ellington was there, Cab Calloway, Ethel Waters, Bill Robinson, and Lena Horne was a chorus girl. I noticed her because she was so pretty. [*Laughter*] The manager of the Cotton Club was Herman Starks. He said, "Do something for the ladies and gentlemen."

We said, "Okay." So we sang a little song and we danced. After we finished, Duke Ellington said, "Oh my, you boys are original."

I said, "Thank you, Mr. Ellington. You're original too." [*Laughter*]

TOR: How long did you work at the Cotton Club?

NICHOLAS: We were there for two years. We were kids. We didn't know about the gangsters who were running the Cotton Club. That was the only reason we could work there. We were two little guys, underage, on stage, and the first show at the Cotton Club was at midnight.

TOR: When did the phone ring to invite you guys to Hollywood?

NICHOLAS: Samuel Goldwyn saw us at the Cotton Club. He wanted us to be in a film with Eddie Cantor called *Kid Millions*. That was our first film in Hollywood, but we'd made some shorts for Warner Brothers in New York.

The first film we did was *Pie Pie Blackbird*, with Eubie Blake and his orchestra and Nina Mae McKinney. It was a half-hour short that we did while we were appearing at the Lafayette Theater.

TOR: How did you feel the first time you actually saw yourself up on the screen?

NICHOLAS: [*Raucous laughter*] Oh, that was real funny. My parents, my sister, my brother, and I went to the theater to see *Pie Pie Blackbird*. I'm watching it and I say to my parents, "I didn't know that I was that good." [*Laughter*] I liked what I saw.

TOR: What were some of the other short films that you did?

NICHOLAS: Oh, we did *The All Colored Vaudeville Show*, with Adelaide Hall, and another short called *The Black Network*. That one was with Nina Mae McKinney too.

TOR: Did Hollywood allow you guys to improvise or come up with steps yourselves? Or did you have to do whatever the choreographers said?

NICHOLAS: No, we didn't improvise. We'd make up a routine that we would do the same way every time. It seems as though every choreographer that we worked with never showed us anything. He'd just tell us where he wanted us to come from, how long it would be, where he wanted us to stand. I had to make up everything because a lot of these choreographers didn't dance. They would just talk about a routine.

TOR: You made quite a few films for Fox, besides *Stormy Weather*, what were they?

NICHOLAS: We were under contract to 20th Century–Fox, and made five movies for the studio before *Stormy Weather*. *Down Argentine Way*, *Tin Pan Alley*, *The Great American Broadcast*, *Sun Valley Serenade*, and *Orchestra Wives*. We made six films for 20th Century–Fox. Before Fox, we made films with all of the studios— Paramount, Columbia, United Artists, Warner Bros.

TOR: Tell me about working on *Stormy Weather*.

NICHOLAS: When we got there, we were wondering what song we were going to perform to. It was "Cocktail Rhythm." I think it was composed by Cab. It starts off with, "the Jim Jam Jump," then he says, "Iggly biggly boo," the band repeats, and he brings us on. We're in the audience and we jump up on this table. Then we jump off the table and go over and slap his hands, like, give him some skin. Then we go right into the dance.

TOR: Did you choreograph that routine also?

NICHOLAS: We choreographed it with Nick Castle Sr. He was the choreographer for most of the films we did.

TOR: He thought of it and you guys just did it?

NICHOLAS: Yeah, we just did it. [*Laughter*]

TOR: Did you look at him strange when he said, "I want one of you to jump off this step, do the splits, and then you jump over him, and do the splits"?

NICHOLAS: A lot of things we did, he knew we could do it. I remember one day, we were rehearsing this song with Glen Miller called "I've Got a Gal in Kalamazoo."

TOR: For the film *Orchestra Wives*?

NICHOLAS: Yes. We were rehearsing and Nick said, "Stop the music! I've got an idea!"

I said, "What is it?"

He said, "I've got an idea where you walk up the wall, do a back flip, and go into a split!"

I looked at him and said, "Are you crazy? What are you talking about?" Then I said, "Wait a minute, let me see you do it." [*Laughter*]

He said, "I can't do it! But I know you can!"

TOR: How many retakes did you have to do on the dance scene in *Stormy Weather*?

NICHOLAS: When we were coming down those stairs, we knew we were supposed to go up that platform and jump down over each other's heads, but we never rehearsed it. When it came time, Nick Castle said, "Don't rehearse it . . . just do it."

TOR: That was the one routine that the Nicholas Brothers didn't get to rehearse?

NICHOLAS: We knew what we were supposed to do! So, we went up on that platform and I jumped to the first step. Then my brother jumped over my head to the next step, and we kept this up until we reached the stage. Then the director yelled, "Cut! That's a print!"

Nick said, "You couldn't get it any better than that."

And I said, "Oh, happy day!" [*Laughter*]

That was in one take, just like you saw it. We only did it one time.

Home of the Brave
United Artists (1949)

"That sensitivity you've got! That's your disease!"
—Doc to Moss

In *Home of the Brave*, Moss is a black soldier during World War II. In preparation for an invasion, he and four white GIs volunteer for a reconnaissance mission to map out a Japanese-held South Pacific island. Once there Moss discovers that the Japanese may not be his only enemy. During the mission, he becomes paralyzed from the waist down and is sent to a hospital for treatment. An examination reveals no physical reasons for his paralysis, and the attending physician tries to get to the root cause of the black soldier's apparent "psychologically produced" trauma.

Through the application of narcosynthesis and regressive hypnosis, Moss eventually reveals his story to the doctor. Told mostly in flashback, the conflict starts the minute a black man reports for duty. We see and hear the initial resentment expressed by some of the other men, including the twenty-six-year-old major in charge, who calls his commanding officer to see if a mistake has been made. He quickly learns that the black soldier not only has the necessary skills and qualifications to do the job, but that he was the only engineer to volunteer for such a dangerous assignment. The other characters include Finch, an old high school buddy and basketball teammate of Moss's. He's unhindered by race and fairly protective of his dark-skinned chum until tensions on the island and questions of loyalty between the two swell to a boiling point. Corporal T.J. is a race-baiting bigot, constantly at odds with the mission's black engineer. Sergeant Mingo is the older, more battle-seasoned veteran of the team. With marital problems awaiting him at home, he tries to keep a lid on the simmering conflicts and attitudes and ensure that the maps get made.

The film skillfully marries the melodrama of war with a tense psychological mystery. We struggle to understand why this black soldier has returned from the mission in a state of paralysis. At first

In *Home of the Brave* GIs hit the beach to map out a Japanese-held island: left to right, Mingo (Frank Lovejoy), Finch (Lloyd Bridges), Moss (James Edwards), and T.J. (Steve Brodie). This was the first film to seriously address racism in the military. (United Artists)

we assume that it is the result of an injury, or of the racism he'd endured in the line of duty, but in the end we find out it's the fear of something much more universal.

Home of the Brave was the first in a series of what became known as "problem pictures" made between 1949 and 1952 that dealt with race prejudice. The others were Elia Kazan's *Pinky* (1949), Louis de Rochemont's *Lost Boundaries* (1950), and Clarence Brown's *Intruder in the Dust* (1952). Previous Hollywood films had

CREDITS: Director: Mark Robson. Producer: Stanley Kramer. Screenplay: Carl Foreman. From the play by Arthur Laurents. Photography: Robert Degrasse. Music: Dmitri Tiomkin. Editor: Harry Gerstad. Art Direction: Rudolph Sternad. Special Effects: J. R. Rabin. 88 minutes B&W. Drama.

CAST: James Edwards (*Moss*), Douglas Dick (*Maj. Robinson*), Steve Brodie (*T.J.*), Jeff Corey (*Doctor*), Lloyd Bridges (*Finch*), Frank Lovejoy (*Mingo*), Cliff Clark (*Colonel*).

commented on the problem on occasion, but had never seriously discussed the topic in such an honest and direct manner. More important, even with the vast number of military- and war-oriented films that had been produced up to this time, the role of the black soldier had been largely ignored.

The film script, by Carl Forman, was fashioned from a Broadway play by Arthur Laurents that was based on the theme of anti-Semitism. That Forman adapted the story without much change to the core resentment, conflicts, and hatred perpetrated against the protagonist shows the universality of the pain and anguish that the evils of prejudice can create, regardless of faith, religion, or skin color. Stanley Kramer, the film's producer, was well known for his hard-edged message films, which would eventually include *The Defiant Ones* (1958) and *Guess Who's Coming to Dinner?* (1967).

Review Summary: According to John Mason Brown of the *Saturday Review*, "When *Home of the Brave* was seen as a play on Broadway three seasons back, its central figure was a Jew. Now, he is a Negro. And the story, though otherwise unaltered, is strengthened by the change."

The film's directing, casting, and acting was applauded by most critics. In *Variety* Kahn said, "It hits hard and with utter credibility." Bosley Crowther wrote in the *New York Times*, "Well produced and intelligently directed by Mark Robson, *Home of the Brave* is a most propitious 'first' in the cycle of Negro-prejudice pictures which Hollywood now has in the works."

One of the few negatives rested with what some considered to be the film's lack of explanation of the main character's ultimate breakdown. According to a *Theater Arts* review, "The prejudice indulged in, and the sensitivity of Moss, seemed dramatically on a juvenile level." The critic argued that in real life Moss, played by James Edwards, probably would have been more prepared or better adjusted to deal with such racist acts. However, as John Mason Brown concludes, "One of the best features of *Home of the Brave* is that it does not preach tolerance and decency directly. It does not have to."

4

Society Profile: 1950–1959

The Coming of Color

By 1950 the black population of the United States had grown to approximately 15 million. New York and California ranked first and second as the states with the largest percentages. Educational accomplishments grew as significant numbers of blacks attended historically black colleges and universities. Nevertheless, there was a large income disparity, with blacks earning a mere 52 percent of the median income of whites.

The post–World War II era again brought the hope for racial progress and social change. Blacks had once again fought bravely overseas, but back home they were still not treated as full equals. Rapid industrialization and mechanization of the agricultural South began to force rural blacks to the cities, and many were being recognized for their great accomplishments. Gwendolyn Brooks won the Pulitzer Prize for *Annie Allen*, a semiautobiographical book of poetry; Ralph Bunche was awarded a Nobel Peace Prize for his work with the 1948 Arab-Israeli dispute; Juanita Hall became the first African American to receive a Tony Award for her performance in the Broadway musical *South Pacific*; and Sugar Ray Robinson knocked out Jake LaMotta to become the middleweight champion of the world.

Segregation and discrimination in the armed forces continued into the Korean conflict. By 1957, blacks made up over 13 percent of the U.S. armed forces, though 80 percent were still serving in all-black units. The majority of these were service support units, but black soldiers were fighting on the front lines as well. Private First Class William Thompson was posthumously honored for his bravery with a Congressional Medal of Honor, the first black to receive the medal since the Spanish-American War.

Many powerful books and plays were written by blacks in this decade. Ralph Ellison's *Invisible Man* won the 1952 National Book Award; James Baldwin's first novel, *Go Tell It on the Mountain*, was published in 1953, and Lorraine Hansberry's Broadway play, *A Raisin in the Sun*, won the 1959 New York Drama Critics' Circle Award.

In 1954, the U.S. Supreme Court's decision in *Brown* v. *Board of Education of Topeka* sent shock waves across the country when it ruled that racial segregation in public schools was unconstitutional. In its wake, most of the northern cities and much of the upper South moved toward school desegregation without violence. Unfortunately, the Deep South was another story. Defiance was often very violent. The Ku Klux Klan openly displayed its deadly opposition, and in the U.S. House of Representatives nearly one hundred congressmen, all from the South, denounced the *Brown* ruling through a "Southern Manifesto." In Little Rock, Arkansas, Governor Orval Faubus issued a series of court orders and personally acted to keep nine black students out of that city's Central High School. President Dwight D. Eisenhower was forced to order in the National Guard to enforce the desegregation plan and protect the students.

On December 1, 1955, Rosa Parks refused to give up her seat on a city bus to a white man. The driver had her arrested, and the Montgomery Bus Boycott was set in motion. The Reverend Martin Luther King Jr. became one of its organizers, and for 381 days more than fifty thousand blacks and others sympathetic to the cause walked, car pooled, or rode bikes and horses to get to work and move around the city. The bus company's profits fell by two-thirds, and many other business establishments lost money, as the Montgomery business community became frantic. The Supreme Court eventually ruled that segregation on buses was in violation of the Constitution. Despite this ruling, however, white opposition to social change would continue to flourish.

In the midst of the boycotts, sit-ins, and protests of the late 1950s, many blacks in the creative arts managed to move forward. Chuck Berry's "Maybelline" and Ray Charles's "I've Got a Woman" both became number-one hits, and Marian Anderson broke the color barrier as the first black to sing at the Metropolitan Opera in New York. Also, paralleling what he'd done on the radio, years before, Nat "King" Cole became the first black to host his own national television variety show. The Alvin Ailey Dance Company was organized in New York, and in Detroit, Berry Gordy Jr. formed Motown Records.

The Jackie Robinson Story

Eagle-Lion (1950)

"Every step forward for our people has started a
fight somewhere. This is a big thing you have to
decide. And not just for you alone. It's a big thing for
the whole colored people."

—Rev. Carter to Jackie Robinson

Jackie Robinson became an influential sports figure when he broke
one of the biggest color barriers in organized sports and became the
first Negro to play baseball in the major leagues. *The Jackie Robinson
Story* chronicles Robinson's life from his childhood to his unprece-
dented breakthrough as second baseman for the Brooklyn Dodgers.

The film begins with a patriotic narration over a group of kids
playing sandlot baseball. Two older white boys hit fly balls for the
younger boys to catch. At the edge of the field, one gloveless black
kid excitedly awaits his turn, but the balls never fly his way.

"How 'bout one?" the young Jackie yells out.

Brooklyn Dodgers owner
Branch Rickey (Minor
Watson) explains his "turn
the other cheek" strategy to
Jackie Robinson (himself) in
The Jackie Robinson Story.
(Eagle-Lion)

The older boys look at each other, and a devious grin crosses the batter's face. He slams a line drive (it's a hardball) directly into the black kid's bare hands. The young Jackie Robinson catches it without flinching, throws it back, and is ready for another. Again and again the batter hits powerful, bone-shattering line drives in the boy's direction, and each time Jackie proves he can take whatever they've got to give. A metaphorical setup, perhaps, but the would-be ballplayer ends up taking a lot more abuse before the film is over. Once the batter realizes the black kid's high level of skill and determination, he goes into the trunk of his car and gives Jackie a tattered old catcher's mitt. He goes from purposely trying to harm the boy to wanting to help. Later, similar scenarios develop where the white fans, and even his own white teammates, gradually turn from a hostile position to one of respect and acceptance.

The film is constructed as a series of biographical events that outline the development of Robinson's trailblazing career. It depicts his personal life with the people who loved him and kept him strong: his long-distance relationship with his sweetheart, Rae, who becomes his wife; his proud and supportive mother and his brother, Mack. As one of life's ironies, big brother Mack may actually have been a better all-around athlete than Jackie. The older Robinson was never given the opportunity, however, and had to settle for a "good job" as a city street sweeper.

Various scenes depict the rough and often rocky road that Jackie had to travel. Late one night, with a black barnstorming team, he is elected to enter a whites-only diner to see if they might be served. Tensions rise as the suspicious white patrons give him the evil eye, until the cook happily agrees to make up some sandwiches to go.

During his first day of training with the Montreal Royals, Jackie is ignored on the field, much as in the opening scene. Once again, his persistence and determination pay off. The lone black ballplayer endures a montage of jabs, gripes, and race-baited harassments, including racial slurs and epithets, followed by petitions, canceled

CREDITS: Director: Alfred E. Green. Producer: Mort Briskin. Screenplay: Lawrence Taylor, Arthur Mann. Photography: Ernest Laszlo. Editor: Arthur H. Nadel. 76 minutes. Drama. NR.

CAST: Jackie Robinson (*Himself*), Ruby Dee (*Rae Robinson*), Minor Watson (*Branch Rickey*), Louise Beavers (*Jackie's Mom*), Joel Fluellen (*Mack Robinson*), Richard Lane (*Hopper*), Harry Shannon (*Charlie*), Ben Lessy (*Shorty*), Bill Spaulding (*Self*), Billy Wayne (*Clyde Sukeforth*), Bernie Hamilton (*Ernie*), Kenny Washington (*Tigers' Manager*), Pat Flaherty (*Karpen*), Howard Louis MacNeely (*Young Jackie*), Lawrence Criner (*Rev. Carter*).

games, hangman's nooses, and a Ku Klux Klan welcoming committee lurking outside the locker-room door.

One of the most crucial and telling scenes occurs when Branch Rickey, president of the Brooklyn Dodgers, explains to Jackie exactly what he will be up against. Jackie asks him, "Mr. Rickey, do you want a ballplayer who's afraid to fight back?"

And Rickey responds. "I want a ballplayer with guts enough not to fight back!"

One of the most touching scenes takes place while Jackie's playing with Montreal. Some hecklers in the stands toss a black cat out on the field with a hangman's noose around its neck for a leash. Jackie angrily stalks toward them and they recoil in fear, thinking that the angry black man has finally had enough. But Jackie pays them no mind. He picks the cat up, carries it over to the dugout, and cares for it. He could take all that they were throwing at him, but he would not allow an innocent animal to be abused as part of his persecution.

The most influential aspect of the production was that Jackie Robinson actually played himself. This gives the film authenticity and makes it a historical document. We know that it is his story, and we accept and respect his courage, and stand in awe at his monumental achievement.

Review Summary: Many of the reviews were mixed. Ira Berkow of the *New York Times* asserted that *The Jackie Robinson Story* was a "limited film," and others expressed similar opinions. In *Commonweal* Philip Hartung complained of "stilted dialogue," while Robert Hatch of the *New Republic* found the film "dull and simplistic," and the *New York Times* implied that there was "too much campiness." A review from *Variety* simply stated that the picture was "not too well made." It also added that the director, Alfred E. Green, seems to have rushed the making of the film for reasons of commercial success. Some critics found the film to be commendable. The *Christian Century* said that it was "awkward, but also sincere." *Commonweal* also noted the film's appeal: "It is interesting that a new biographical film which was made on an inexpensive budget, and with a script that is no masterpiece of writing, succeeds so well in vivifying its main character and situation." Many reviews that were generally positive contended that *The Jackie Robinson Story* offered a good presentation of race issues, and that, as an actor, Jackie Robinson made the film genuine. Some noted that he did a good job, while others thought him too reserved.

Carmen Jones

20th Century-Fox (1954)

"The wind's blowin' me in another direction . . . ain't
no use arguing with the wind."

—Carmen to Sgt. Brown

Carmen Jones is a modernized version of *Carmen,* Georges Bizet's
nineteenth-century opera. Oscar Hammerstein turned the story into
an all-black, Broadway musical in 1943, and Twentieth Century–Fox
chief Darrell F. Zanuck contracted Otto Preminger to translate the
hit musical to the silver screen.

In this classic but modernized tale of romance, betrayal, and
tragedy Carmen is transformed from a cigarette factory worker into
a parachute factory worker during the war, the Spanish corporal
becomes a GI, and the toreador is morphed into a champion boxer.
When Carmen gets into a fight with one of her coworkers, she is
arrested, and Joe is the military policeman assigned to take her into
custody. On their way to the lockup, Carmen tries her best to
seduce Joe, but he thwarts her at every attempt. He has a sweetheart, Cindy Lou, and he's just a "true-blue" kind of a guy.

Everything changes when a fight with Sergeant Brown, his pain-
in-the-ass C.O., ends in tragedy and Joe is forced to go AWOL with
Carmen. He gives in to his desires and in time wants to possess
her totally. But the hot-to-trot vixen soon tires of Joe and his
"never-leave-the-room" sense of paranoia. While socializing at a
local roadhouse, Carmen catches the eye of Husky Miller, a popular prizefighter, and the doomed triangle begins. With encourage-
ment from her good friends Frankie and Myrt, Carmen joins Husky's
entourage, and they all take a train to Chicago. But the sun, fun,
and new scenery don't last long. A crazed Joe catches up with
Carmen at one of the pugilist's crowded prizefights, and as always,
the tragic mulatto must die.

The on-screen chemistry between Dandridge and Belafonte was
hot enough to melt the film's emulsion, and they became Hollywood's first black on-screen sex duo. The classic score was rich

Carmen (Dorothy Dandridge) is accosted by Joe (Harry Belafonte), her jilted lover in *Carmen Jones*. Dandridge would receive an Academy Award nomination for her fiery performance. (© 1954 Courtesy of 20th Century-Fox Film Corporation. All rights reserved.)

and powerful. Songs like Carmen's "I Go for You, but You're Taboo," Husky's "Stand Up and Fight," and Frankie's "Beat Out That Rhythm on the Drums," take Bizet's music and Hammerstein's lyrics to a different level altogether. The film took the 1955 Golden Globe Award for Best Film: Musical/Comedy and was nominated for Best Original Score at the 1954 Academy Awards.

CREDITS: Producer-Director: Otto Preminger. Screenplay: Harry Kleiner. From a book by Oscar Hammerstein. Photography: Sam Leavitt. Editor: Louis R. Loefler. Music: Georges Bizet. Lyrics: Oscar Hammerstein. 105 minutes. Musical. NR.

CAST: Dorothy Dandridge (*Carmen Jones*), Harry Belafonte (*Joe*), Olga James (*Cindy Lou*), Pearl Bailey (*Frankie*), Diahann Carroll (*Myrt*), Roy Glenn (*Rum*), Nick Stewart (*Dink*), Joe Adams (*Husky Miller*), Brock Peters (*Sgt. Brown*), Sandy Lewis (*T-Bone*), Mauri Lynn (*Sally*), DeForest Covan (*Trainer*), with the singing voices of Le Vern Hutcherson, Marilynn Horne, and Marvin Hayes.

Dorothy Dandridge earned an Academy Award nomination for Best Actress, the first ever for a black woman. A well-publicized behind-the-scenes story is that Otto Preminger, the film's director, initially rejected Dandridge for being too much of a classy, pretty girl. When she returned the next day, in costume and in character, she not only won the part but some of his personal time and interest as well.

Review Summary: The critics had mainly positive things to say about *Carmen Jones*, from its exciting musical score to the fluid direction and staging. Although it was regarded as pure commercial packaging, most critics gave the movie a thumbs-up.

Dorothy Dandridge is often cited for her outstanding performance as Carmen. In *Commonweal*, Philip Hartung described her as "a vital, hip-swinging, sensational beauty whose fiery acting style makes her one of the most vivid Carmens of our day."

Jay Carr of the *Boston Globe* wrote, "Dandridge looks terrific! Sashaying across the screen with sexual confidence, commanding any space she occupies."

Variety called Preminger's direction "a deft touch, blending the comedy and tragedy easily, and building his scenes to some suspenseful heights." Moria Walsh of *America* said the movie was "a happy wedding of sight and sound combined with Preminger's fluid staging, the caliber of the music itself, and Hammerstein's pungent and colloquial lyrics."

In *Commentary*, well-known black writer James Baldwin expressed a very different take on the film, protesting that the characters' singing sounded "ludicrously false and affected, like antebellum Negroes imitating their masters." Baldwin also reminded viewers that the movie made an important statement, because it related "less to Negroes than to the interior life of Americans."

St. Louis Blues

Paramount Pictures (1958)

"There's only two kinds of music in the world. The
Devil's and the Lord's!"

—Rev. Charles Handy to church choir

St. Louis Blues is based on the life and the music of composer W. C.
Handy (1873–1958). Handy became known as the father of jazz
music, the only true art form to have originated in America.

The son of a strict, "fire and brimstone" preacher, Handy had a
hard way to go. As a child, he played organ for church services
and would add a few upbeat riffs that came naturally to his finger-
tips. The young Handy would be harshly reprimanded by his father
and scolded for bringing the devil's music into the House of the
Lord.

The natural beats and rhythms of the world give inspiration to
the aspiring musician. The chants of the laboring dockworkers and
the sounds of horse hooves clapping against the dusty ground help
to develop Handy's unique sense of timing. He saves up 250 pennies to buy the horn he sees in a pawn shop window, only to be
devastated when his father hurls it beneath the wheels of a moving
wagon. When the horn is crushed, so are the young musician's
dreams. We flash forward. Handy returns home from college with
plans to fulfill his father's high hopes for him. He becomes a
teacher, but is quickly fed up with giving piano lessons at twenty-
five cents a pop, while deep inside, his music begs to come out.

One night he goes into a nightclub where the voluptuous GoGo
Germaine is rehearsing. He plays some of his music for her.
Impressed, she gets Blade, the club's owner, to hire him. This brings
serious conflict into the Handy home, as well as concern and uncer-
tainty from Elizabeth, Handy's fiancée, in regard to the extent of his
relationship with the nightclub singer. The tug-of-war between the
musician's sense of right and wrong is unbearable, and as he tor-
ments himself, he loses his eyesight. Now blind, Handy feels that he

W. C. Handy (Nat "King" Cole), the father of jazz music, experiences temporary blindness as Elizabeth (Ruby Dee) leads the way in *St. Louis Blues*. (Paramount Pictures)

is being punished for the music he has created, and as a show of repentance, he returns to the church. Meanwhile, GoGo has traveled the country performing and recording his music. Its popularity explodes onto the American culture, and its influence is felt, absorbed, and adopted by countless other musicians. Finally, GoGo performs Handy's music in a special concert at Carnegie Hall, where it is welcomed and recognized as the original musical art form that it is.

The film's all-star cast was lead by Nat "King" Cole as William C. Handy. Already a popular singer and songwriter, Cole had been

CREDITS: Director: Allen Reisner. Producer: Robert Smith. Screenplay: Robert Smith, Ted Shereman. 93 minutes. B&W. NR.

CAST: Nat "King" Cole (*W. C. Handy*), Eartha Kitt (*GoGo Germaine*), Pearl Bailey (*Aunt Hagar*), Cab Calloway (*Blade*), Ella Fitzgerald (*Herself*), Mahalia Jackson (*Bessie Mae*), Ruby Dee (*Elizabeth*), Juano Hernandez (*Charles Handy*), Billy Preston (*Young Handy*).

previously featured with his musical trio in the films *Killer Diller* (1947) and *China Gate* (1957). He'd played himself in *The Nat King Cole Story* (1955), and years after his leading role in *St. Louis Blues*, would play a strolling minstrel in *Cat Ballou* (1965).

Eartha Kitt, who portrays the sultry and talented GoGo Germaine, would go on to perform on stage, in television, and in other films. She would star in *Anna Lucasta* (1959) opposite Sammy Davis Jr., and become internationally known as "The Cat Woman" in the 1960s television series *Batman*.

Pearl Bailey was Aunt Hagar. She began her career singing with the Cootie Williams and Count Basie big bands, and had made her stage debut in the play *St. Louis Woman* in 1946. Her other film roles include *Carmen Jones* (1954), *That Certain Feeling* (1956), *Porgy and Bess* (1959), *All the Fine Young Cannibals* (1960), and *The Landlord* (1970).

Cab Calloway, as Blade, played the overbearing nightclub owner in a straight, dramatic fashion. It was a far cry from his usual scat-daddy "hi-de-ho" musical performances in movies like *Stormy Weather* (1943), and his many musical film shorts.

Billy Preston, who played the young Handy (and the organ rather well, too), would grow up to have a successful music career of his own with hit records such as "With You, I'm Born Again," and "Will It Go 'Round in Circles?"

Review Summary: The film received generally mixed reviews, and a number of critics were not pleased with it. Leonard Feather, in the *Los Angeles Times*, complained that it was "a patronizing biography of composer W. C. Handy. The cardboard characters were given dialogue to match." Jack Garner, of the *Gannett News Service*, called it "dramatically suspect with great musical performances."

As for the story line, Bosley Crowther wrote in *Variety*, "It is really a rather silly, tedious notion of emotional conflict that Robert Smith and Ted Shereman have used for the core of their screenplay and it is presented with neither style nor subtlety." As for the music, Crowther continued, "Some fairly well done musical numbers are few and far between, and add up to a piteous accounting of the works of W. C. Handy, and the oldtime Memphis jazzland atmosphere."

The film's title, taken from Handy's most famous song, was originally used as a film title in 1929 for a twenty-minute short film featuring blues singer Bessie Smith.

RUBY DEE

By phone from Emmalyn II Productions Offices
New Rochelle, New York
July 12, 2000

TOR: How did you land the role of Elizabeth in *St. Louis Blues*?

DEE: I forget who asked me to do it, but what I had been doing in several films was working with people who were not actors. Like Joe Lewis, Jackie Robinson, and like Nat Cole, who was basically a singer. Maybe I was called to do the film because I didn't have such a strong, overwhelming personality of my own in those days. I really was just sort of in the story to push the plot along and be the romantic interest.

TOR: What was it like being on the set?

DEE: I remember I was just fascinated doing this part with Nat because he was a singer and a musician, and of course my life sort of revolved around actors. Although I knew a lot of singers, I wasn't one who was deep into music. I was fascinated by his celebrity, and being around people like Pearl Bailey, Mahalia Jackson, Eartha Kitt, and all of the music type people.

TOR: So how did Nat Cole do as an actor?

DEE: He did very well. I liked him. I liked his simplicity. He seemed like the "real deal." I could believe him in the role.

TOR: So he gave you what you needed to play off of him?

DEE: Well, I didn't need anything, but for the director to be happy. [*Laughter*] And to not get in Nat's way. That's about all . . . and to be supportive.

TOR: Even though he was a singer, did his acting just come naturally?

DEE: I just remember that the director was always making suggestions about what he should do with his hands: Nat was a pianist, and so when he was singing he would play for himself—just being a singer was something that came to him later.

TOR: What was it like working with Eartha Kitt?

DEE: Oh, I just loved it. I loved her because she was so flamboyant [*Laughter*] and musical. She seemed so very sure of herself. She could command the atmosphere, and I liked that about her.

TOR: It seemed like her character, GoGo Jermaine, could be very intimidating.

DEE: Oh, I used to love the way she would walk around the set and ask for this and that and make known what she had to have. I just thought it was wonderful. Now they'd call her a diva, I guess, but then they used other words. [*Laughter*] And I said, oh, my goodness . . . oh, to be a diva. . . . oh, to be a bitch! It's so exciting and so marvelous. The set came alive when Eartha was around.

TOR: Did you have any scenes with Cab Calloway?

DEE: No. But I did get a chance to meet him on many occasions, because he lived up on Westchester. At events and benefits, Ossie and I would often bump into Cab.

The musicians, you know, were the aristocracy of the arts. The music people have a certain self-assurance that I really admired. They were accepted for what they did, and they set standards.

TOR: How influential do you think that film was in illuminating the importance of W. C. Handy's music and getting it out to a broader audience?

DEE: Oh, I just think it was wonderful that somebody saw fit to do it. And that Nat was chosen to be Handy. I don't know how to really measure stuff like that, but my own assessment was that people wanted to know about the author who had written so many popular songs.

5

Society Profile: 1960–1969

A Separate Cinema

The 1960s began with the Voting Rights Act in full effect. President Dwight D. Eisenhower had signed the bill in 1957, but there was still much open opposition to blacks exercising their right to vote. In the wake of this and other widespread racial discrimination, the momentum of the civil rights movement of the 1950s spawned the Black Power movement of the 1960s, which shifted emphasis from the concept of nonviolent resistance to "freedom by any means necessary."

The median income for blacks had risen to 55 percent, even though their unemployment rate was twice as high as that of their white counterparts. Police brutality was common, and racism was still a major factor in black-white relationships.

The years 1960–1975 would become known as the Vietnam War era. At least 16 percent of the young men drafted were black, yet blacks made up only 11 percent of the nation's population. In this war, however, blacks would train, fight, and die side by side with whites in a fully integrated army. By this time, 73 percent of black Americans were living in big cities, and the term "black urbanization" became a catch-all phrase for deteriorating inner-city ghettos. At least 75 percent of the working blacks in the cities held menial jobs, and despite being employed, they were still among the nation's poorest citizens.

Some progress had been made through *Brown* v. *Board of Education*, which had ruled in 1954 that school segregation was unconstitutional, but many problems remained. In some places the level of education for black children was three years behind that of white children, and most schools in the South were still segregated.

Some of the most promising achievements for blacks in the

1960s came in the realms of sports and politics. While the rest of the country battled hatred and injustice here at home, at the 1960 Olympiad in Rome, Italy, many black athletes were battling fierce competition in track and field, and ten black champions brought home medals for the United States.

Wilma Rudolph brought home three gold medals, including the hundred-meter, Rafer Johnson won the gold in the decathlon, and Cassius Clay in boxing. Clay would later change his name to Muhammad Ali and become one of the greatest and most charismatic heavyweight champions of all time. These three triumphant Olympians would later be honored and recognized in film and television as well. Wilma Rudolph's accomplishments would be heralded in the made-for-television movie *Wilma* (1977). Rafer Johnson would act in several films, including *Sergeant Rutledge* (1960), where he played a Buffalo Soldier. Ali would play himself in the autobiographical film, *The Greatest* (1977).

In politics, Andrew Hatcher became the highest-ranking black federal employee as President John F. Kennedy's associate press secretary. Thurgood Marshall, chief counsel for the NAACP, was appointed to the U.S. Supreme Court, and on Capitol Hill, the number of blacks elected to congress was up to fourteen.

Blacks were also busy in the world of entertainment. Harry Belafonte was the first to win an Emmy for his television special, *Tonight With Harry Belafonte* in 1960, and three years later Sidney Poitier became the first black to win the Best Actor Oscar for his role in *Lilies of the Field* (1963). James Earl Jones earned a Tony Award for his portrayal of boxing champion Jack Johnson in the Broadway play *The Great White Hope*, and comedian Bill Cosby landed a costarring role on the television series *I Spy*. Cosby would win an Emmy for Best Actor in a dramatic series.

On August 28, 1963, more than 250,000 concerned Americans participated in a massive civil rights march on Washington. From a podium at the base of the Lincoln Memorial, Dr. Martin Luther King Jr. delivered his famous "I Have a Dream" speech. While it was a high point of hope for serious change, this triumph of the spirit was followed by the bombing of the Sixteenth Street Baptist Church in Birmingham, Alabama. The church was a key meeting place for civil rights and voting rights advocates, and four little black girls attending Sunday school were killed. This horrendous event marked a major turning point for the civil rights movement. On March 7, 1965, more than 700 people attempted to march from Selma to the state capital in Montgomery to protest continued resistance to the voting rights laws. Despite their peaceful intent many were tear-gassed, beaten, and arrested by Alabama state troopers, and one was killed.

Black Muslim leader Malcolm X separated from the Nation of Islam to form the Organization of Afro-American Unity. While on a holy pilgrimage to Mecca, he had seen a profound and different light, and he returned to America fighting for "human rights" rather than "civil rights," arguing that hatred would not bring about the peace and freedom that he sought. The following year, he was assassinated as he spoke at the Audubon Ballroom in Harlem. Some of the many films portraying Malcolm's life are Woodie King Jr.'s docudrama, *Malcolm X: Death of a Prophet* (1991), Spike Lee's *Malcolm X* (1992) with Denzel Washington as El Hajj Malik El Shabazz, and Orlando Bagwell's documentary *Malcolm X: Make It Plain* (1994).

Despite the eventual passage of the Civil Rights and Voting Rights acts by Congress, the country was in a state of racial chaos. Riots erupted in Chicago, Cleveland, Watts, Newark, Harlem, and Boston. In 1968, rejecting the "turn-the-other-cheek" politics of some black leaders, the Black Panther Party was formed in Oakland, California. The goal of its founders, Huey P. Newton and Bobby Seale, was to bring about a revolutionary change in the adverse conditions affecting black people in the United States.

The Kerner Commission Report on Civil Disorders warned that America was rapidly becoming two societies, one black, one white, both separate and unequal.

As the 1960s came to a close, the Reverend Dr. Martin Luther King Jr. was assassinated on April 4, 1968, as he stood on a motel balcony in Memphis, Tennessee.

Sergeant Rutledge

Warner Bros. (1960)

"Yeah, it was all right for Mr. Lincoln to say we were
free, but that ain't so! Not yet. Maybe someday, but
not yet!"

—Sergeant Rutledge to Lieutenant Cantrell

Sergeant Rutledge was brought to our attention only after we had
begun work on this book. Our list had already been made, but
once we saw *Sergeant Rutledge* on the American Movie Classics
cable channel, we decided to add it to our selections.

The film tells the story of a Buffalo soldier from the all-black
Ninth Cavalry unit who has been charged with the rape and double
murder of a white girl and her officer father. Wise enough not to
wait around and try to convince authorities that he didn't do it, he
goes AWOL, but is eventually captured and brought back in chains
to face the charges.

The events are told in flashback through the various eyewitness
reports during the court martial. As the events are replayed through
these individual testimonies, we slowly get the picture of what actually happened. We know Rutledge is not guilty, but we constantly
wonder who is.

One witness is Mary Beecher, who has just returned to the area
after a twelve-year absence. She has arrived late at night and her
father is not at the train station to meet her. But Rutledge is there,
wounded, and all alone. The stationmaster has been killed by renegade Indians, who might still be in the area. She and he make it
through a turbulent night until Lieutenant Cantrell, Rutledge's commanding officer, tracks him down to bring him in. Another witness
is Skidmore, who is part of the search party. He's an older, battle-
weary soldier who asks his comrade, "If you didn't do it, why did
you run?" And the answer is simple. As an ex-slave, Rutledge knows
that when a black man is confronted with the rape and murder of
a white woman, the truth and the facts don't mean a thing; his

Lieutenant Cantrell (Jeffrey Hunter, left) and Captain Shattuck (Carleton Young, right) debate the guilt or innocence of buffalo soldier Sgt. Braxton Rutledge (Woody Strode, center). (Warner Bros.)

accusers would have lynched first and not even thought about asking questions. When the real killer is finally rooted out, Rutledge returns to his position as "top soldier" of his unit.

The film is very much about the cavalry, the soldier's code of conduct, and doing things "by the book." There are some exciting battle scenes between the Buffalo Soldiers and the band of renegade Indians, and just the hint of a love story between Cantrell and Beecher, but it's more of a vehicle than a destination.

CREDITS: Director: John Ford. Screenplay: James Bellah. Willis Goldbeck. Producers: John Ford, Willis Goldbeck, Patrick Ford. 111 minutes. Western. NR.

CAST: Woody Strode (*Sgt. Braxton Rutledge*), Jeffrey Hunter (*Lt. Tom Cantrell*), Constance Towers (*Mary Beecher*), Carleton Young (*Captain Shattuck*), Juano Hernandez (*Sgt. Matthew Lake Skidmore*), Willis Bouchey (*Col. Otis Fosgate*), Billie Burke (*Mrs. Cordelia Fosgate*), Fred Libby (*Chandler Hubble*), Toby Richards (*Lucy Dabney*), Judson Pratt (*Lieutenant Mulgreen*), Bill Henry (*Captain Dwyer*).

Encouraged by the success of *The Defiant Ones* (1958), which featured Sidney Poitier and Tony Curtis as chained fugitives on the run, Hollywood was drifting back to the idea of the black "problem" picture. Willis Goldbeck, an accomplished writer-director, came up with the idea of combining a race theme with a western, and *Sergeant Rutledge* was born.

Veteran director John Ford was well known for his "John Wayne" westerns, and though it was said that he had a genuine sympathy for the civil rights struggle, his own racial tolerance was occasionally called into question. His films often depicted American Indians as bloodthirsty savages and African Americans as lovable, lazy coons. Warner Bros. prescreened *Sergeant Rutledge* for several civil rights groups and received positive responses, but the picture was marketed as a "story of suspense" instead of an "action-packed western" and did poorly when released.

Despite its failure at the box office, the film's star, Woody Strode, received unanimous accolades and acclaim. While much respect has been paid to the dignified roles of blacks at the time as played by Sidney Poitier, and rightly so, when it comes to the honest celebration of powerful and positive images of black men in film, Woody Strode too often has been overlooked. One of the most powerful single images of a black man ever filmed has to be the shot of Rutledge, standing guard on a desert hillside, carbine in hand, illuminated by the flickering campfire. His proud, statuesque form embodies the lyrics being sung by his men about the legend of Captain Buffalo, an incarnation of the strongest and finest in the tradition of the black soldier: "Said the Private to the Sergeant, 'Tell me, Sergeant, if you can. Did you ever see a mountain come a-walking like a man?' Said the Sergeant to the Private, 'You're a rookie, ain't you, though? Or you'd be a-recognizing Captain Buffalo.' "

Years later, Strode would admit that he never got over the role he played in Sergeant Rutledge. "It had dignity," he said. "You never seen a Negro come off a mountain like John Wayne before."

Review Summary: "I hope no one shows this movie to Martin Luther King," Robert Hatch wrote in the *Nation*, not because he considered it a bad movie, but because the ending was so patronizing and trite. So go most reviews of *Sergeant Rutledge*; critics loved it and they hated it.

As a John Ford film, the movie was given the benefit of the doubt in most cases. In *Commonweal* Philip Hartung wrote, "As a movie, *Sergeant Rutledge* is uneven, with some suspenseful courtroom scenes, some very exciting battle sequences, and some character sketches that only pad the running time. But for its eloquent plea for justice for a minority group, *Sergeant Rutledge* deserves both attention and applause." In the *New York Times Film Reviews*, Howard Thompson called it "a good picture, thoughtful, well acted, biting, interesting and stimulating."

According to Don Thompson in *McGill's Survey of Cinema*, "*Sergeant Rutledge* is certainly not one of Ford's masterworks; only Strode's personification of the noble Rutledge and Burke's superb performance as the flighty Mrs. Fosgate are of much interest. The film is worthy of attention, however, because it deals courageously with a problem as old as America itself."

A Raisin in the Sun

Columbia Pictures (1961)

"Now you say after me! In my mother's house. There
is still God!"

—Lena to Beneatha

A Raisin in the Sun is a rich and introspective film that delves deep
into the hearts and minds of its characters. Based on Lorraine
Hansberry's Broadway play of the same title, it was called "multi-
movement cinema" at the time of its release because of its vast
array of timely and culturally diverse topics.

Walter Lee Younger is a man with dreams. He is a chauffeur
for a wealthy white doctor, but he needs more out of life and
craves the opportunity to get it. He lives in a two-bedroom, second-
floor apartment with his wife, son, mother, and sister, with barely
enough room to breathe.

"I tell you I gotta change my life because I'm choking to death,
and all you say to me is 'eat these eggs,'" he says to his hard-
working wife, Ruth. She's also tired of being stuck in the same old
rut, but has more tolerant and realistic ideas about how to get out.

Walter Lee's sister, Beneatha, is a fresh, energetic medical student in search of love, social status, and her self-identity. Vying for
her time and her heart are two male college students, each cut from
a different cloth. George Murchison is an upper-class preppy type in
what Walter Lee calls "faggoty white shoes." Joseph Asagai is the
proud African who wants to whisk her away to his homeland as
one of his wives. "There is but one true feeling that a man need
have for a woman, and that I have for you," he tells her. But
Beneatha is not about to give up her life, or her independence, to
become part of anybody's harem.

Lena Younger is the strong, stoic matriarch of the family. She's
waiting for a $10,000 check from her deceased husband's insurance
settlement. Lena plans to use the money to move her family out of
their South Side Chicago tenement and into a house where every-

The Younger family, left to right, Ruth (Ruby Dee), Lena (Claudia McNeil), Beneatha (Diana Sands), and Walter Lee (Sidney Poitier), grapple with the difficulties of making a better life for themselves in *A Raisin in the Sun*, based on Lorraine Hansberry's award-winning stage play. (Columbia Pictures)

CREDITS: Director: Daniel Petrie. Producers: David Susskind, Phillip Rose. Screenplay: Lorraine Hansberry. Based on her stage play. 127 minutes. Drama. NR.

CAST: Sidney Poitier (*Walter Lee Younger*), Claudia McNeil (*Lena Younger*), Ruby Dee (*Ruth Younger*), Diana Sands (*Beneatha Younger*), Ivan Dixon (*Joseph Asagai*), John Fiedler (*Mark Linder*), Louis Gossett (*George Murchison*), Stephen Perry (*Travis*), Joel Fluellen (*Bobo*), Roy Glenn (*Willie Harris*).

one will have his own room, and she can plant a garden in the backyard. When she finally finds her dream house, it's in an all-white neighborhood where she is not wanted. Regardless, the family makes plans to move.

When the check comes, Walter Lee usurps the money to invest in a liquor store with two friends, Bobo and Willie. The deal falls through, and Walter's dreams, along with Lena's trust in her son, are dashed. Down but not out, Walter Lee comes up with a solution, and in doing so regains his self-respect and his dignity in the eyes of his family.

All the actors, with the exception of the young son, brought their characters from the Broadway stage to the screen. As an ensemble cast, they encompass so many authentic dreams, fears, beliefs, and values that you can't help but feel that at least one is speaking directly to you or for you. They reach, fall, bounce, clash, and rebound from their failures and disappointments only to dream again.

If hope, faith, determination, and self-redemption are somehow the keys to a better life, then *A Raisin in the Sun* could be a how-to guide for success.

Review Summary: Many critics discussed how difficult it is to transform theater-based performances into motion pictures. "In all fairness," Arthur Knight noted, "*A Raisin in the Sun* was the exception to such a rule." As the theatrical format was followed in the film, critics debated about whether the shift was effective. Stanley Kauffman in the *New Republic* called the script "commonplace" and "occasionally ludicrous," but said the film performances were "excellent." According to Philip Hartung in *Commonweal*, it was highly dramatic that almost all the action takes place in a three-room Chicago flat so that the audience could "feel the discomforts and indignities of five people living too close together in cramped, sunless quarters [where] the effect is too confining."

Many reviews discussed the strong thematic content Hansberry covered in the film, noting that *A Raisin in the Sun* presented complicated and controversial ideas that touched the audience and generated love rather than hate. *Time* wrote that Hansberry's script "has the towering merit of presenting the Negro not as a theatrical stereotype, or a social problem, but as an all-too-human being."

Black Like Me

Continental Distribution Co. (1964)

"Take away a man's identity . . . his face, his color . . .
what's left?"

—John Horton to his wife

Someone once said, "If people knew what it felt like to be on the
other side of a situation, they wouldn't do to other people some of
the ugly things that they do." *Black Like Me* takes this statement to
heart; it crosses that line and goes beyond the barriers to actually
experience what life is like on the other side.

The story is based on a highly successful book by John Howard
Griffin, a white novelist who, with the help of a drug, turned his

After darkening his skin to research a story from the other side of race relations,
journalist John Finley Horton (James Whitmore) hides from white thugs in *Black
Like Me*. (Continental Distributing Co.)

skin black and traveled the South under an assumed identity to experience racial prejudice firsthand. As a black man, "John Finley Horton" finds himself harassed by a bus driver, chased by two white thugs for no apparent reason, discriminated against when trying to find work, and he comes up against a white lady in a ticket booth with the meanest "hate stare" you'd *never* want to see. He painstakingly discovers the knowledge that he seeks, and experiences the troubling reality of being black in America.

The film plays out in a series of encounters that John has while on his journey, and his conversations with the various black people he meets are real and insightful. There's Bert, the bootblack, who tutors him in the art of passing for black; Bill Mason, a Good Samaritan, who warns him of "what a mess of trouble may be had by just looking too hard at a white woman," even if she's on a billboard advertisement; Mrs. Townsend, the owner of a local diner, who informs him that mankind originated in Africa—"they didn't bear us . . . we bore them!" she tells him. Frank Newcome, an older gentleman who invites John into his home, is well aware of the degradation that's been perpetrated against his people, but reasons that "If blacks hated white people, we would be dragged down to their level, and ruined for sure."

At a low point, when he's about ready to give up, John goes to see Eli, a white, liberal publisher and friend. In disbelief, he says to him, "I don't know how they've stood it all their lives." And Eli calmly replies: "It's simple. They have no choice."

The film marked the directorial debut of Carl Lerner, who was a film editor in New York, and he collaborated on the screenplay with his wife, Gerda, a historian. One of the most interesting aspects of the film is the device of the recurring shots of the white divider lines going down the middle of the road. They pop up here

---

CREDITS: Director: Carl Lerner. Producer: Julius Tannenbaum. Screenplay: Carl and Gerda Lerner. Based on the book by John Howard Griffin. Photography: Victor Lukens, Henry Mueller II. Editor: Lora Hayes. Music: Meyer Kupferman. 107 minutes. Drama. NR.

CAST: James Whitmore (*John Finley Horton*), Lenka Petersen (*Lucy Horton*), Dan Priest (*Bus Driver*), Walter Mason (*Mason*), John Marriott (*Hodges*), Clifton James (*Eli Carr*), Roscoe Lee Brown (*Christophe*), Sorrelt Booke (*Dr. Jackson*), Richard Ward (*Burt Wilson*), Stanley Brock (*Salesman*), Will Geer (*Farmer*), David Huddleston (*Man in Car*), Thelma Oliver (*Georgie*), Robert Gerringer (*Ed Saunders*), Sarah Cunningham (*Mary Saunders*), Eva Jessye (*Mrs. Townsend*), P. J. Sidney (*Frank Newcomb*), Al Freeman Jr. (*Tom Newcomb*), Ralph Dunn (*Priest*).

and there as John takes the bus or hitchhikes from town to town, and in the end, rich in experience, his skin almost back to normal, we see him walk across that white divider line and back to "his side" of the street.

Review Summary: The critics were not kind to *Black Like Me*. Many thought it a hodgepodge of events that did not hang together well. James Harrison of *Christian Century* suggested that the movie's major flaws were rooted in the book: first, that it was impossible for "Horton" to really know how African Americans feel because he could go back to being white anytime he chose. And second, that without the experience of growing up and being nurtured in black culture, Horton did not have the emotional defenses or the determination of a black person. Harrison added that the film fell short of helping its audience to feel what goes on in the heart of the Negro, who lives in a society that does not fully accept him. But despite a predominantly negative review, he concluded that the movie was "worth seeing."

Carl Lerner, the film's director, received countless criticisms about the film's casting, its documentary style, and its staging. In The *New Republic*, Stanley Kauffmann wrote that Lerner's film was "slickly made, preachy, and false." In the *Saturday Review*, Hollis Alpert said the screenplay "turned to caricature what might have been vastly compelling."

James Whitmore, a good actor, was apparently considered not well suited for the role. Several critics mentioned that his black coloring looked phony and that his acting seemed staged. Bosley Crowther of the *New York Times* called his performance "ponderous and overzealous."

Nothing but a Man

Nothing but a Man Company (1964)

"You've been stoopin' so long, Reverend, you don't
know how to stand straight anymore . . . you're just
half a man."

—Duff Anderson to Rev. Dawson

When it comes to rich, black stories on film, the independently produced *Nothing but a Man* exudes a quiet dignity. It tells a simple
story of Duff Anderson, a railroad section hand who falls in love
with Josie, a schoolteacher in a small southern town. Despite his
coworker's ridicule and their advice against it, he leaves his good-
paying, always-on-the-road job and tries to settle down.

As if wrapping up loose ends, Duff goes into Birmingham to
look up his estranged father. Will Anderson is a bitter, one-armed
drunk who has apparently never shown his son any love. He lets
Duff know that he has little respect for the institution of marriage,
and despite the support shown to him by Lee, his caring mistress,
Will seems to have no respect for her or women in general. On his
way back out of town, Duff stops in to see about his own illegiti-
mate son and finds that he has been virtually abandoned by his
mother and left to live in squalor with relatives. Not really sure that
the child is even his son, Duff leaves money for the boy's care and
promises to send more.

Now married, Duff takes a job at a local mill that openly takes
advantage of its black workers. It's a good job, but he's labeled a
troublemaker when he suggests to his coworkers that they should
"stick together." One of the men blabs, and when put to the test,
Duff chooses to walk away rather than recant his statement. He
searches for another job, only to find he's been blacklisted. As the
pressure mounts, Duff questions the choices he's made. Leaving the
railroad, falling in love, getting married, and standing up for his
beliefs—all the things he should be proud of are now bringing him
grief.

His father-in-law, a prominent preacher who is always out to keep the racial peace, arranges a job for Duff at a local gas station. He works hard and does his job, but when he doesn't "Yah-suh, boss" and grin in the face of an overbearing white customer, he is labeled "uppity." The unhappy customer returns with a few of his friends, and they threaten to burn the gas station down unless Duff is fired. He is out of work again. Josie informs him that she is pregnant, and it all becomes too much. He packs his things and leaves with a smug "Like I said, baby, I'll write you," and heads off to Birmingham. But life in the big city is no better. Will has been on a drinking binge and becomes very ill. Duff acknowledges the painful emptiness of their relationship and realizes that it's too late for them, but that he doesn't have to repeat the past. He goes to collect his son and returns to Josie. Unsure of what lies ahead, Duff's ready to face his responsibilities like the man that he is.

Nothing but a Man is an inspiring film that radiates pride and warns against the death of the spirit. It's a dark, solemn film, and very few of the characters ever laugh or even smile. Yet the strength and subtleness of the performances all somehow ring true. Despite the invisible chains of fear and accommodation that seek to hold him in bondage, Duff Anderson is too strong-willed and determined not to succeed.

Michael Roemer and Robert Young, TV documentarists and former Harvard classmates, made the film with $230,000 and a six-person crew. Along with Robert Rubin, they not only produced the film, but also served as its director, cameraman, and sound recordist. The production was shot in New Jersey, and the terse, documentary look and feel of the film adds to its authenticity. It debuted at the Venice Film Festival as the only American film in competition, where it won the Prix San Giorgio and the City of Venice Prize.

CREDITS: Director: Michael Roemer. Producers: Michael Roemer, Robert Young, Robert Rubin. Screenplay: Michael Roemer, Robert Young. 92 minutes. B&W. NR.

CAST: Ivan Dixon (*Duff Anderson*), Abby Lincoln (*Josie Dawson*), Julius Harris (*Will Anderson*), Gloria Foster (*Lee*), Martin Priest (*Driver*), Leonard Parker (*Frankie*), Yaphet Kotto (*Jocko*), Stanley Greene (*Rev. Dawson*). Helen Lounck (*Effie Sims*), Helene Arrindell (*Doris*), Walter Wilson (*Car Owner*), Milton Williams (*Pop*), Melvin Stewart (*Riddick*).

Former roaming railroad worker Duff Anderson (Ivan Dixon) and Josie Dawson (Abby Lincoln) share a happy newlywed moment in the powerful, independently produced *Nothing but a Man*. (Courtesy of the Academy of Motion Picture Arts and Sciences)

Initially, Young sent the script to Sidney Poitier, who turned it down. But Ivan Dixon merged into the role of Duff Anderson as if it were written for him, winning the Best Black Actor Award at the First World Festival of Negro Arts. Previously, Dixon had portrayed the role of Joseph Asagai, the African student in love with Beneatha Younger, in both the Broadway stage play and film version of Lorraine Hansberry's *Raisin in the Sun*. He is perhaps best known for his role as Communications Officer Kinchelow on the television series *Hogan's Heroes*. Dixon went on to direct in both film and television. His films include *Trouble Man, The Spook Who Sat by the Door*, and *Percy and Thunder*. In television, he directed multiple episodes of *Magnum, P.I., The Rockford Files*, and *The Waltons*.

Nothing but a Man was Abbey Lincoln's first dramatic role. Well known as a jazz singer and stage performer, she would go on to star in *For Love of Ivy* (1968) with Sidney Poitier.

Review Summary: *Nothing but a Man* received praise from many critics for its strong social and political message. While the film proposed no real answers to the questions it raised, it was considered a stunning picture of racism. Kevin Thomas of the *Los Angeles Times* said it "succeeds as a damning portrait of social injustice, because it is first of all a work of art, the unpretentious kind that's warm and real and doesn't call attention to itself."

Several critics noted the social maturity and directness of the film. According to Bosley Crowther in the *New York Times*, "The splendid thing about this picture is the simplicity and honesty with which the conflict is drawn . . . the clarity and naturalness of the performance, and the absence of the usual sentimental clichés."

Guess Who's Coming to Dinner

Columbia Pictures (1967)

"You and your whole lousy generation believes the
way it was for you is the way it's got to be! And not
until your whole generation has laid down and died
will the dead weight of you be off our backs!"

—John Prentice to his father

Controversial for its time, *Guess Who's Coming to Dinner* opens with
light, happy music that accompanies a plane landing at the San
Francisco International airport. A giggly, interracial couple exits the
plane, seemingly unnoticed by any passersby. They hail a cab and
go to an upscale art gallery where Hilary, a polite but rather nosy
employee, welcomes the couple. Hilary is happy to see her boss's
daughter, Joey Drayton, and is openly curious about her dark-
skinned companion, Dr. John Wade Prentice. Joey's mother is not at
the gallery, so the two hop back into the cab and head for the
Drayton home.

We soon learn that Joey is a college senior and has just returned
from a vacation in Hawaii, where she met John, and they fell in love.
The black research doctor is many years her senior, a widower, and
very concerned about the racial implications of their relationship.

As they arrive at the Drayton mansion, Tillie, the black maid, is
the first to openly show disapproval. "I don't care to see a member
of my own race getting above himself," she tells John, like the
proverbial crab trying to pull another one back into the basket.
Joey, having been raised by Tillie practically since birth, can't understand her opposition to the relationship. The mother, Christina, is
shocked at first, but once she realizes her daughter's complete happiness, quickly comes to terms with the situation. Matt, her newspaper publisher husband, is another story. Supposedly a left-wing
liberal, he reacts against his professed beliefs and cannot accept the
interracial relationship. Christina tries to explain to him that when
they taught their daughter not to be prejudiced, they did not add,

Dr. John Prentice (Sidney Poitier, standing) confronts his future in-laws Matt Drayton (Spencer Tracey) and Christina (Katharine Hepburn) in the controversial *Guess Who's Coming to Dinner*. (Columbia Pictures)

"But don't ever fall in love with a colored man." John calls his parents in Los Angeles to tell them the news, and they decide to fly up to meet their future daughter-in-law. He has not told them the full story, however.

Later, in a wonderfully poetic scene, Hilary, the nosy employee from the art gallery, shows up to get the scoop about what's going on. Appalled at the mere thought of the miscegenation that's about to take place, she expresses her personal concern for the "horror" and "anguish" her employer must be going through. In return, Christina politely escorts Hilary out of the house to her car, where she promptly fires her. Meanwhile, longtime family friend Monsignor Mike Ryan comes to the house to find out why Matt had canceled their afternoon golf game. Undaunted by the politics of the scenario, he is surprised at his liberal friend's show of conservative values and tries to lend his objective and unbiased support.

John's parents arrive at the airport and are more shocked and upset by the situation than the white parents. Back at the house, each side tries to rally support for its cause. The couples are split by gender on both sides of the equation; the fathers are in full agreement on the con side, while the mothers are positively pro. In a quaint, understated scene on the patio, Mrs. Prentice explains her thoughts to Matt in a way that she hopes he can understand. "I believe that men grow old," she tells him. "And when sexual things no longer matter to them, they forget it all . . . forget what true passion is." The real conflict, however, is between John and his father. Mr. Prentice is determined to make his son see the error in his thinking, but John stands firm and rejects his father's outdated beliefs.

Eventually, after much thought and searching his old, hypocritical soul, Matt comes to the conclusion that the important thing is how Joey and John feel about each other. He vows to rally with the mothers to work on Mr. Prentice's attitude, and they all sit down to eat dinner.

Guess Who's Coming to Dinner was the last film in which Spencer Tracy and Katharine Hepburn appeared together as a team; Tracy died just nineteen days after principal photography was completed. The film received ten Academy Award nominations. Both Tracy and Hepburn were nominated, and when Hepburn won, she accepted her Oscar for both of them. William Rose won an Oscar for his screenplay, and Beah Richards was nominated for Best Supporting Actress.

As mild as it appears today, the film created a whirlwind of controversy when it was released in 1967. Its statement is really quite bland and optimistic in comparison to, say, Spike Lee's *Jungle*

CREDITS: Producer-Director: Stanley Kramer. Screenplay: William Rose. Photography: Sam Leavitt. Music: Frank De Vol. Editor: Robert C. Jones. 112 minutes. Drama. NR.

CAST: Sidney Poitier (*John Prentice*), Spencer Tracy (*Matt Drayton*), Katharine Hepburn (*Christina Drayton*), Katharine Houghton (*Joey Drayton*), Cecil Kellaway (*Monsignor Ryan*), Roy E. Glenn Sr. (*Mr. Prentice*), Beah Richards (*Mrs. Prentice*), Virginia Christine (*Hilary St. George*), Isabell Sanford (*Tillie*).

Fever (1991). In researching this selection, we were amused at how some of the reviews of the time blasted *Guess Who's Coming to Dinner* for its weak depiction of the couple's "physically aloof, giddy and child-like, loving but sterile unconsummated relationship." As if the studio heads would have allowed anything else.

Review Summary: Critics agreed that *Guess Who's Coming to Dinner* employed the feeling of light entertainment while grappling with a very serious issue of the period: interracial marriage. It tied into the old cliché: "I've nothing against Negroes, but would I let my daughter marry one?" While many critics praised the film's social message, they also criticized the acting and the script for its preachy tone. Ann Birstein wrote in *Vogue*, "The actors are left looking wooden and uneasy."

In the *Los Angeles Times*, Mark Chalon Smith said, "There's no way it's a great movie, significant yes, but really too glib, too frothy for its own good."

The *Motion Picture Guide* calls it a lame melodrama in which "the script is unimaginative and hortatory . . . a Kramer crusade that backfires." Leo Lerman summed it up nicely in *Mademoiselle*: "There's so much to criticize, its old-fashioned story apparatus, its unadventurous film technique. But somehow *Guess Who's Coming to Dinner* is beyond that sort of serious cinematic criticism, for it is an honest attempt to help, to further the cause of integration: it is on the side of right."

The Learning Tree
Warner Bros. (1969)

"I think sometimes, if the people in the world were
made up of colors, instead of just black and white, it
would be a happier world."

—Uncle Rob to Newt

The Learning Tree is the emotional and moving tale of Newt
Winger, a black teenager growing up in Cherokee Flats, Kansas, in
the 1920s under Jim Crow laws and segregation. He comes of age
and learns about life, dreams, racial hatred, and the haunting
inevitability of death.

The film opens as a whirling tornado traps young Newt out in
a wheat field. He's rescued by Big Mabel, a concerned and voluptuous brothel worker, who ushers him to shelter in a nearby barn.
The storm enacts the winds of change, and the night Newt spends
with the older woman signals the beginning of a rite of passage.

Although he continues the young and carefree mischief of stealing apples from a neighbor's tree, and swimming butt-naked with
his friends at the swimming hole, a series of events begin to steal
away Newt's innocence and force him to face the cold, cruel world
of reality. His mother, Sarah, is his bastion of wisdom and provides
him with his sense of strength and moral courage. Uncle Rob,
although blind, sees the world more clearly than most people with
sight, and he shares this perspective of the world with his curious,
inquisitive nephew. Newt's nemesis is a bad seed named Marcus, a
troubled boy raised without a mother and neglected by his hap-
less, downtrodden father. Marcus has it in for Newt, and the two are
constantly at odds. Lurking in the background is the ominous figure
of Sheriff Kirky, a hotheaded, racist lawman with a propensity for
shooting black men in the back.

At church one Sunday morning, Newt meets and falls in love
with Arcella, the new girl in town. But the couple is betrayed by
Chancey, a wealthy white friend who takes a stand against segre-

Newt Winger (Kyle Johnson) and his pals (Carter Vinnegar, Stephen Perry, and Bobby Gross) enjoy a lazy afternoon as Big Mable (Carol Lamond) says, "Hi." *The Learning Tree* was based on director Gordon Parks's autobiographical novel. (Warner Bros.-Seven Arts)

CREDITS: Writer-Producer-Director: Gordon Parks Sr. Based on his novel. Photography: Burnett Guffey. Music: Gordon Parks. Editor: George R. Rohrs. Art Director: Edward Engoron. Set Design: Joanne MacDougall. 107 minutes. Drama. PG.

CAST: Kyle Johnson (*Newt Winger*), Alex Clarke (*Marcus Savage*), Estelle Evans (*Sarah Winger*), Dana Elcar (*Sheriff Kirky*), Mira Waters (*Arcella Jefferson*), Joel Fluellen (*Uncle Rob*), Malcolm Atterbury (*Silas Newhall*), Richard Ward (*Booker Savage*), Russell Thorson (*Judge Cavanaugh*), Carol Lamond (*Big Mabel*), Peggy Rea (*Miss McClintock*), Sandra Sharp (*Prissy*), Kevin Hagen (*Doc Cravens*), James "Jimmy" Rushing (*Chappie Logan*), Dub Taylor (*Spikey*), Felix Nelson (*Jack Winger*), George Mitchell (*Jake Kiner*), Stephen Perry (*Jappy*), Philip Roye (*Pete Winger*), Hope Summers (*Mrs. Kiner*), Carter Vinnegar (*Seansy*), Bobby Gross (*Skunk*), Zooey Hall (*Chancey Cavanaugh*).

gation, only to turn around and take advantage of Arcella, thus proving precisely how liberal he is willing to be. Later that summer, Newt witnesses a murder, for which an innocent white drunk is accused. Realizing the trouble that would ensue if a black man had done the killing, he remains silent about what he saw, until his parents encourage him to reveal the truth, no matter what the consequences. They are severe.

The people, influences, joys, and misfortunes Newt encounters become his learning tree. At times his lessons are hard and bitter, but often they are just plain fun.

Kyle Johnson was a seventeen-year-old Hollywood High School student when he was cast as the twelve-year-old protagonist. He convincingly brought Newt Winger's troubled character to the screen and carried the film with a sincere innocence. The sensitive depiction of a caring family, respect for elders, moral values, the support of the church and community, and the importance of making proper decisions are key plot points that even today make this film an important social statement.

The Learning Tree was the first theatrical feature-length film financed by a major Hollywood studio to be directed by an African American. The world-renowned still photographer, author, musician, poet, athlete, and artist Gordon Parks was fifty-six when he accepted this historic opportunity. Now known as "the Renaissance Man," he produced, scored, and wrote the screenplay for the film from his highly successful autobiographical first novel.

Review Summary: Reviewers admired the multiple talents of Gordon Parks and commended the cast as well chosen. While a few complained that the story was unreal, others, such as Philip Hartung in *Commonweal*, disagreed, explaining that Warner Bros. had made an effort to feature realistic Negro culture and themes by signing Parks. In *Motion Picture Review* the varying racial attitudes of both whites and blacks were cited as critical to the complexity of the film's focus and such complexity was said to rarely exist in similar works. There were a number of concerns about the use of clichés, excessive melodrama, and listless directing.

GORDON PARKS

Mayflower Hotel, Washington, D.C.
April 18, 1998

TOR: Is it true that *The Learning Tree* was the first film directed by an African American to be produced by a major Hollywood studio?

PARKS: Yes.

TOR: How did that come about?

PARKS: My first autobiography, *The Learning Tree*, had become a bestseller, and several people had approached me about doing a film of it. I said, "Fine. If you can raise the money, you can buy the rights." One, after great difficulty in raising the funds, went so far as to suggest that I change all the characters to white people. "Of course not," I said, "there wouldn't be that much of a film, and not much of a story." Some time later, I had just returned from Paris, when I got a call from John Cassavetes.

TOR: The actor?

PARKS: Yes. I had made friends with him on some other occasion, some assignment. He called from Hollywood and said, "I've just finished reading *The Learning Tree* and was wondering if you'd like to direct a film of it?"

I said, "That'll be fine, John, but you know there are no black directors in Hollywood—and I don't think there are going to be any black directors in Hollywood for the major studios."

So he said, "Can you get out here in a couple of days? I want you to meet the son of the man who runs Warner Brothers/Seven Arts. We're not speaking to each other because we've had some odds on the film I'm on, but I'll introduce you to him, and I think he's stupid enough to do it." [*Laughter*]

TOR: Did he use those words?

PARKS: He was just kidding of course. [*More laughter*]. So I said, "All right, John. I'll get out there." So I arrived in Los Angeles and John introduced me to a young man named Kenny Hyman and left. Kenny was the son of Elliott Hyman, who was running the studio. John didn't say good-bye to Kenny or anything. So Hyman gave me a seat and pulled out *The Learning Tree* and *A Choice of Weapons*, which was my second autobiography, and said, "Which one would you like to do first?" I said to myself that this guy was giving me some kind of Hollywood hype. I looked at him and smiled, and I think he recognized my doubt in my look at him.

He said, "I'm serious, very serious. I've read both books and I think that one of them should be made into a film."

I said, "If you are serious, *The Learning Tree* should be the one. That's my very first novel, and it's more graphic in a photographic sense."

He said, "Fine, I would like for you to direct it."

I smiled again, and said, "Uhmp."

He said, "I still don't think you believe me."

I said, "I believe you, but I do have my doubts."

TOR: You wore a number of different hats on the project. How did that come about?

PARKS: Very quickly. He then asked me, "Who would you like to write the screenplay?"

I said, "I don't know any screenwriters out this way so I couldn't suggest one."

He said, "Well, why don't you write it? You wrote the book."

I smiled again. I said, "Fine."

Then he said, "Now Cassavetes tells me that you're a composer. I would suggest that you compose the music for the film."

I said, "Why not?" and smiled again.

TOR: Wow, did you think it was Christmas?

PARKS: I didn't think it would happen so fast. This was five minutes after Cassavetes left.

TOR: Did it excite you or make you nervous?

PARKS: I didn't have time to give it any serious thought. I frankly didn't believe him.

Then he said, "Since you're going to be the first black director to do a film for a major studio, I think you're going to have to have a lot of clout. You're going to have to be completely in control. So, I suggest again that you act as producer on the film . . . the complete boss."

So I said, again, "Why not? Fine."

TOR: So, on your first Hollywood film production, you were set to write, produce, direct, and score the film all at once?

PARKS: I didn't actually take it that seriously until I saw it on the wires across America that Warner Bros. had chosen the first black director for a major studio in Hollywood. When I signed the contracts, I started to believe it.

TOR: Where did you get your directing experience?

PARKS: I didn't have any experience as a director, or a screenwriter, or a composer for film, or a producer. So it all fell on me at once. And it was a load never dropped on any director in Hollywood, white or black.

TOR: Do you think they may have wanted you to take on too much and possibly fail?

PARKS: No. I think that Kenny Hyman just loved the novel so much. He'd seen my photographic work, and he had the confidence that I had a good eye. I had written and worked for *Life* magazine for a number of years, and I had experience with actors of all sorts, some of the finest actors and actresses in the world. So that was in my corner. I hadn't taken time out to be frightened about it. I said, here's an opportunity opening up, and I'm going to take advantage of it.

TOR: How did the process continue from there?

PARKS: First thing he did was to invite me to lunch with five producers who worked for Warner Bros., and said I can use either one of those persons as someone to guide me. Of the five he introduced me to . . . one didn't bother to shake my hand or even say too much to me, which was Bill Conrad. He was pretty well known in TV. So we had lunch and we left.

Hyman called me later and said, "Well, who would you like?"

I said, "Well, I think I want Conrad."

He said, "That ornery son of a bitch?" Just like that. He said, "Why did you choose him?"

I said, "I want to be his boss!" [*Much laughter*]

TOR: How did he like that?

PARKS: Conrad was as surprised as anybody else. I went to his office. He had a beautiful office. He pulled out a bunch of cigars and offered me one.

I said, "No, I don't smoke."

He said, "What do you know about making films?"

I said, "Nothing. That's why you're here. That's why I chose you as my assistant."

Conrad admired Orson Welles, and I think wanted to be like him. He wanted to be a composer, he wanted to direct a film himself . . . and I was this black monster doing everything he wanted to do, so he seemed to have a built-in resistance to me.

Finally he said, "Okay, let's begin." He pulled a matchbox out and took two matches. He placed one to the right of the box, and one to the left of the box, and he said, "The box is the camera, which would you say is camera right?"

I pointed to the right.

He said, "Which is camera left?"

I pointed to the left.

He switched the box around and said, "Now which is camera left and camera right?"

I again pointed and said, "Camera left, camera right. It's simple."

He said, "You learn fast."

I said, "There wasn't much to learn. Any idiot could've told you that." So he was thwarted there. Then he went on to asking, "Have you had any experience with actors?"

"Yeah, a few."

He said, "Like who?"

I said, "Like Ingrid Bergman," and named a few other great actors, and he said, "Oh, I see. Fine, fine, fine . . . then I think we'll get along."

So we did all right until one day I had gotten my crew together for the first time. He came in, stood in the back of the room, and one of the technicians that I had hired was asking me how much water power we would need for the storm. And Bill says, "You're not gonna get that."

I said, "What do you mean we're not gonna get that?" I thought he was kidding.

He said, "No, I'm serious, we can't take that kind of equipment all the way to Kansas."

I said, "We'll get it."

He said, "I said you wouldn't!"

And the crew looked at me as if to say, "What are you going to do?" I said, "Bill, I want you to leave here immediately. And if you don't leave immediately, I'm going to throw you out." I weighed about two pounds; he weighed about two hundred and fifty pounds. [*Laughter*] So he stormed out, and the crew smiled. A few clapped and said, "Good for you."

TOR: Was that all there was to it? Was there some kind of recourse later?

PARKS: He came back about noon. And Susana, the secretary, said [*in accent*], "Gordon, Bill Conrad is here." I said, "Send him in."

He came in and said, "Look, I want to apologize for what I did."

I said, "I think I deserve an apology."

Meanwhile, Dana Ellcott, a big strong guy, came into the office and said to Susana, "I want to see Mr. Parks about the role of Kirky."

So she came in and said, "Dana Ellcott is here about the role of Kirky."

I said, "Did you tell him we've chosen someone for that?"

"I did, but he insists on seeing you."

So, he burst in the door, cursing, and using some of the words out of the screenplay. And after he said it . . . he kicked Bill in the shin!

And I said, "You're hired! I've been wanting to do that all day!"

[*Laughter*] That's how Dana Ellcott got the job of Kirky.

TOR: The film has a powerful racial message. How was it received?

PARKS: When the film *The Learning Tree* opened on Broadway, it had a strange effect on the audiences—especially the whites. They were all puzzled when they came out. It was sort of phenomenal for whites in regard to this kind of film because of the mixture of black and white . . . and my mother, who in the end was sort of the inspiration for the whole film . . . and the way she encouraged her son to stand up for what is right sort of stunned everybody. And they just sort of stood around talking to each other after the film was over. They didn't leave the theater. I didn't know how they really accepted it, nobody did . . . even the studio was puzzled.

However, the Library of Congress voted it one of the twenty-five most important films ever made. And so now it's in the registry, and it's being shown around the country. And I'm proud of that.

6

Society Profile: 1970–1979
The Blaxploitation Era

By 1970, four out of every ten African Americans lived in urban areas, and the black residents in Atlanta, Newark, Gary, and Washington, D.C., made up more than half of the population in those cities. White flight was well under way as white families fled to the suburbs, leaving the inner cities to "the darkening community." Along with this increase in urban residency, home ownership among blacks was on the rise, as well as high school graduation rates for black youth.

In an effort to avoid desegregation, whites created great numbers of private schools. An estimated four hundred were established, and to address this issue, the NAACP filed a lawsuit asserting that the Department of Health, Education, and Welfare was not adequately enforcing school integration. In response, Robert Finch, the department secretary, proposed a cut in tax exemptions to help eliminate the problem.

Richard Nixon was in the White House, and he was not considered a friend of blacks. His retreat from desegregation and liberalism caused the NAACP to label him "anti-Negro." In 1971, the Supreme Court ruled that busing and redistricting were legal and acceptable ways for integration to be achieved in American schools. Nixon didn't agree and signed a bill that prohibited the use of busing to accomplish racial integration. The battle continued until 1980, when President Jimmy Carter vetoed an antibusing amendment by Senator Jesse Helms that would have barred the Justice Department from bringing legal actions to require school busing.

As the seventies continued, more black politicians than ever before won success in local and national elections. Shirley Chisholm became the first black woman to enter the race for the presidency of the United States. The cities of Dayton, Ohio, and Newark, New Jersey, each elected their first black mayors, and Ronald V. Dellums of California, Ralph Metcalfe of Illinois, Parren J. Mitchell of Maryland, and Charles Rangel of New York were elected to the U.S. Congress.

At opposite ends of the spectrum, two new black television images emerged—Tony Brown's *Black Journal,* a cutting-edge news and issues program, and the *Flip Wilson Show,* which had a comedy-variety format and often featured the show's host in drag. Large Afros, bell-bottom pants, and platform shoes were the fashion of the day. In literature, popular poetry began to flourish with Maya Angelou, Gwendolyn Brooks, and Nikki Giovanni at the forefront. Making the transition from page to screen, Ernest Gaines's successful novel *The Autobiography of Miss Jane Pittman,* starring Cicely Tyson in the title role, became an award-winning television movie.

Unemployment for blacks remained twice as high as for whites, with almost 32 percent of black teens unable to find jobs. Several civil rights organizations were formed to protest this inequity, including the Reverend Jesse Jackson's Operation Push (People United to Save Humanity). Studies were begun that looked at the disproportionate number of blacks in the country's prisons and jails, and suggested that their disproportionate lack of employment might be related to that fact. Another study showed that families with women as head of household were more likely to be in poverty than the traditional nuclear family headed by a man.

In sports, Jim Brown and Gale Sayers were inducted into the Football Hall of Fame, and Josh Gibson, Satchel Paige, and Willie Mays were inducted into the Baseball Hall of Fame. Bill Russell, Wilt Chamberlin, and Oscar Robinson became inductees into the Basketball Hall of Fame.

In 1976, Jimmy Carter was elected president based on his receiving 94 percent of the black vote, and his church in Plains, Georgia, immediately dropped its eleven-year-long ban on black attendance. Carter was very proactive in the cause for civil rights. He appointed nineteen blacks to his White House staff and another thirty-seven to key executive positions. Black mayors were elected in the cities of Atlanta (Maynard Jackson), Compton, Calif., (Doris A. Davis), Los Angeles (Thomas Bradley), and Detroit (Coleman Young). In the Motor City, WGPR, the first black-owned television station, began broadcasting. Its formation was organized by an investment group headed by Dr. William V. Banks.

One of the most outstanding achievements ever, blending literature and television, was the TV miniseries based on Alex Haley's ancestral saga *Roots*. Aired in February 1977, it ran for eight consecutive nights and attracted more than 80 million viewers each night, becoming the most watched series of all time. Haley won a Pulitzer Prize and a Spingarn Medal, and *Roots* went on to earn nine Emmy Awards, more than any other television series.

The 1970s ended with American schools still widely segregated. The National Center for Health released statistics suggesting that white Americans were expected to live longer than black Americans, and that black women on average would outlive black men by more than nine years.

The House Select Committee on Assassinations found that J. Edgar Hoover, one-time head of the FBI, tried to discredit slain civil rights leader Dr. Martin Luther King Jr.

Sweet Sweetback's Baadasssss Song

Cinemation Industries (1971)

> "Life is tough, baby. A real struggle from the womb
> to the tomb!"
>
> —Gambling Man to Sweetback

Sweet Sweetback's Baadasssss Song was the brainchild of its maverick producer, director, and star, Melvin Van Peebles. This avant-garde, part-pornographic, part-action thriller, now cinematic icon, was the first film that showed a brother actually stickin' it to "the Man."

A homeless child (played by the filmmaker's son, Mario) is taken in by the women of a bordello. The boy performs menial chores for his room and board until one slow day, one of the ladies of the house decides to "show him the ropes" (so to speak). In the process, the lad acquires the nickname of Sweetback, and grows up to become a top performer in live sex shows. One night, two crooked detectives stop by the sex show to collect their payola. They also need someone to ride along with them, and Sweetback gets the nod. He's forced to watch as the cops brutally beat a black militant named Mu-Mu. Initially cool and aloof, Sweetback suddenly turns on the cops, using his handcuffs as a weapon, and saves the revolutionary's life.

For the rest of the film Sweetback is a fugitive on the run, stopping only for help, and sex, and often both. A variety of cinematic techniques made the film fresh and unique for the time. Odd camera angles, superimpositions, reverse-key effects, box and matting effects, rack-focus shots, extreme zooms, stop-motion and step-printing, and an abundance of jittery handheld camera work all helped to express the paranoid nightmare that the fugitive's life had become.

The music and soundtrack with credits to Earth, Wind & Fire slowly build a psychotic audio landscape, juxtaposed against jazz, gospel, and poetry segments peppered with childlike rhymes reminiscent of schoolyard chants. *Sweetback* was shot in twenty days

116

In *Sweet Sweetback's Baadasssss Song,* Sweetback (Melvin Van Peebles), a popular live sex-show performer turned cop killer and fugitive on the run, seeks help from the wife of a friend (Rhetta Hughes). The Cinemation Industries release ushered in a new wave of action-packed black films in the 1970s, and Van Peebles become known as the Godfather of Soul Cinema. (Courtesy of the Museum of Modern Art)

on a $500,000 budget, and grossed more than $10 million in its first year of release. A few months after *Sweetback* hit the big screen, MGM released Gordon Parks's detective thriller *Shaft* (1971), and when *Superfly* (1972), directed by Gordon Parks Jr., was released by

CREDITS: Writer-Producer-Director, Score, and Editor: Melvin Van Peebles. 97 minutes. Drama. X.

CAST: Melvin Van Peebles (*Sweetback*), Simon Chuckstar (*Beetle*), Hubert Scales (*Mu-Mu*), John Dullaghan (*Commissioner*), West Gale, Niva Rochelle, Rhetta Hughes (*Old Girlfriend*), Nick Ferrari, Ed Rue, Johnny Amos (*Motorcycle Guy*), Lavelle Roby, Ted Hayden, Mario Van Peebles (*Young Sweetback*).

Warner Brothers, the black cinematic trio of *Sweetback, Shaft,* and *Superfly* firmly established a new genre of black film for a hungry new black audience.

Despite the rampant stereotyping and negative images of pimps, pushers, hookers, and street thugs that these films have become known for, it was the first time black Americans could actually see people who looked like them up on the screen in a variety of subjects and genres. There were the Supermen: *Shaft, Superfly, Hit Man, Trouble Man, Hammer, Truck Turner.* And the Superwomen: *Foxy Brown, Cleopatra Jones, Sheba Baby, Lady Cocoa.* Horror films: *Blacula, The Watts Monster,* and *Blackenstein.* Family films: *Sounder, Sparkle, Bustin' Loose.* Message movies: *The Spook Who Sat by the Door, The River Niger, Cornbread, Earl and Me.* Buddy pictures: *Uptown Saturday Night, Three the Hard Way, Cooley High, Cotton Comes to Harlem.* And romance: *Claudine, Thomasine and Bushrod, Aaron Loves Angela,* and *Mahogany.* These black films saved Hollywood from going bankrupt during a major financial slump, yet once the audience began to demand more positive images, Hollywood simply cut off the tap.

Melvin Van Peebles's first feature film, *Story of a Three Day Pass* (1967), attracted the attention of Columbia Pictures when it premiered at the San Francisco Film Festival, and they signed him to write and direct *Watermelon Man* (1969). Twenty years later, he and his son, Mario, would make *Identity Crisis* (1989). The production was written, produced, and directed by the father and son team, and they were also its stars. They would collaborate again on *Panther* (1995), about the rise and fall of the famed Black Panther Party in the late sixties and seventies.

Another independent visionary who cannot go unmentioned here is Rudy Ray Moore, who starred in a series of karate-packed, rock-'em sock-'em, black-avenging-hero flicks, beginning with *Dolemite* (1975). Directed by D'Urville Martin, the comedy-gangster film exposed the underside of disco nightlife and, much like *Sweetback,* has now reached cult status. Moore quickly folloed with the sequel *Dolemite 2: The Human Tornado* (1976), *Disco Godfather* (1976), and *Avenging Disco Godfather* (1976), which he directed himself. *Dolemite* is probably best remembered for Moore's rendition of the classic street poem "The Signifying Monkey."

Review Summary: At a time when many movies were losing money at the box office, *Sweet Sweetback's Baadasssss Song* became a blockbuster. Kevin Thomas in the *Los Angeles Times* described the film as "a series of earthy vignettes, where Van Peebles evokes the vitality, humor, pain, despair and omnipresent fear that is life for so many African Americans."

Many of the reviews addressed Van Peebles's exceptional business sense and how Hollywood was forced to take notice. Louis Parks in the *Houston Chronicle* explained, "For the first time, Hollywood saw the power of the African American audience and realized how profitable it could be to give black viewers movies they really wanted to see." Commenting on the film's unique look and style, he added, "The editing has a jazzy, improvisational quality, and the screen is often streaked with jarring psychedelic effects that illustrate Sweetback's alienation."

Technically, the picture was criticized for a variety of things including poor lighting, tedious murky scenes, negative women's roles, a limited performance by Van Peebles, and the exploitation of black cultural stereotypes. Stephen Holden in the *New York Times* called it "an innovative, yet politically inflammatory film."

Shaft

Metro-Goldwyn-Mayer (1971)

"Don't let your mouth get your ass in trouble."
—Shaft to militant

Shaft was Gordon Parks's second feature-length film, and the profits it generated helped to save MGM from financial ruin. The hardhitting, action-packed, life on the New York City streets, private-dick flick gave us our first black, kick-butt action hero. (Note: Sweetback is generally considered a black, kick-butt *anti*hero).

John Shaft is a private investigator who gets hired to find a Harlem gangster's kidnapped daughter. Bumpy Jonas, the gangster, isn't totally up-front about the circumstances surrounding his little darling's disappearance but wants her found at any cost. "I can always get more money," he tells Shaft through watering eyes, "but I only got one baby." Meanwhile, rumblings of an impending gang war has gruff police lieutenant Vic Androzzy very concerned. After interrogating Shaft about how and why one of Bumpy's henchmen took a swan dive out of his fourth-floor office window, he makes a deal for the private eye's release if he will keep him informed about what's going on out in the streets.

After following up several false leads, Shaft relies on his gut instincts and finally learns the truth about what's going on. He enlists the help of Ben Buford, an old friend, and his group of black militants to pull off his plan. Down for the cause and the money, together they stage a dramatic rescue of the girl from her white Mafioso-type captors.

Shaft broke new cinematic ground on many levels. The new black audience in the seventies was hungry for more assertive images more in keeping with the hard-earned civil rights gains that were constantly being fought for. *Shaft* portrayed a black man that had never been seen on the movie screen before. His cool, in-control demeanor and the way he maneuvered on both sides of the color line with confidence and dignity, using his connections, risking his

Private detective John Shaft (Richard Roundtree) looks down the barrel of a mobster's machine gun in *Shaft*. The film helped save MGM from financial ruin. (Metro-Goldwyn-Mayer)

CREDITS: Director: Gordon Parks Sr. Producer: Joel Freeman. Screenplay: John D. F. Black, Ernest Tidyman. Based on the novel by Tidyman. Photography: Urs Furrer. Music: Issac Hayes. Editor: Hugh A Robertson. Art Director: Emanuel Gerard. 98 minutes. Drama. R.

CAST: Richard Roundtree (*John Shaft*), Moses Gunn (*Bumpy Jonas*), Charles Cioffi (*Lt. Vic Androzzy*), Christopher St. John (*Ben Buford*), Gwenn Mitchell (*Ellie Moore*), Lawrence Pressman (*Sgt. Tom Hannon*), Victor Arnold (*Charlie*), Sherri Brewer (*Marcy*), Rex Robbins (*Rollie*), Camille Yarbrough (*Dina Greene*).

life, and taking no crap from anybody, made him a consummate professional worthy of respect and admiration. The street vernacular of the script was sharp, cool, and enticing. It had schoolkids across the country wearing leather jackets, calling each other "baby," and trying to talk with a hip, Harlem street twang.

The film's theme song and music score was written by Issac Hayes and performed by Hayes with the Bar-Kays and Movement. It won a 1971 Academy Award, the first "Music Award" Oscar ever to go to an African American. Parks was also nominated for his directing.

MGM followed this black blockbuster with two sequels, *Shaft's Big Score* (1972), and *Shaft in Africa* (1973). Neither was as successful as the original. A short-lived television series was also based on the Shaft character. *Boyz 'N the Hood* writer-director John Singleton would do a remake of *Shaft* in 2000, starring Samuel L. Jackson as the new generation Shaft.

Review Summary: Most critics agreed that the main purpose of *Shaft* was to entertain, and it did that well. According to Moira Walsh, in *America*, John Shaft, played by Richard Roundtree, was a successful cross between Sam Spade and James Bond. In *Time*, Jay Cocks wrote that the film was a "fast-moving pleasure that kept things going at such a headlong pace that the movie hardly pauses for breath."

Another main issue among reviewers involved the film's look and the photography. Some expected director Gordon Parks's experience as a still photographer to translate into a more exceptional product. In *Newsweek*, S. K. Obenbeck called the camera work insipid, with endless tracking shots . . . overhead pans . . . and sexual clichés. Oberbeck suggested that *The Learning Tree* had more "pictorial lushness" and that at times *Shaft* looked "downright tacky."

Many reviews were more complimentary. In *Motion Picture Guide* Murf said, "Parks' concentration on the humanistic elements of Shaft, [brought] some depth to the super slick detective, showing other sides to his personality."

GORDON PARKS

Mayflower Hotel, Washington, D.C.
April 18, 1998

TOR: How were you selected to direct *Shaft*, and what was the studio's initial attitude about the project?

PARKS: I think that after the success of *The Learning Tree*, MGM came to me. I read the screenplay and I said, "Well, I don't like it." The guy who wrote the book, Ernest Tidyman, had also written the screenplay. It was too condescending. They said, "Well, if you do it, change the screenplay." I said, "In that case I'll do it."

TOR: What part did *Shaft* play in the so-called "blaxploitation" era?

PARKS: I never associated *Shaft* with black exploitation. It was not exploitation. Who exploited who? I always go wild a little bit when they put it in that category. Why is having a black hero who for the first time stood up for what he believed and fought the system ... why call it an exploitation film? It wasn't an exploitation film. He was a good-looking, bright young detective who defied the white system. He even told blacks who did wrong, like Bumpy Jonas, whose daughter was kidnapped by the white mob, he said, "I don't like you any more than I like them because you're just as bad as they are. You're out there robbing black people. I dislike you, too." So Shaft is a guy who stood up for his rights ... Why they would put him in a black exploitation category, I don't know.

TOR: Did any black crew work with you on *Shaft?*

PARKS: Yes. In fact, as I did on *The Learning Tree*, I hired a lot of black people to work behind the camera for the first time. At first, they told me at Warner Bros., "We're not going to be able to find any black people because they don't have the experience." So I said, "Let's try." And they tried, and they found about five. And by the time I did *Shaft*, I had about ten black people working in key positions behind the camera.

TOR: What was the audience's initial response to *Shaft* and what kind of influence on society do you think it's had?

PARKS: Jim Albray, the head of the studio, was a tough guy. He said, "Gordon, you've got a hell of a success on your hands. Now I want you to take it to England and show it to the English press."

I said, "Okay, Jim." They called Jim "the Cobra," because he was so tough. And I went to England, and there was a press conference. One of their reporters asked [*in British accent*], "Mr. Parks, I say, a . . . really . . . a . . . what does *Shaft* really mean anyway?" [*Laughter*] I said, "Well, it sort of means, Up yours!" [*More laughter*] Another one of these reporters asked [*still in accent*], "Now, these tough blokes walking around calling each other 'mother,' What's that?"

I said, "Look, we have a couple of ladies in the audience, and it's very difficult for me to tell you what that other word is. [*Laughter*] But I'll tell you how many letters are in it and you can figure it out." Everybody laughed about that time because they had already figured it out.

Recently, Susan, my young friend here, who is from England, said that when she was growing up people used to say "Mutty" all the time. So I asked, "Mutty? Mutty what?" She said that her friends used to call each other that and when she asked why, she was told, "It's from that film *Shaft*. It means Mutty . . . Mutty Fucker!" [*Much laughter*]

Buck and the Preacher

Columbia Pictures (1972)

"I ain't gonna live in this land no more! The war
ain't changed nothin' or nobody. It's like a poison
soaked into the ground."

—Ruth to Buck

Buck and the Preacher, the directorial debut for monumental film
star Sidney Poitier, showed an important part of history that seldom
appeared in American history books.

The story takes place just after the Civil War. Buck, a former
Buffalo Soldier, is a dedicated wagon master determined to lead a
wagon train of pioneering freed slaves westward to their new
home. While he is off negotiating for food, provisions, and safe
passage through the Indian territories, the wagon train is attacked
by white bounty hunters. Ruthless, murderous, and in the pay of
southern landholders, they are determined to turn the black settlers
back so they can return to work in the cotton fields of Dixie. Several of the pioneers are killed, and their money is stolen.

Without the money for food and supplies, their future looks
bleak, but Buck will not let them down. "I gave them my word," he
tells the Reverend Willis Oaks Rutherford, an eccentric con man
who carries his faith (and a loaded gun) in a hollowed-out Bible.
The two men join forces to track down the killers and retrieve the
settler's life savings. They find the desperadoes drinking and gambling at a nearby town brothel and a shoot-out ensues. When it's
over, most of the bad guys are dead, and it's discovered that much
of the stolen money has been spent. The town sheriff rounds up
some men and goes after our heroes turned outlaws. The posse
includes one furious bounty hunter who survived and will stop at
nothing to get his revenge.

On his way back to the wagon train, Buck stops off at his
ranch. It's all too quiet, and his woman, Ruth, is nowhere in sight.
The posse has beat him home and has been planning an ambush,

but Buck reads the signs and barely escapes, in a hail of bullets. Since all of the men in town are out looking for them, Buck and the Preacher decide to rob the town bank to recoup some of the stolen money. They enlist Ruth's help and pull off the heist, but on their way out of the bank, they see the posse riding into town . . . and the posse sees them.

A chase ensues, but once they cross into Indian Territory the sheriff halts his posse, reluctant to risk the lives of his men. This extra time is used by Buck and the Preacher to take cover in the hills. The bounty hunter takes over the posse and continues his relentless pursuit.

Poitier directs a tense and exciting firefight, in which the mean old bounty hunter gets his comeuppance. The film ends happily, with the wagon train reaching its destination and Buck, Ruth, and the Preacher riding off into the sunset.

At first the well-known western filmmaker John Sargent was slated to direct, but he was replaced because of some friction with one of the film's stars. Poitier stepped up. Now in the director's mode, Poitier would often work both sides of the camera, acting and directing. *A Warm December* (1972) was his second film, with Esther Anderson, and he went on to work with Bill Cosby in the highly popular comedy trilogy of *Uptown Saturday Night* (1974), *Let's Do It Again* (1975), and *A Piece of the Action* (1977). Poitier would also go on to direct the crossover film *Hanky Panky*, featuring Gene Wilder, in 1982, and *Ghost Dad* (1990), again with long-time friend and collaborator Bill Cosby.

Thomasine and Bushrod (1974) was another popular black western of the time. It starred the real-life duo of Vonetta McGee and Max Julien as a black Bonnie and Clyde. They robbed banks with six-shooters instead of tommy guns, and rode away on horseback instead of in Model T cars.

CREDITS: Director: Sidney Poitier. Producer: Joel Glickman. Screenplay: Ernest Kinoy. Based on a story by Kinoy and Drake Walker. Photography: Alex Phillips Jr. Music: Benny Carter. Editor: Pembroke L. Herring. 102 minutes. Western. PG.

CAST: Sidney Poitier (*Buck*), Harry Belafonte (*Preacher*), Ruby Dee (*Ruth*), Cameron Mitchell (*Deshay*), Denny Miller (*Floyd*), Nita Talbot (*Mme. Esther*), John Kelly (*Sheriff*), Tony Brubaker (*Headman*), James McEachin (*Kingston*), Clarence Muse (*Cudjo*), Lynn Hamilton (*Sarah*), Doug Johnson (*Sam*), Errol John (*Joshua*), Ken Maynard (*Little Henry*), Pamela Jones (*Delilah*), Julie Robinson (*Sinsie*), Enrique Lucero (*Indian Chief*).

Over the years, dozens of John Wayne and Alan Ladd–type set-
tling-the-West films had been made, and every now and then one
might have had a black cook or blacksmith. But it is a fact that
blacks also settled the West, organized wagon trains, homesteaded,
founded cities, and, unfortunately, even fought Indians on occasion.
In its portrayal of blacks in the old West, *Buck and the Preacher* has

Ex-buffalo soldier and wagon master Buck (Sidney Poitier, left) and con
artist and man-of-the-cloth "the Preacher" (Harry Belafonte) prepare to rob
a bank to recoup a wagon train's stolen funds, in *Buck and the Preacher*.
(Columbia Pictures)

the highest degree of historical significance since *Sergeant Rutledge* (1961) and the black westerns with "the Bronze Buckeroo," Herbert Jeffrey, in the late 1930s.

Review Summary: The critics were mixed in reviewing *Buck and the Preacher.* Gordon Gow in *Films and Filming* called it "breezy stuff and highly entertaining." Gow said Poitier and Belafonte's presence "lifted the comedy aspect into quite a tolerable caper, if perhaps a little obviously show-bizzy underneath the period realism."

During the period of blaxploitation, the film had taken a unique direction into the western genre, yet the characters tended to fall into the same prominent categories: bad guys, good guys, and women in the typical background roles. The review in *Motion Picture Guide* is quite negative. "Stereotypes abound in this foolish, witless western, a production misusing the fine black talent in its cast."

In *Blacks in American Films and Television,* Donald Bogle explained that once Poitier replaced the original director, he turned the picture over to Belafonte. "Poitier himself sleepwalks through most of the action, somber and heroic, but lifeless," he wrote, "while Belafonte gives his most robust and idiosyncratic performance." Bogle concluded that the film was "rousing entertainment with a certain degree of historical significance and political thought."

Blacula

American International Pictures (1972)

"Uh, uh! You ain't getting this nigga' in no graveyard
tonight!"

—Michele to her husband, Dr. Thomas

It's eighteenth-century Transylvania, and African Prince Mamuwalde
is on a diplomatic visit to Count Dracula's castle to discuss ways of
stopping the slave trade. Dracula has an eye for Mamuwalde's beautiful wife and decides to have the African princess for himself. He
disrespects the prince by offering to buy her from him, and when
Mamuwalde recoils at the insult, Dracula bites his neck and curses
him to life as an undead.

Two hundred years later, two gay interior designers purchase
the contents of Dracula's castle, including a coffin found resting in
a secret chamber. They transport their new belongings to a warehouse in Los Angeles, where they begin to unpack and inventory
their acquisitions. When the coffin is opened for a quick look
inside, Blacula is finally released to quench his thirst for fresh
blood. In the process, he creates many more blood-gorging vampires out of his helpless victims, and they begin to wreak havoc on
the City of Angels.

Dr. Gordon Thomas gets involved when bodies that were once
dead keep disappearing. He realizes there is something wrong and
is determined to find out what it is. He attends a wake for one of
the deceased with his wife and sister-in-law, Tina, who just happens
to be the reincarnation of Blacula's beautiful wife. Mamuwalde pursues Tina for her heart, not her blood, and she instinctively knows
that the story the vampire tells her of their past together is true.
Mesmerized by his powers of seduction, she agrees to rejoin him
and to stay at his side forever. Meanwhile, the victims keep piling
up and then disappearing. The police scoff at Dr. Thomas's absurd
theories as to what's going on—until they go to check out the
warehouse. They fight with the horde of freshly made vampires,

Accursed African prince and creature of the night Mamuwalde (William Marshall) relishes a tender moment with Tina (Vonetta McGee), his reincarnated wife, in *Blacula*. (American International Pictures)

CREDITS: Director: William Crain. Producer: Joseph T. Narr. Screenplay: Joan Torres, Raymond Koenig. Photography: John Stevens. Music: Gene Page. Editor: Allen Jacobs. Art Design: Walter Herndon. 92 minutes. Horror. PG.

CAST: William Marshall (*Blacula*), Vonette McGee (*Tina*), Denise Nicholas (*Michelle*), Thalmus Rasulala (*Gordon Thomas*), Gordon Pinsent (*Lt. Peters*), Charles McCauley (*Dracula*), Emily Yancy (*Nancy*), Lance Taylor Sr. (*Swenson*), Ted Harris (*Bobby*), Rick Metzler (*Billy*), Jitu Cumbuka (*Skillet*), Logan Field (*Barnes*), Ketty Lester (*Juanita*), Elisha Cook Jr. (*Sam*).

and even burn the warehouse down, but Mamuwalde escapes. In a final chase scene, Tina is mortally wounded. "What is left for this cursed creature?" Blacula laments, then ascends a darkened staircase and opens a door that leads to the light of day. It is his final sacrifice to be with the woman he loved and lost so many years before.

Directed by William Crain, *Blacula* was the first prominent black horror film. Earlier films in the genre included *Voodoo Devil Drums* (1934), by Toddy Pictures Company, and *Professor Creeps* (1942). *Professor Creeps* was produced by Jed Buell, the man who brought us *Harlem on the Prairie*, the first black western, in 1938. Buell's creepy flick featured a dark-skinned Bela Lugosi.

Review Summary: Apparently very few critics thought *Blacula* worthy of review. The reviews we did find recognized that the film was created in the midst of the blaxploitation era, but, nevertheless, critics were not pleased.

Donald Bogle in *Blacks in American Films and Television* called it campy; "This is perhaps passable TV-type entertainment, but clearly what's needed is also clearly what's missing."

Richard Weaver in *Films and Filming* said that *Blacula* seemed to "reach rock-bottom, and needs a more tolerant sense of humor than usual, to be endured." Weaver was also highly critical of the film's technical nature. He discussed the atrocious makeup, the bad photography, and noted a general lack of sensitivity in the film. "He ain't dead or alive, we've just put him out of his misery," he suggested as a suitable line of dialogue from the film, which could also be used as its epitaph. "Totally unconvincing on any level; someone should lay garlic at the studio door, cross themselves, and pray that Blacula is never resurrected." Weaver's prayer was ignored; *Scream Blacula Scream* was released in 1974.

The Spook Who Sat by the Door

United Artists (1973)

> "A black man with a mop, tray, or broom can go
> damn near anywhere. And a smiling black man is
> invisible."
>
> —Turk to recruits

The Spook Who Sat by the Door opens as a white senator, concerned about the lack of black support for his reelection campaign, charges the Central Intelligence Agency with racial discrimination as a political ploy. The call immediately goes out for a few good black men, and the recruitment process begins. Hell-bent on tripping up the candidates and kicking them all out, those in charge of the training process find that one applicant has passed all their mental and physical requirements, as well as avoided all of their cleverly laid traps and snares.

The first colored agent for the CIA is assigned to the position of Reproduction Section Chief and given a no-frills office in subbasement 3. As the copy machine operator, he has plenty of time to take visiting diplomats on guided tours of the facilities, thus demonstrating the success of the agency's intensive integration efforts.

Through it all, Agent Dan Freeman plays the game. He knows his role, plays it well, and even tells a female coworker, "I want to be the best reproduction chief the CIA has ever had." But all this time he's learning, growing, and storing away his priceless cache of knowledge, experience, and tactical training with greater aims in mind. He resigns after five years to take a higher-paying position— as a social worker.

Freeman returns to his hometown of Chicago and, once there, rallies the new members of his old street gang, the Cobras, and passes on his covert guerrilla-war training. His plan is to amass an army of freedom fighters to take over the country, all the time knowing that his ragged group of urban hoodlums would never be suspected of doing the things they are about to do.

During a riot, police detective Dawson (J. A. Preston, center) signals for reinforcements as ex-CIA agent turned militant social worker Dan Freeman (Lawrence Cook, right) and an unidentified player look on, in *The Spook Who Sat by the Door*. (United Artists)

Racial tensions are high, and it all comes to a head when Shorty, a small-time drug pusher, is shot and killed by the police. A riot ensues, and the National Guard is called in to quell the disturbance. The Cobras go into action. They begin broadcasts of their revolutionary message from an underground radio station and steal

CREDITS: Director: Ivan Dixon. Producers: Ivan Dixon, Sam Greenlee. Screenplay: Sam Greenlee, Melvin Clay. Based on Sam Greenlee's novel. Photography: Michel Hugo. Music: Herbie Hancock. Editor: Michael Kahn. Art Director: Leslie Thomas. 102 minutes. Drama. PG.

CAST: Lawrence Cook (*Dan Freeman/Turk*), Paula Kelly (*Queen*), Janet League (*Joy*), J. A. Preston (*Dawson*), Paul Butler (*Do-Daddy Dean*), Don Blakely (*Stud Davis*), David Lemieux (*Willie*), Jack Aaron (*Carstairs*), Byron Morrow (*General*), Beverly Gill (*Willa*), Bob Hill (*Calhoun*), Martin Golar (*Perkins*), Kathy Beck (*Doris*), Stephen Ferry (*Colonel*).

an arsenal of weapons from the local armory. At a loss for any decisive leads, Dawson, a detective with the police department, goes to his old college buddy, the social worker Freeman, for information on the street that may lead to the capture of Uncle Tom, the man behind the troublemaking voice on the radio. Trust, suspicion, and betrayal lead to confrontation and murder.

In the end, Freeman has to do things he does not want to do, but he does them in the name of freedom. The Cobras, having trained factions of their covert organization in most major cities, escalate their revolution for freedom and begin the fight for social change. Over the sound of news reports describing the many organized uprisings that seem to be flaring up throughout the country, the ex-spook raises his wineglass in a solitary toast to the offensive that he has begun.

Reluctantly released by United Artists, *The Spook Who Sat by the Door* attracted lines that went around the block at the back-alley theaters in which it was booked. Weeks later, after a National Guard armory in California was robbed (much in the same way that had been depicted in the movie), the film was snatched off the screen and pulled from distribution.

[I had never heard of the film until I attended a Los Angeles screening at the Black American Cinema Society's 1982 Black Talkies on Parade film series. I was totally blown away by what was on the screen. Until *The Spook*, every movie I had ever seen that dealt with issues of race seemed to take on an attitude of "Woe is me, I'm black and catching hell in America . . ." And they would end with "I'm still black, still catching hell (perhaps not as much), but maybe . . . someday?" *The Spook* sidestepped all of that and confidently stated: "Here's the problem—here's a possible solution."
—TOR]

Review Summary: This was another film that apparently defied criticism, as we could find very few reviews of it. The opinions in those that were available were mixed. The fact that the main character was not the typical, ebonic-speaking superstud was a plus where most critics were concerned. Paula Hankins in *Cinéaste* wrote that Lawrence Cook gave an excellent performance and described him as "a warm, sensitive, intelligent man who made it through the tough training for the CIA . . ." Hankins was disappointed in the female characters, suggesting that one was a whore and the other a bitch. She also observed that "There is not a single woman in the [film's] guerrilla bands. One of the characters might as well have said that black women have no role to play in the struggle."

Meyer Kantor wrote in the *New York Times* that the movie had a number of flaws, including a lack of respect for the enemy, the system, and its ability to defend itself, a lack of respect for human life, and the portrayal of anger without reason. Kantor added, "Dixon, the black actor turned director, keeps the action moving and the screenplay crackles with the wit and heat of men of anger. It is the failure of [the scriptwriters] Greenlee and Clay to present a clear indictment of white society's treatment of third world people that causes the film to drift from meaningful outrage to senseless, James Bond–like violence."

Kantor concluded that *The Spook Who Sat by the Door* was a valuable response to oppression. "For all its excesses, it sounds a warning to an overstuffed goose of a society that it is swimming in a sea of despair, with the tide rapidly rising."

IVAN DIXON

By phone from his home in Maui, Hawaii
June 7, 1998

TOR: How did Sam Greenlee's novel *The Spook Who Sat by the Door* make it to the big screen?
DIXON: I read it and decided I wanted to do it. It was the first and only thing I'd wanted to do as a film.
TOR: So you were the one who actually spearheaded the production?
DIXON: Yes. I guess I read it in 1968 or '69, and it took me until 1972 to put it together. It turned out that Sam Greenlee came out to Los Angeles to see somebody about making his book into a film. Either they turned him down, or he turned them down. I found him, had a talk with him, and he sold me the rights.
TOR: How did the two of you go about seeking financing?
DIXON: I paid him for the rights, personally, out of my own pocket. Then we set out to try to find money to make the movie. We went to various agencies and studios trying to sell the project.
TOR: How receptive were they?
DIXON: None were receptive, of course.
TOR: Was it the subject matter?
DIXON: In the beginning most of those people had not read the script, but when we would leave it with them, they would imme-

diately turn it down. But at the same time, I was going to other people, in other areas, that I hoped would finance it.

TOR: People like who?

DIXON: I went to middle-class and upper-class blacks and tried to raise money. The Johnsons of Chicago, John, George, and Al . . .

TOR: Of Johnson Publishing?

DIXON: That's John Johnson. George Johnson has the beauty products, and Al Johnson is the Cadillac dealer. They're all millionaires.

TOR: All Johnsons with money, huh?

DIXON: And none of them gave me a dime.

TOR: Were they interested at all? Or did they just turn you down flat?

DIXON: Actually, I can't recall, but I really think they turned me down flat. They were not really interested in filmmaking, or if they were, they were not sure if they should invest in me or not. I also went to A. G. Gaston, Spalding & Cox, of North Carolina Mutual, and various other people with money.

TOR: Did you ever think about giving up?

DIXON: By that time, I was also going to other countries. I went to Algiers and tried to get the money from the Algerian government, the Algerian filmmakers. I had spoken with Locdah Amedah, who is the most famous Algerian filmmaker, and head of Algerian film production. They promised me help, and then nothing came of it. I went to them because they had financed *Z* or *Zed.*

TOR: The Costa Gavras film?

DIXON: Yes. They had financed that, and since it was a very revolutionary type of film, I thought maybe they would come up with the dough for *The Spook.* I returned home with the idea that I had some money coming from them, at least partial support, and they just completely backed out.

TOR: And then?

DIXON: I tried raising money from Africa. Particularly the Nigerians, and the Ghanaians too. The Ghanaians turned me down completely. I had spoken to a man at the Bank of Nigeria, in London. Kisarugi Rotini was his name. I'm not sure of the spelling, but use it anyway, they'll know who I'm talking about. Anyway, he said there was some money that was being held by "the Boys," meaning the generals and the army. And they had something like $400 million in the Nigerian Bank in London, and in a Swiss bank. He said the Boys were coming to London to meet with him, and he would explain the project to them, and they would come up with the money and everything would be cool.

So, the Boys came to London. They told me later that they were in a back room of the bank having a meeting. There were ten or twelve guys. And all of a sudden, this white man walked into the room. They said they don't know how he even got through security. But he came in the room and said, "I'm here from the American government. We hear you are about to do business with a gentleman named Dixon . . . you do not want to do business with this gentleman." And he turned and walked out.

TOR: Ouch!

DIXON: [*Laughter*] They said the Boys looked at each other and got the hell out of there! [*More laughter*]

TOR: So with even the U.S. government coming out against you, what kept you going?

DIXON: This is what was told to me. It was never proven it actually happened.

TOR: So it might have been an excuse?

DIXON: Perhaps. Anyway, I kept on trying to raise money. Finally, I found a black attorney in Los Angeles who said he would help me—Tom Newsome. He decided to go directly to the people. Not the blacks who had money, but the ones who didn't have a lot of money. We started asking people who had maybe saved $5,000 or $10,000 and would like to risk some, or all of it, if they could invest it with us.

We found we had to raise it in $25,000 increments. So what we did was put these people together. Like if a guy had $5,000, and a lady had $10,000, that was $15,000 . . . and then if somebody else added up to ten . . . we'd put them together. And we pulled together all of these $25,000 investments. And that's how we raised the money.

TOR: What was the budget that you were going for?

DIXON: The budget was $750,000. We had set it up through limited partnerships that were legal and bona fide and everything. We had gotten an accountant. And we had people all over the country who were investing with us, which was very interesting. One schoolteacher who had saved about $25,000 gave us $12,000. We had a lady who worked for the county who had saved $7,000, and she lent it all to us. There was another lady whose husband had left her his real estate business. She had quite a bit of money, and she wanted to invest . . . $25,000 at first, then later invested another $25,000.

TOR: That must have made you feel good.

DIXON: Yeah, it made me feel good . . . but it made me feel awful when I lost it. We started the movie when we had $48,000. We decided to go with it because we had so many promises of money that we thought more should come in as people saw us doing it. Which was a stupid move on our part. Really a naive kind of move. So we started the film and managed to scrape up about $600,000 while shooting.

TOR: Was that enough?

DIXON: No, we needed $750,000. So at the point where I did not have the next week's salary to pay the crew, I stopped work . . . we shut down.

TOR: How did you get the additional money?

DIXON: We cut together some of the footage and showed it to various studios. It was a lot of action footage, and they thought that being in the early seventies, during the blaxploitation films, they figured it was another blaxploitation film. It looked good, the action was good, camera work was good.

TOR: No one remembered you from before when you were trying to raise money?

DIXON: Not at all, nobody knew, or nobody paid any attention. And what happened was that . . . we showed it to David Picker at United Artists, and he bit. He said, "Here, take the money, $325,000 to finish the film, and we will distribute it." Of course, it was a sucker's distribution deal, because they had all the rights, because they put up the money to finish it. But by then we were all happy just to finish it. So we just let them have it essentially . . . and that was the end of that.

TOR: So once the film was completed, how did United Artists like it?

DIXON: Well, we got a big screening room and screened the film for about forty people from the studio. Now, it's got talking scenes with philosophy, and story lines with meaning.

TOR: Which was not what they anticipated?

DIXON: Right. It was a totally different film from what David Picker surmised it to be. And of course, he was terribly embarrassed. At the end of the screening, nobody said anything. There was absolute silence. They all just kind of looked at each other. And then several of them went off in a corner and talked. Nobody said anything to me. Later Picker came over and told me that the film needed to be recut. "It's too long and it has many problems."

TOR: Problems with what?

DIXON: He didn't say the story line, but the flow of the film. They gave me an editor and he was supposed to help me to reedit the film. Of course, I wouldn't do anything that he said, except I did take some minutes out of some scenes and made it shorter.

What they were trying to do was to take all that stuff out that the Spook was saying. Everything that was indoctrinating these kids with CIA tactics, so that they could actually begin an underground skirmish. They wanted most of that out. But I instructed them that the ending could not be changed and that was in our deal. They also asked me to remove some of their names from the credits. I did that.

TOR: Then they accepted the film?

DIXON: They had no choice. By contract, they had to open *The Spook* in thirty-six cities.

TOR: Where was the premiere?

DIXON: They opened it in New York, and it made $500,000 in the first week or something like that. It was really a remarkable thing.

TOR: How much promotion did they put out?

DIXON: They put out quite a bit of promotion. They really did. They had to, it was contractual.

TOR: So, despite the film's content, they did want to make their money back?

DIXON: No, they didn't want to make their money back. They just wanted to satisfy the contract and get out of it. What happened was, David Picker was fired because of this film. Yeah, he was set out, and he was the head of United Artists at the time. He was rolled over into an independent producer and the rest of them took over. TransAmerica, who owned United Artists, immediately took their logo off the film. They didn't want anything to do with it.

TOR: What was their attitude after it made so much money in its first week?

DIXON: A few weeks after it opened in Los Angeles, the armory—I believe it was in Compton—was robbed. And the robbery took place the same way that the robbery of guns took place in the movie. [*Laughter*] They stole one hundred M-1 rifles. The only thing was that they didn't get the firing pins, so the guns were useless.

TOR: Do you think the robbery was inspired by the film?

DIXON: It could have been a ploy. I have no idea what really occurred. But the picture in the paper looked almost like a production still from the film. [*Laughter*] Anyway, a few weeks after that, ninety pounds of plastic explosives were stolen from Fort Ord. And then, a few weeks after that, the Simbionese Liberation Army started its little uprising. The film was due to open here in Hawaii the same week that the S.L.A. kidnapped Patty Hearst . . . suddenly the film was impounded and disappeared.

TOR: They thought *The Spook* was causing all this stuff?

DIXON: Right. But it was only lightly blamed. They wanted to keep it from becoming too controversial, so people wouldn't have too much interest in it. We finally ended up threatening to sue and finally signed an agreement that if they gave the film back, totally, all the prints and everything, we would not sue them. Then we tried to self-distribute the film, and no theaters wanted it.

TOR: Judging from the initial box office response *The Spook* received, how do you think the film would have done if it had received a legitimate release and distribution?

DIXON: I think it would have done very well monetarily. You can compare any film that started out like that with an uproar at the box office. In the black neighborhoods, people came out of the theaters and told their friends, and more people came. It really scared Hollywood.

TOR: The main thing that impressed me about *The Spook* was that at least it offered a solution to the problem.

DIXON: It really wasn't a real solution, I've got to tell you. It was a fantasy. But it was a fantasy that everybody felt, every black male particularly. Most black men in this country have probably said to themselves, "I'd like to kill all those M-Fs," you know? [*Laughter*] It's just what we have felt after all of the bullshit that we as a people have been put through in this country. And I felt that the opportunity was there to express the feelings of these people, let them get their feelings out through *The Spook*. And that's what I was doing with this film.

Coffy
American International Pictures (1973)

"As long as people are deprived of a decent life,
they're gonna want something to just feel good with.
And nothing's gonna change that except money and
power. That's what I'm after, baby . . . the power to
change things for our people."

—Brunswick to Coffy

Coffy was the first film to elevate a black actress to Superwoman status, and Pam Grier, as the title character, went from being an office receptionist to becoming the undisputed Queen of the blaxploitation film.

When her kid sister is coaxed into trying heroin, and then purposely hooked, Coffy wages her own personal campaign of vengeance. Tough and street-smart, she uses her voluptuous body, along with a loaded shotgun, to methodically work her way up the drug food-chain ladder. She goes from the junkie to the dealer to the supplier, all the way up to the H.H.I.C. (Head Honkey In Charge).

The hard-edged production maintains all the violence and not-so-positive screen characters that the "soul cinema thrillers" of the seventies have come to be known for. There's the pitiful junkie who got Coffy's sister hooked, his perverted dealer, who trades drugs for sex, and Carter, the smitten policeman, who is nearly beaten to death for having convictions. King George is a loud-dressing, drug-dealing pimp, with an insatiable appetite for money and white women. And Brunswick is Coffy's militant, down-for-the-cause, politically minded boyfriend, who betrays her, leaves her for dead, and is later found in the company of a white woman. Even Coffy herself (while apparently in a sort of a stress-induced trance) does some pretty seedy things in the name of getting even. But pimps, hookers, thugs, and drug dealers were Hollywood's black images of choice at the time.

The voluptuous Coffy (Pam Grier) is a mild-mannered nurse who becomes a revenge-seeking hooker in *Coffy*. (American International Pictures)

CREDITS: Writer-Director: Jack Hill. Producer: Robert A. Papazian. Photography: Paul Lohmann. Music: Roy Ayers. Editor: Charles McClelland. Art Director: Perry Ferguson. 91 minutes. Drama. R.

CAST: Pam Grier (*Coffy*), Booker Bradshaw (*Brunswick*), Robert DoQui (*King George*), William Elliott (*Carter*), Allan Arbus (*Vitroni*), Sid Haig (*Omar*), Barry Cahill (*McHenry*), Morris Buchanan (*Sugar-Man*), Lee de Broux (*Nick*), Bob Minor (*Studs*), John Perak (*Aleva*), Ruben Moreno (*Ramos*), Carol Lawson (*Priscilla*), Linda Haynes (*Meg*).

Just as black men identified with the male heroes played by Richard Roundtree (*Shaft*, 1971), Fred Williamson (*Hammer*, 1972), Bernie Casey (*Hit Man*, 1972), Jim Brown (*Slaughter*, 1972), and music man Isaac Hayes (*Truck Turner*, 1974), which allowed them to vicariously experience feats of superhuman machismo on the screen, many black women have identified with and rooted for the assertive and independent Pam Grier playing Coffy.

The film's success inspired a series of Grier star vehicles including *Foxy Brown* (1974), *Sheba, Baby* (1974), and *Friday Foster* (1975). After a long layoff in the eighties, Pam Grier revived her acting career in the 1990s with roles in *Original Gangstas* (1996), where she teamed up with other blaxploitation alums to save a town from a street gang that's run amuck, *Mars Attacks* (1997), *The Faculty* (1998), and her outstanding performance as the title character in Quentin Tarantino's surprisingly neglected *Jackie Brown* (1998), which has become a cult film in Europe.

Review Summary: Among the handful of reviews that we have found for *Coffy*, the opinions of the critics differed significantly. Whit Williams in *Variety* was firmly positive; he not only rated *Coffy* as an overall good action film, but applauded Pam Grier in the title role. On the other hand, Michael McKegney in the *Village Voice* spent much of his review discussing what he perceived as the predictability and hypocrisy of the film's story line. He also (justifiably) questioned the harsh, sadistic nature of the picture's violence, as well as the audience's celebration of it.

Donald Bogle, in his *Blacks in American Films and Television* discussion of the movie, reflects upon the legacy of *Coffy*. According to Bogle, the film, which made Pam Grier into a B-movie star, was criticized by many black intellectuals but supported by many feminists at the time of its release. Bogle goes on to note that Coffy's character is not flawless and that one cannot deny the senseless violence of the film, but he seemed to find a redeeming factor in the comedic campiness of *Coffy*.

Many reviews mentioned the physical beauty of Pam Grier, a quality that seems to have enhanced the very nature of the film.

Claudine

20th Century-Fox (1974)

"I've actually avoided success. Because when you're
successful and rich, people will envy and hate
you . . . I want people to love me."

—Roop to Claudine

In the midst of all the black action-packed, cinematic offerings of
the time, *Claudine* gazed unflinchingly into black social issues and
single-parent dating in Harlem. It is a film about family, for family.
And much like a northern-based urban contemporary version of
Sounder (1972), it's a film for all ages and audiences.

Claudine is a single mother trying to raise her six children while
trapped in a welfare system that will not allow her to succeed. It
forces her to lie and cheat just to survive (with an outside job as a
domestic), and discourages her telling the truth, for which she
would surely be punished. She meets Roop, who works as a
garbage man and is struggling through a complex life of his own.
Together, they both enhance and threaten each other's existence.
Claudine's public assistance eligibility is jeopardized by whatever
financial support Roop might provide, and as a divorced man who
is behind on child support payments of his own, six additional
mouths to feed is a costly sacrifice.

Their rocky but sincere affair is further complicated by the various problems, needs, attitudes, and actions of Claudine's children.
Her eldest son, Charles, is protective of his mother and disapproves
of this new suitor in her life. He's frustrated with the world he sees
around him and involves himself with the impending struggle for
revolutionary change. The teenager Charlene is confused about her
own self-worth, while at the same time beginning to give in to her
physical impulses with regard to the opposite sex. Adolescent Paul
skips school to hang out and shoot dice with the wrong crowd.
The three younger siblings are just trying to be kids in a rough and
deprived world that demands too much of everyone.

On a family stroll through their Harlem neighborhood, Claudine (Diahann Carroll, center left) and Roop (James Earl Jones, center right) happily hold hands with Claudine's six children, left to right, Patrice (Yvette Curtis), Paul (David Kruger), Charles (Lawrence Hilton-Jacobs), Charlene (Tamu), Lurlene (Socorro Stephens), and Francis (Eric Jones), in *Claudine*. (© 1974 Courtesy of 20th Century–Fox Film Corporation. All rights reserved.)

Unlike the majority of films that deal with some sudden tragedy or existential influence that comes into a happy home and threatens to tear a loving, affluent family apart, *Claudine* deals with real-life, kick-you-in-the-butt problems—paying the bills, putting food on the table, and the sheer difficulty of surviving in a tough and often unfair inner-city world. Despite the serious subject matter, the film delivers a lot of laughs and was considered to be a new-style, 1970s black romantic comedy.

CREDITS: Director: John Berry. Producer: Hannah Weinstein. Screenplay: Tina and Lester Pine. Photography: Gayne Rescher. Music: Curtis Mayfield. Editor: Luis San Andres. Art Direction: Ben Kasazkow. Set Design: Ted Haworth. Costume: Bernard Johnson. 92 minutes. Comedy/Drama. PG.

CAST: Diahann Carroll (*Claudine*), James Earl Jones (*Roop*), Lawrence Hilton-Jacobs (*Charles*), Tamu (*Charlene*), David Kruger (*Paul*), Yvette Curtis (*Patrice*), Eric Jones (*Francis*), Socorro Stephens (*Lurlene*), Adam Wade (*Owen*), Harrison Avery (*Minister*), Roxie Roker (*Mrs. Winston*), Mordecai Lawner (*Process Server*), Terry Alexander (*Teddy*).

Directed by John Berry, a returning McCarthy-era exile, *Claudine* is a gritty, heartfelt story with strong, thought-evoking performances. Diahann Carroll received a 1974 Academy Award nomination for Best Actress, and Curtis Mayfield's music, as performed by Gladys Knight and the Pips, should have been recognized as well; it became one of the first soundtrack albums to make big bucks for a movie outside the box office. Even now, listening to timeless songs like "On and On," "Mr. Welfare," and "Make Yours a Happy Home" still get heads to bopping and fingers popping.

Review Summary: Most reviews commented on the fact that *Claudine* was a welcome relief from the majority of black films produced during the period, and this comment from *Variety* says it all: "Claudine isn't, and praise be for that, another blacksploitation job, complete with glorification of low life, violence, and the attendant short-term emotional blowout." Although it dealt with contemporary urban black family life, the focus was on well-defined black characters who were smart and funny at the same time.

And one reviewer located the film's significance in what some considered to be stereotypes. Judith Crist in *New York* wrote: "They're wise to their particular situation in black poverty, to limited opportunities within the stereotypes that they and society have created, from the mythology of the black woman as perpetual propagator, to that of the black man as the stud who drops his seed and disappears. But they happen to be people who love, and who therefore, find each other worth the coping."

JAMES EARL JONES

At the Willard Hotel, Washington, D.C.
October 15, 1998

TOR: The early 1970s brought action-packed films like *Shaft, Super Fly, Trouble Man, Hit Man,* and *Hell Up in Harlem.* How did a story like *Claudine* make it out of all that?

JONES: It didn't make it "out" of that. *Claudine* was an idea that came about when three people got together. The late Diana Sands, the late Hannah Weinstein, and James Grant, an attorney. They created a company called Third World Productions. They had intended to do several films—all they got done was *Claudine.*

TOR: Why weren't any of the other films made?

JONES: Oh, several reasons . . . Death was one of them.

TOR: Ms. Sands?

JONES: Yes, and later Ms. Weinstein.

TOR: Were you their first choice for Roop? Or did you have to audition?

JONES: You know I wasn't the first choice, don't you?

TOR: [*Laughter*] No, I don't.

JONES: Well, I certainly was not the first choice. The first choice was Bernie Hamilton.

TOR: The Captain from the *Starsky and Hutch* television series?

JONES: Yeah. And Diana Sands was the first choice for Claudine. At some point—and it's kind of a mystery in a way, as it came to me—Diana knew she was ill. I don't think she shared it with anybody except her family.

At that time, I was engaged in *King Lear*. She gave me a call and said, "Jimmy, why aren't you in this movie?" I said, "I'm involved in this play right now." So, she said, "Think about it," and we hung up. Later on, the director, John Berry, who is a friend of mine from our Athol Fugard play days, called me and said, "Jimmy, we'd like to engage you for this film. Bernie is doing it, but we would like for you to do it."

I assumed that things had been worked out between the production and Bernie Hamilton, and I said, "Well, John, I have to finish *King Lear* before I can think about anything." He said, "We'll work it out." What had happened was that Diana decided to pull her own coup d'état in a way. She wanted to get Diahann Carroll in to replace herself, and me in to replace Bernie, which was the final result.

TOR: Was there friction behind that move?

JONES: Bernie called me one day and was outraged that the change had been made that way. I didn't know what to say to him because I thought it had been worked out. But it was Diana Sands's wish, so there wasn't much further argument about it.

TOR: It seemed that you and Diahann Carroll were perfect casting and very easily could have been the first choices.

JONES: That was Diana Sands's vision. It didn't just happen all at once; it was step by step. I was brought in first, over Bernie's objections, and Diana Sands and I rehearsed together for a while. She wanted the young children playing the roles to think that she was continuing.

TOR: How was the chemistry between you and Ms. Sands?

JONES: Although Diana and I never had a romantic relationship, I had kissed her before, in our younger days. [*Chuckle*] Diana Sands—I've told my wife this too, but—Diana was the best kisser I've ever had the occasion to kiss. She had a wonderful kiss . . . I can't explain it. It was like . . . eating wonderful fruit that you've never had before. But when I kissed her in the rehearsals for the film, it wasn't the same. Something was odd . . . I thought, maybe it was my bad breath? I realized later that she was in so much pain she could barely say her lines. She was dying but didn't want anybody to know.

TOR: Was the story idea her concept?

JONES: I don't really know. Tina and Lester Pine, who wrote the script, had the family living in Watts, California. At what point they changed it? I have no idea, but they adapted it for New York, for Harlem. Claudine was a welfare mother who worked as a housekeeper in the suburbs with a bunch of kids with different fathers. At the time, Diahann Carroll was known for her glamour. And so they had to get Diahann to push her hair back off of her very square forehead and wear clothes that would disguise her great figure . . . and sort of knock-knees, you know? [*Laughter*] And she was willing to deglamorize herself and transform herself into Claudine.

TOR: Would your character in *Claudine* be considered your first romantic lead role?

JONES: [*Very thoughtful*] I don't know. I never looked at myself as a romantic leading actor. I'm a character actor and I have been since I was twenty-five years old. I never think of those categories, really. I'm primarily a stage actor as well. I'm a farm boy from Mississippi, and I never wanted to present any other kind of image. I had a chance to play *Shaft*. I read the galleys before they made it into a screenplay and I said, "I'm a farmer . . . This street talk is something that I don't really know. So it's not really fair for me to try and present myself as a "street dude." I tried to be honest about it and passed up a great opportunity, in terms of a career move. But I said, "That is not me."

TOR: Getting back to *Claudine*. Do you have a favorite scene in the film?

JONES: Oh, boy . . . there were so many of them. The scene where we catch Milhouse, the mouse. When we're in bed, and that kissing scene was one of my favorites also, as well as the first time I ever got butt-naked in front of a camera.

TOR: That reminds me of the bathtub scene. I remember the bathtub scene from *Super Fly* and it really had an effect on me. I was only fourteen or fifteen at the time, so that was pretty exciting stuff. But when Claudine was taking a bath at your apartment and fell asleep in the tub, I remember how respectfully that scene was played out.

JONES: I think Roop, like me, was originally a country boy. You didn't grab at the woman, you courted her, and you tried not to make a fool of yourself. Nevertheless, he did all the time. The kids were laughing at him and taunting him for the way he dressed, and he didn't care. His object was to win this woman. But he courted her more or less as a country bumpkin, trying to be cool.

TOR: What was his attitude about taking on the responsibility of the five kids?

JONES: Very difficult, as it would be with anybody. He was having enough problems dealing with his own kids from a divorce ... alimony ... but he took them on because of his love for their mother, and in a way his love for them too. He'd gotten to know them, and except for the oldest son, they had grown to accept him. He liked those kids, her children, her family, so he married a family.

TOR: That's definitely an important vision, even today.

JONES: Yeah, it doesn't happen in films too often. Usually in films, whether you're talking about ethnic films, or any kind of films, they'll deal with the fracture of family, rather than the cohesion of family. And I accept that because good plays are often about conflict. And good drama is all about conflict. And that conflict is often drawn out of negative social energies.

TOR: What was the audience response to the film?

JONES: I don't know how to measure audiences with motion pictures. We all worked for SAG minimum, which was just a few hundred dollars a week back in those days. But a trickle of money always comes in from *Claudine*, a trickle. It doesn't pay my bills, but it shows that people still watch it. They rent the videos, whatever. It was a well-watched film. It was not a blockbuster, but it was a well-watched movie.

Cooley High

American International Pictures (1975)

"This is for the brothers who ain't here . . ."

—Cochise to his partners as he pours
libations

Cooley High could be considered an anthem to black youth. You don't have to have personally experienced the exploits of this rowdy group of inner-city teenagers from Edwin G. Cooley Vocational High School to understand and identify with their problems, struggles, needs, dreams, and desires.

We fade in on high-angle aerial views of the Chicago skyline. The Supremes croon their hit song "Baby Love" to the opening title sequence, and each subsequent shot brings us closer in to the city. We are visually transported from the glistening skyscrapers to the dull housing projects on the other side of the elevated tracks. It's a Friday morning, the last school day before the weekend.

Cochise is a basketball star awaiting an athletic scholarship to Grambling University. He stops by to pick up his friend Preach for school, but Preach doesn't even want to get out of bed. Preach is naturally smart but has little interest in going to college, or high school either for that matter. Once at school, the boys pull a prank to sneak out of class and start their weekend early. They're joined by Pooter and Tyrone, and they decide to hang out at the city zoo for a day filled with horseplay, laughter, jive street vernacular, and lots of "yo' Momma" jokes. The foursome enjoy a fun time amongst the birds, reptiles, and wild animals until Pooter gets hit with a wad of gorilla shit.

From there, Preach and Cochise take to smooching with their girlfriends in a darkened apartment hallway. (Flashback: Anyone who couldn't identify with this scene had either too-strict parents or a low libido.) One girl is willing, the other is not. "I will if she will," Cochise's girl, Johnny Mae, says. Perhaps a cliché dilemma, but so true.

High school pals Cochise (Lawrence Hilton-Jacobs, left), Preach (Glynn Turman, right), and Tyrone (Joseph Carter Wilson, standing) prepare to celebrate some good news with an illicit bottle of wine in *Cooley High*. (American International Pictures)

CREDITS: Director: Michael Shultz. Producer: Steve Krantz. Screenplay: Eric Monte. Photography: Paul Van Brack. Music: Freddie Perren. Editor: Christopher Holmes. Art Direction: William B. Fosser. 107 minutes. Drama-Comedy. PG.

CAST: Glynn Turman (*Preach*), Lawrence Hilton-Jacobs (*Cochise*), Garrett Morris (*Mr. Mason*), Cynthia Davis (*Brenda*), Corin Rogers (*Pooter*), Maurice Leon Havis (*Willie*), Joseph Carter Wilson (*Tyrone*), Shermann Smith (*Stone*), Norman Gibson (*Robert*), Maurice Marshall (*Damon*), Steven Williams (*Jimmy Lee*), Christine Jones (*Sandra*), Jackie Taylor (*Johnny Mae*), Lynn Caridine (*Dorothy*), Mary Larkins (*Preach's Mother*).

Cochise goes home smiling and finds his baby nephew playing in the toilet. He caringly collects the infant and notices a soaked envelope floating in the commode. It's a letter, addressed to him, from Grambling University.

Cochise's scholarship has come through, and he'll be heading for college. It's time to celebrate with his boys and a bottle of cheap wine. His partners are proud and happy for him, but they scoff at Preach's plans to head for Hollywood after graduation, to become a screenwriter. Once the wine is gone, they take their celebration to a "quarter party" being given by Dorothy, one of their classmates. Young people are busy doing "the jerk" to Martha Reeves and the Vandellas' hit, "Dancing in the Streets," and all is fine until trouble-maker Damon shows up. When he sees Cochise doing a sultry slow grind with his girlfriend to Smokey Robinson's "Oooh, Baby, Baby," the fight is on. It quickly becomes a free-for-all, and needless to say, Dorothy won't be giving another party any time soon.

After the fracas, Cochise and the boys drink more wine, smoke a joint, and sing doo-wop on a street corner. Stone and Roberts, a couple of street hoods, drive up in a ragged Cadillac and offer the guys a ride that will change their lives forever. The car is stolen, of course, and there's a police-car chase, jail, an interrogation, and a big misunderstanding when Preach and Cochise are released and the other two are not.

From there, the story escalates into a web of mistrust, betrayal, and revenge. The ending is tragic and heart-wrenching, and has left many a tear at many a matinee screening, but the upbeat Four Tops tune, "Reach Out: I'll Be There," which plays over the end credits, lets us know it's gonna be all right.

The jam-packed 1960s Motown sound track really helped to anchor the film to its time period. The songs are like a musical time machine, and "It's So Hard to Say Good-bye to Yesterday," the moving ballad that's played over the final scene, sung by G. C. Cameron, seems to say it all.

Cooley High was a welcome relief from the violent, action-packed, rock-'em-sock-'em blaxploitation films of the period. And unlike the 1990s string of black-boys-coming-of-age-in-the-inner-cities flicks such as *Boyz 'N the Hood* (1991), *Juice* (1992), and *Menace II Society* (1993), it showed that the sixties were a simpler time, with more innocence, more fun, less stress, and fewer bullets.

"Sometimes you have to use violence to offset what you want to say," director Michael Shultz observed about the perceived violence in *Cooley High*. "It had violence, but that wasn't the substance of the piece. It made you feel this tremendous loss of potential in black youth; it never condoned violence. It made you feel so sorry that that kind of action had to take place. And a lot of films today don't."

In addition to its tremendous box office success, the film helped to launch the careers of many of its talented actors. Glynn Turman, who had already starred in *Five on the Black Hand Side* (1973), would continue to play starring roles in films such as *J.D.'s Revenge* (1976) and *The River Niger* (1976). Lawrence Hilton-Jacobs was fresh off the set of *Claudine* (1973) when he was cast, and would go on to do many other films, but his real popularity came as a "sweat hog" on television's *Welcome Back Cotter*. Garrett Morris, who portrayed Mr. Mason, the tough but caring schoolteacher, went on to be an original member of the Saturday Night Live Not Ready for Prime Time Players. Steven Williams, who portrayed Jimmy Lee, the sharply dressed trickster pimp, would go on to do television's *21 Jumpstreet*, *The X-Files*, and the BET comedy series, *Linc's*. Actor-director Robert Townsend made his film-acting debut in *Cooley High*'s gym scene.

The female characters seemed to receive very little respect throughout the film, and in its wake Hollywood failed to show them any respect as well. Unlike so many of the male actors, none of the actresses went much further in their careers. In regard to the disappointing female images, however, the portrayal of Preach's mother, a hardworking single parent of three who was in over her head but still fighting the odds, was a strong counterbalance. Mary Larkins, who played the role, came off as a real person and a moving character.

Review Summary: The energetic, youthful performances were key to the reviews for *Cooley High*. Glynn Turman and Lawrence Hilton-Jacobs are praised again and again for their superb portrayals of Preach and Cochise. Director Michael Shultz and script writer Eric Monte receive both praise and criticism. Lawrence Van Gelder in the *New York Times* said, "Impressively written by Eric Monte and directed with an almost unwavering sense of pace by Michael Shultz, *Cooley High* pulsates with the careless exuberance of youth and captivates with characterizations and incidents presented not for the sake of nostalgia, but out of the kind of understanding that cherishes and makes peace with the past." Margo Jefferson in *Newsweek* complained that "Eric Monte's script is astutely colloquial, but clumsily plotted, and director Michael Shultz occasionally plays for cheap laughs that will strike many viewers as patronizing." In the *Village Voice*, James Walcott called the movie "loose, rowdy, tough, and sentimental, alternately lucid and unfocused, a movie divided against itself, it's the best American comedy so far this year."

LAWRENCE HILTON-JACOBS

Hilton-Gateway Hotel, Newark, New Jersey
May 7, 1999

TOR: What awakened your interest in acting?
HILTON-JACOBS: I think I just wanted to always do it. I had a cousin, Sunny Davis, who was staying with us when I was a kid . . . maybe seven, eight years old, for a while. He was a singer from the Virgin Islands, which is where my family is from, St. Thomas, Virgin Islands. And he had a record out, and he had managers calling the house, and every time we got a phone call I got excited because there was a real show-business person on the other end. And when I saw the record, and I saw his name on the label, I was like . . . "Aaahhhhhh!"
TOR: How did you go about landing the part in *Cooley High?*
HILTON-JACOBS: *Claudine* was my first feature film. And I auditioned for that. I had nothing, no agent, no appointment . . . nothing. But I heard about it, so I showed up. They must have seen about, maybe, twenty-five or thirty guys, but it looked like nine million to me. I mean they were there all day! I was the last person, and rest in peace, the guy who was the casting director, Charlie Briggs, came out. And you could see he was exhausted. And he looked at me and said, "Whadda you want?"
    And I was like, "I. . . . I . . . I wanted to read."
    Charlie said, "Come on in."
    And I was like, "Oh, man, this is the way it goes," and I went in. I originally read for the part of Tommy Blackwell, the boyfriend of the older sister, which they cut out of the movie. They brought me back on a callback and it worked out.
    So *Claudine* happened, and about nine or ten months later the movie was out. The American International people had seen it and were considering me for a part in *Cooley High,* but their

concern was that I had played such an edgy kind of a guy, and my character in *Cooley High* wasn't that kind of a guy. You know how they do in show business, and it's dumb, dumb, dumb . . . but it goes on. If you play one role . . . that's gotta be you and that's you for life! When it was *Cooley High* time, they were like, "Charles from *Claudine* was a militant guy . . . and we don't know about that." But it finally worked out.

TOR: How old were you then?

HILTON-JACOBS: I had just turned twenty-one.

TOR: Though they had you in mind all along, do you know if they had been considering anyone else?

HILTON-JACOBS: I think they read a lot of actors. I know a lot of guys who read for the part of Preach. In fact, a friend of mine, Leon Pinkney, he was my real tight buddy back in those acting days. We used to work a lot together from extras on. He and I were down to the wire and he got called first, and they said, "You're going to play Preach, who was called Reverend at the time. The original name was Reverend, and the original name for Cochise was Genghis, like "Genghis Khan," but they didn't want to use the real names to protect the innocent, you know? They didn't want to get sued. But anyway, we had gotten cast. So he called me, and I got the message and I called him back, and he said, "Man, brother, did you get your part? 'Cause I got mine."

I said, "I just found out too!"

We went to a Puerto Rican store, we got some food, we were eating arroz con pollo. We thought we was on! And a few days later, Glynn Turman became available, and they dissed my man, straight up!

TOR: They wanted Glynn Turman from the get-go?

HILTON-JACOBS: They wanted Glynn, and Glynn had worked with Michael a couple of times. They had also done *What the Wine Sellers Buy* on Broadway. And they had done *Ceremonies in Dark Old Men* as a TV special, and they wanted him for *Cooley High*, but he was unavailable for a moment. Know what that means . . . [*rubs his fingers together*] unavailable? And so they were able to work it out.

TOR: How much of the Cochise character was you?

HILTON-JACOBS: The womanizing part! [*Laughter*] Anytime you play any kind of a character, you definitely lend yourself to it. You have to go to your own sensibilities first, and then you try to create. I could relate to Cochise because at the time I did the movie, I was not out of high school that long—maybe five years—and remembered having those kind of carefree, fun times.

TOR: How was it on the set? Any difficulties?

HILTON-JACOBS: Not really. Just overzealous things happened while we were doing the car chase scene. We had to shoot some things twice: the car chase scene and the scene in the school, and where we get into the fight in the movie theater. The first time we filmed in the movie theater they used real sixteen-year-olds next to us and it didn't work because we look old. So they had to refilm that entire scene and get some older, thug-looking cast members to even it out. [*Laughter*]

And when we did the car scene the first time . . . and this is how you know magic can happen on a movie set: We did the car scene in a big area that's called the Area Crown—it's all modern now, but it was all swampy and dumpy back when we did *Cooley High* in 1974. Michael Shultz was trying to get, like, real reactions out of us. And we were coming round some bridge where Glynn was supposed to drive the car . . . and this ragged old '64 Cadillac was holding on by luck. And what Michael didn't tell us was that when Glynn comes around a blind corner . . . he had put a garbage can in the middle of the road. And we had camera equipment mounted on front of the car, and lights, so you couldn't really see. And Glynn was like a maniac driving this thing . . . he's flooring it all the way. And he turned that corner, man . . . and the acting was over! [*Laughter*] Because this big thing was in the way, and Glenn yelled, "WHAT THE FUCK ARE YOU DOING, SHULTZ!" And I was laughing my butt off, and Glynn said, "I'm paid to *act* scared, not *be* scared!" And so they had a little shouting match.

But I'm saying the magic of it is that, a lot of that footage when they shot it, got fogged. The film got underexposed or something . . . it didn't come out. So we had to refilm the whole thing. And what happened when we filmed it another day is we had a different attitude. I guess because we had done it, we kinda knew what we were going for, and this time we were extra self-conscious that there'd be no garbage cans in the middle of the street that we don't know about. And we're all in the car, and Glenn's driving crazy, and the cops are chasing us, and we're all laughing.

What happened is the guy who played Robert, he got so scared that he kept saying Glynn, instead of Preach. He said,

"You're going too fast, Glynn! You're going too fast! Watch out, Glynn!" And we just lost it, right? We were cracking up. But we were still trying to keep it going because the cameras were filming. So, you see Glynn trying not to crack up driving, and I'm in the back and I don't give a damn. It was just the funniest thing, and that's one of the most special moments in that movie.

TOR: Did anybody have any idea at the time, that you guys were making a film that would become such a classic?

HILTON-JACOBS: No, you never know that. What happens is you go off and you do a job. And you try to do a good job, and hope it's going to be a good film. We were excited about it and all that, but the response? Some things kinda fell into place. When they finished the movie, for instance, we had no idea what they were going to do sound track–wise. But the Motown idea came up, and by putting in that music, authenticated it. It just got a whole other life.

TOR: The music helped everyone relate to and identify with those characters and those situations?

HILTON-JACOBS: I think it's more than the characters. I think those fresh, untarnished kind of times, and the fun of it, the freeness of it, is really the key. The characters were just having innocent fun . . . it wasn't like we were saying "Fuck you, mutha fucker! I don't like your lips! Bang! Yo' shoes are better than mine!" You know, it wasn't that kind of a thing.

TOR: I'm sure you're very aware of the many tears that Cochise's demise has produced in theater audiences.

HILTON-JACOBS: My mother, for the first maybe ten, eleven, twelve years, could not watch the end of that movie. Because as far as she was concerned, that was her kid. And my older sister, Louise, was the same way. They would just break up.

TOR: How does it feel to have played a character who is capable of bringing about that kind of emotion?

HILTON-JACOBS: I never get used to it. When I see someone's response, especially to *Cooley High*, that's the Black National Anthem movie for black people. They respond to it, and I see sincere joy in a lot of people's faces. I just try to roll with it.

TOR: Even young kids today still relate to the film and those experiences, don't they?

HILTON-JACOBS: A new generation has picked up on it, maybe because a lot of the younger singers, even the rappers, are into it. They really promote things like *Cooley High* or *Dolemite*, or people from back in the day. They bring these things out now and it's a whole new audience. Boyz II Men doing "It's So Hard to Say Good-bye to Yesterday," and having an album out called "Cooley High Harmony," definitely brought new attention to the movie. Plus, the movie is on TV every two hours, so that may have something to do with it.

ERIC MONTE

On the phone from his home in Burbank, California
July 27, 1998

TOR: The end of *Cooley High* tells what happened to the main characters, as if the film were based on a true story. Is it?

MONTE: I wanted the movie to have an autobiographical feel, so one of the things I did was to leave out a plot . . . and at the end, by saying, "This is what happened to these people," also give it a biographical feel. But it was fiction.

TOR: What prompted you to tell this story?

MONTE: I was working with this guy named Steve Krantz. He was trying to figure out a project that we could do together. So he took me to see this movie called *The Education of Sonny Carson*. And when we walked out of there, he was like, "See, Eric, that's real black."

I was like, "No, it's not." I said, "Man, look . . . I lived in the projects in Cabrini Green in Chicago. So you can't tell me what real black life is. I said, "That was not a real black story. All it showed was the negative side of black life. It didn't show any of the positive. When I was growing up in the projects? Yeah, we had hard times and we were hassled by the police . . . but I also had some of the best times I ever had in my entire life. And I met some of the best friends that I've ever had in my entire life." So Steve rented a recording studio and we went in and I talked about my life for four hours a day for two days. Then he cut it down to a twenty-minute tape and sent it around to the studios.

Columbia and American International Pictures both wanted to buy it. And he decided to go with A.I.P. because he'd have more control. So that's when I started writing *Cooley High*.

TOR: So the story was inspired by some of your personal experiences?

MONTE: As I mentioned before, I wanted it to have an autobiographical feel—so I left out a plot. When they started shooting on October 1, 1974, Sam Arkoff called me up and said, "Eric, we got a problem! I just read the script and I just realized that it doesn't have a story . . . you've gotta put a story in it."

And I said, "Look, you're a professional moviemaker who has made hundreds of movies over the years. You've been involved with this script every day for a year, and it just now dawned on you that it doesn't have a story? You're a professional, Sam. Do you think that some amateur sitting in the theater is going to watch it in an hour and a half and realize that there's no story? It's not going to happen."

He was like, "Eric, it's gotta have a story. You can't have a movie that doesn't have a story."

I said, "Okay, Sam. Send me the script, and I'll put a story in it."

So he sent me the script and I tossed it on my dresser and kept on going about what I was doing. In the twenty-something years that that movie has been out, only two people have ever come up to me and said, "There's no story in that movie."

TOR: I can't say that because I saw a lot of stories in the film.

MONTE: You saw stories, but there was no plot.

TOR: Not even the coming of age? Dealing with society and peer pressure?

MONTE: Those are not plots. A plot is . . . the protagonist wants or desires something . . . and the antagonist interferes with that person accomplishing his goals or whatever. Without a protagonist, antagonist, and a goal . . . you don't have a plot. And *Cooley High* didn't have any of that.

TOR: You're right, somebody has to say no. But even with the Lawrence-Hilton Jacobs character wanting to go to college and getting the basketball scholarship, that wouldn't be considered a goal?

MONTE: Where's the antagonist?

TOR: It ended up being Stone and Robert.

MONTE: No, no . . . that was just an incident that happened. There was nothing or nobody there trying to keep him from reaching that goal. It wasn't there. They didn't even know he wanted to go to college.

TOR: The Garrett Morris character kept telling Preach to get his act together and stay in school.

MONTE: But Preach didn't have that goal.

TOR: Right, right.

MONTE: You see, all that stuff happened, but there was no plot. The plot is in your mind, not in the film.

TOR: Were you on the set during production?

MONTE: Only once. I went there to talk to Michael Shultz because they were trying to credit him and Steve Krantz with writing the movie, and they hadn't written it. I'd had a lot of problems with people ripping me off for credit prior to that. And I wanted to talk to Michael to ask him not to fight for the writing credit and not to try to cheat me out of my credit.

TOR: Did Michael Shultz have your vision in mind in the way he directed the film?

MONTE: Michael set up with me for, like, two or three months while I did the final draft. And I told him how it needed to be shot. And he had the expertise to go out and be able to do that.

TOR: What was the initial audience reaction to the film?

MONTE: They loved it. I had always believed that it would be a hit because there had never been a black movie, never any movie like *Cooley High*. A plotless movie had never been done before. A movie that showed black life as it really was. I knew black people were going to eat it up. It played in a Chicago theater that sat 4,000 people—eight shows a day to standing-room-only audiences, from June 15 until after Thanksgiving of 1975. And the amazing thing was that it managed to do that without any television ads. We didn't have any national billboards or none of the kind of stuff black movies get today. It was all word of mouth.

TOR: How much did the film change from the script to the screen?

MONTE: The opening scene changed a little bit, where they pulled the kids out of the class. And they cut out a scene in the middle where I showed Stone and Robert stealing the car. But outside of that, basically they shot exactly what I wrote.

TOR: The line at the end of the film where Preach pours the wine on the ground and says, "For the brothers who aren't here," was that a line that you guys used back in the day at Cabrini Green, or did you just come up with it?

MONTE: [*Laughter*] When I wrote that, they did it in the alley first, "This is for the brothers who ain't here. There's a whole lot of brothers who's dead or in jail and we gotta give 'em props." I did that to set up the scene in the graveyard. I made up that line because I wanted Preach to do something that people would recognize from something that happened earlier in the film. Since that movie has come out, I've seen it in other black movies, and I've seen it in so many rap music videos . . . it's incredible.

TOR: It's interesting that you made it up in light of the emergence of a Pan-African kind of culture, and the opening of various events with pouring a "libation" for the ancestors. When I first saw the African ritual of pouring libations to the ancestors, I said, "Oh, that's where that line in *Cooley High* came from."

MONTE: A friend of mine told me just recently that Africans pour out libations. But I had no idea at the time I wrote that movie.

TOR: *Cooley High* is the project that really launched your writing career, isn't it?

MONTE: When *Cooley High* came out, I knew it was going to be a big hit and I was going to be able to do whatever I wanted to do. So when it was a bigger hit than anyone had imagined, ABC decided they wanted to make *Cooley High* into a series. And I was into "The only way that I will be involved is if I can produce it under my own production company. I don't want white guys in charge and telling me what to do on a black show." So ABC said, "Okay."

I pitched four ideas for the pilot. They said I needed to hire some producers who had done it before, and they hired these two guys named Sal Turtletaub and Bernie Hornstein. I went away, came back, and they had a script on this thing that said, "Torrid Productions." I said, "Who's Torrid Productions?" Sal Turtletaub and Bernie Hornstein had gone out and formed a company with Bud Yorkin. ABC signed a deal to do my pilot for "What's Happening" with that company, pushing me out completely.

TOR: Did you have anything on paper? Any legal recourse?

MONTE: Yes, I did. And so I filed a lawsuit, and that got me black-listed.

MONTE: Yeah . . . I created *Good Times*, George and Louise of *The Jeffersons*, and *What's Happening*, which was the television series based on *Cooley High*. And they cheated me out of all of that.

TOR: You came up with the ideas and concepts and they took them? Or did you at least get paid for it?

MONTE: I got credit for *Good Times*, but not for *The Jeffersons* or *What's Happening.*.

TOR: What types of projects are you involved in now?

MONTE: I'm doing my life's story, my autobiography. It's called *From Good Times to Cooley High and Back.*

TOR: Do you have an idea of when it will hit the shelves?

MONTE: It's not going to hit the shelves. I'm going to sell it on the Internet.

TOR: What's next after that?

MONTE: I have fifty projects on my computer. And I have some incredible projects too. Anyway, I wrote a book on Nat Turner, and I did his life as a love story. It's an incredibly beautiful love story. And out of everything that I've done, I think it's by far my best piece of work.

TOR: Does Hollywood still have its doors closed to you?

MONTE: I don't know. I'm into not asking anybody to do anything else for me . . . ever again in life. I've got it and I'm going to put it out. Since the Internet, it's irrelevant whether they want to do my work or not.

TOR: As far as getting to the audience?

MONTE: That's right. I don't have to go to a studio or a network or a publishing house. I can put it out there and I can notify people that it's there, and it's up to them whether they want to buy it or not.

Author's Note: Eric Monte's Web site: www.valentinelove.com

Countdown at Kusini

DST Communications/Columbia Pictures (1976)

Shot in and around Lagos, Nigeria, *Countdown at Kusini* is set in the fictitious African country of Fahari. Political intrigue and revolution drive this hard-edged melodrama, spiced with a taste of romantic adventure. Red Salter, an African-American jazz musician on tour, becomes involved in the country's struggle for independence when he becomes emotionally entangled with Leah Matanzima, a beautiful rebel. Ernest Motapo, a guerrilla leader, must be smuggled out of

Theater poster for *Countdown at Kusini*, from DST Telecommunications. The film was produced and financed by the Delta Sigma Theta Sorority, Inc.

the country after it's learned that a mercenary assassin has been hired to kill him. The colonialist-backed multinational corporation behind the plot is about to lose millions of dollars if the freedom fighter's revolutionary plans succeed.

Countdown at Kusini was financed by the Delta Sigma Theta sorority, the largest black women's service organization in the United States. The sorority wanted to make a different kind of movie, one that reflected the organization's deep concern for high moral and social values rather than the typical blaxploitation yarn being produced at that time. They hoped to encourage positive connections between black Americans and Africa, and to dramatize the need for solidarity between black people throughout the world in their struggle for freedom and dignity.

The organization planned to raise the film's budget through fund-raisers and the solicitation of its members' contributions, marketing the final product directly to their guaranteed audience. The logic was that if all 85,000 members bought tickets at, say, five dollars each, and took their husbands, lovers, family, friends, and even their children, a financial windfall at the box office would be assured. It didn't happen, because the film's distributor pulled it and shelved it two weeks after it opened.

Unfortunately, we have never seen the film and no one seems to know what happened to it; we include it here because it represents a pioneering effort in the modern history of black film. The Deltas took a bold and futuristic step when they organized their subsidiary, DST Telecommunications, with the purpose of not only entering, but becoming a dominant force in the film and television marketplace. DST's president, Lillian Benbow, saw an opportunity to produce, control, and profit from the multitude of black images that were suddenly being dumped onto the market at an alarming rate. Hollywood studios were making big bucks off many of these films, which was just the way they wanted to keep it.

What Delta Sigma Theta tried to do was brave, historic, and precedent-setting. If their plan had been allowed to succeed, DST Telecommunications would probably be a media powerhouse today, and there is no telling what kind of impact such efforts might have had on the industry if other organizations had followed the Deltas' bold example.

Review Summary: Among the reviews, both praise and criticism abound. The cinematography of the Nigerian countryside by lensman Andrew Laszlo was highly commended, as was the handling of many of the film's action scenes. Also praised was the sound track by African musician Manu Dibango, and the fact that many local Nigerian actors and crew members were involved in the produc-

---

CREDITS: Director: Ossie Davis. Producers: Ossie Davis, Ladi Ladebo. Screenplay: Ossie Davis, Ladi Ladebo, Al Freeman Jr. Based on a story by John Storm Roberts. Photography: Andrew Laszlo. Music: Manu Dibango. 99 minutes. Drama. PG.

CAST: Ruby Dee (*Leah Matanzima*), Ossie Davis (*Ernest Motapo*), Greg Morris (*Red Salter*), Tom Aldredge (*Ben Amed*), Michael Ebert (*Charles Henderson*), Thomas Baptiste (*John Okello*), Jab Adu (*Juma Bakari*), Elsie Olusola (*Mamouda*), Funso Adeolu (*Marni*).

tion. Keith Baird in *Freedomways* described the film as a clear-cut adventure-romance story and applauded what he saw as a beautiful African scenario that functioned well within the plot. He also had high praise for the musical score.

On a more negative note, despite some praise, Kevin Thomas in the *Los Angeles Times* found problems with the plot, characters, and directing of the movie. And Donald Bogle in *Blacks in American Films and Television* complained of a "rambling narrative," criticizing the casting and the slowness of the film's action.

OSSIE DAVIS

On the phone from his office in New York
January 28, 1999

TOR: The Delta Sigma Theta sorority's financing of *Countdown at Kusini* was a landmark event for a service organization in the 1970s. How did that come about?

DAVIS: Ruby and I were approached by the two top ladies in the Delta structure at that time . . . Lillian Benbow, who was the president, and Dr. Jeanne Noble. They came to us and said that Delta was interested in making a film and asked us to be involved. I happened to have a son-in-law at that time who was interested in filmmaking and he had rights to a story called "Countdown at Kusini." We talked back and forth and Ruby and I agreed, and it wasn't the wisest thing we ever did, but we had what we thought was sufficient motivation.

TOR: Which was?

DAVIS: Our son-in-law was a Nigerian, and we thought that if we went to Nigeria and used his connections, a lot of our cost could be subsidized or would come to us in-kind and we could make the film at a very minimal cost. So we went to Nigeria, and ultimately, after many trials and tribulations, we did make a film called *Countdown at Kusini*. We brought it back, we put it into distribution, but it didn't stay too long. Ultimately, it went the way of films that failed at that time.

TOR: Was it your decision to write, star, and direct the film?

DAVIS: We entertained options and possibilities and made decisions based upon what we thought we could do. We ended up with me rewriting the script, directing . . . for which I was originally assigned, acting, and ultimately, and this is where the great disaster came . . . being the producer.

A producer has certain talents and responsibilities. He's got to raise the money and make sure that it is dispensed in a practical way. He has to know how to budget a film, he has to know how to keep within the budget, and his job is to ride herd and see that all of this is done. I had neither the talent nor the inclination to do all that.

TOR: I take it directing and acting in the film presented a whole other set of distractions?

DAVIS: Yeah, and since the production was in Nigeria, that was another problem. Producing in Nigeria is totally different than producing in the United States. And many of the promises that my then son-in-law made, such as his capacity to get actors in Nigeria to act at minimum, and be able to go into villages and get the cooperation of the whole village for nothing, turned out not to be the case. We wound up acquiring a great deal of costs that we did not anticipate. Ultimately, we had to settle for much less than the film deserved.

TOR: I read that some of your Nigerian backers pulled out at the last minute, so a lot of the money that you thought you had didn't come at all.

DAVIS: That is true, but at the same time, I wasn't paying as much attention as I should have. In other words, I wasn't the producer, except in terms of having to assume the producer's responsibility. Paying for things out of my pocket, or something like that. So it was a labor of love, but love ain't the right way to make a motion picture.

TOR: So the result was that you could not shoot all of the scenes that you needed to?

DAVIS: That is essentially what did occur, but you have to understand the larger picture—the philosophy behind Delta Sigma Theta, the strategy they thought that they could use and how it did not work—to understand the true importance of *Countdown at Kusini.* It wasn't the greatest film in the world, but the most important thing about the venture is the questions it poses and the lessons it teaches.

TOR: And what were they?

DAVIS: Delta acted on the theory that it had a controlled market.

TOR: Its membership?

DAVIS: Right. Assuming that Delta had X number of members, and assuming the price of a ticket was seven dollars, X times seven dollars would give you the amount of money that market could provide you. All you would then have to do was to make sure that your budget didn't overrun your market expectations. As a matter of fact, if you knew how to economize, you could serve your own market, make a profit, and maybe turn around and make another film. So the film didn't necessarily have to be a big box office smash in terms of the regular marketplace. All it had to do was to satisfy the needs of the Delta membership. If each Delta member could be counted on to come to the film and bring husband and friends . . .

TOR: Then it should make a profit and be self-supporting.

DAVIS: Right, and that is where the experiment was eminently worthwhile. But, unfortunately, it did not work out.

TOR: Why not?

DAVIS: For two basic reasons. One was that the Delta organization was better geared to the *openings* of the film. They filled the theaters on these occasions. Important people came to these premieres, from state governors on down. It's what happened after the opening that Delta wasn't quite prepared for, which was, how to keep the people coming to see the movie on Monday, Tuesday, and Wednesday when you've blown your wad on the opening-night gala.

TOR: They didn't have any money left to put into P.R. and advertising?

DAVIS: Here's the situation. Delta . . . Lillian Benbow, Ruby, and I, went out to see the head of Columbia Pictures, David Begelman. Begelman not only knew Ruby and me, but he used to be our agent. We showed him the film. He said he liked it and Columbia would distribute it. To that end, he pledged to subsidize all the prints, which distributors do, and to give us, I think, $300,000 for promotion and advertising. Now, we only got, I think, about $75,000 to advertise and try to get the people to the box office.

TOR: What happened to the rest?

DAVIS: Now, David Begelman—and this is a presumption that I have no proof of—he had the job of selling Columbia Pictures' product to the exhibitors. He'll go to them and say, "I've got this big film here, called . . . "whatever"? But in order for you to get this film, you have to also take these dogs here." In other words . . .

you've got to take *Countdown at Kusini*. And the exhibitor, in order to get the big film, will agree to take it, not that the distributors didn't give it time to be supported.

Now, when the exhibitor gets the film, the gala goes well, and it makes money for one or two days, and then there's a drop at the box office. The exhibitor, having fulfilled his commitment to put the dogs out, snatches the film away and puts something else in its place. By the time Delta could gear up and get their membership to go see the film, it is no longer there. So Delta was caught up in how the Hollywood system operates; they have their own ways of doing things out there. Even if Delta used all of its resources, we were still at the mercy of exhibitors, who had other things in mind. Before word of mouth could get going, the exhibitor pulled the film, and there was no way we could get him to bring it back.

TOR: If the theater owners had left the film out there longer, or given the Deltas time to get their membership together and then rereleased the film, do you think it could have been financially successful?

DAVIS: It could have made money for the Deltas, it could have made money for the exhibitors, and it could have made money for Columbia. But the exhibitor? . . . What do they care about the Deltas trying to build up a black audience?

TOR: Maybe that's what they didn't want to happen?

DAVIS: Absolutely. The Deltas could have gone to the distributors and said, "Look, here's what we plan to do, this is how much time it's going to take, let's make a deal . . ."

TOR: Why didn't they do that?

DAVIS: If they had had slick Hollywood representation, they might have. They could have come out of this thing and made money like other independent film companies had done. But the Deltas are the Deltas. And God knows that Ossie and Ruby are just Ossie and Ruby. We didn't know what the hell was going on either. We were at the mercy of people who were advising us, either as do-good enthusiasts or hard-nosed cutthroats. In the end, we got the distribution, but we couldn't maintain it long enough for the Delta's strategy to take hold.

TOR: That's a revelation, because I had been led to believe that it was a bad film and people just didn't support it, not that the distributors didn't give it time to be supported.

DAVIS: One of the reasons Ruby and I agreed to participate was that we understood that what Delta had to offer was control over its own market. Not only were the Deltas established in the United States and the West Indies, but they were established in Africa too. If we could have gotten a situation where they were allowed to bring their forces to bear, and support the box office for a week or so . . . Meanwhile, they're on the phone to the churches, and the schools, and beating the drums . . . you know? And then there's all this talent. Greg Morris, Ossie Davis, Ruby Dee in the film . . . and the music of Manu Dibango in the film. We had many ways to go, and I've seen films that were worse than the one that we had.

TOR: And I'm sure they got much more opportunity to stay on the screen.

DAVIS: And they made money. They were the types of films that exhibitors liked to associate with black folks, so they got that kind of sympathetic treatment. But in this instance neither Delta, nor I, nor anybody connected with *Countdown at Kusini* was prepared to play the game in a knowing way. Anyway, the situation with *Countdown at Kusini* is such a corkscrew story that it needs to be carefully presented to the public. The Deltas—they put money into it and they never got it back. The Delta membership never fully understood what was happening, and there was no way to explain it to them.

TOR: On the other hand, do you think that if *Countdown at Kusini* had turned a profit, that other organizations would have followed Delta's lead and maybe created a black Hollywood?

DAVIS: Very much so, very much so.

TOR: How was it collaborating with Al Freeman Jr. on the script?

DAVIS: It was wonderful. And it wasn't only on the script. Al was our first choice to play the lead. When we went to Nigeria the first time, until our money ran out, we were shooting with Al. But the funds ran out and we came back to the States. When we regrouped, Al was working in the ABC Daytime Soap, *One Life to Live*. We couldn't use him again, so we got Greg Morris.

TOR: Is the film available at all now, say, on video?

DAVIS: I don't know where the film is now. It belongs in little bits to the various people who put money into it. Different people and sources have put liens on it, so where it is at the moment, I don't know.

TOR: It seems that with the rereleases and remastered screenings of films like *Gone With the Wind* and *Grease*, that *Countdown at Kusini* would be an interesting film to bring back and share with audiences today, especially with the progressive themes it had.

DAVIS: You know with cable, the market for films is insatiable. A lot of stuff is going to come back that might not have had an immediate appeal when it first came out. I don't know what the legal ramifications would be, but somebody, somewhere, owns it, but God knows who that somebody is.

DR. JEANNE NOBLE,
TWELFTH NATIONAL PRESIDENT, DELTA SIGMA THETA SORORITY, INC.

At her home in New York City
February 10, 1999

TOR: How did Delta Sigma Theta get into the business of making movies?

NOBLE: Lillian Benbow, who was then national president, and I, along with Lynette Taylor, who was executive director of the sorority, conceptualized an Arts and Letters Commission, and I was appointed National Chair. The idea came to us when we realized that many distinguished Deltas were actresses and performers in various areas of the arts. We thought it would be a good idea to pull them all together into some entity that could advance the arts and letters, especially as it relates to black people. In the 1970s, remember, there were all those blaxploitation films that were coming out, and a lot of negativism around our images.

TOR: So, take us back. How did it happen? In what meeting or conversation did someone first suggest that Delta Sigma Theta should make a film?

NOBLE: I can't remember the precise moment, but I do remember it was Lillian Benbow, the national president, who was the real mover and shaker. She was one of the most daring, and bold, and venturesome leaders that I have ever worked with. I don't think any of us, either before her or after her, have had that charismatic quality of galvanizing women to do things. I don't know if I alone would have had the nerve. Ruby would not have had the nerve; Ossie would not have the nerve. We began on Lillian's nerve. She said, "I don't want to bring all of these distinguished women together around some small, hokey-pokey idea, or something that perhaps a local chapter could do alone. Let's give them something to reach for! Something that will make a real difference." Then she said, "If we could just produce our own movie . . ."

And I remember we all looked at her and said, "What is she talking about?" Now, on this commission, there were people like Ruby Dee, Ellen Holly, Lena Horne, and Leontyne Price. We're talking about socially conscious women who have world-class images and who are hugely successful. We're not talking about artists who put their names on something and never show up. So Lillian wanted some project that was big enough for them to be interested in.

TOR: About what year was this?

NOBLE: Around 1972 . . . '73 . . . something like that.

TOR: Once Ms. Benbow convinced the commission to do a film, what was the next step?

NOBLE: The word got out, and the first script we looked at was a beautiful story by a black woman. I can't remember her name now, but it would have been filmed in someplace like Jamaica. But we thought there was a little too much symbolism.

TOR: So people were submitting works for consideration?

NOBLE: I can't even tell you what all we could have picked up and bought. We looked at Zora Neal Hurston's *Their Eyes Were Watching God*, and we said we didn't think this was the film— quite possibly because of the dialect.

At some point, we looked at Ruby and we said, "Surely there must be some film or some idea that you might have." So they presented *Countdown at Kusini*, and we liked the script. We liked it because we thought that filming it in Africa would be positive. [*Laughter*] Shirley Barnes, who was serving on the commission, and who is now an ambassador to one of the African countries, said, "Do you know how difficult it will be to film in Africa?" We hadn't a clue. But Ossie had been to Africa and had a big name there. We thought that they had enough connections and of course there was a kinship between us black Americans and Africans.

TOR: How was the money raised for the film?

NOBLE: By sheer force of persuasion. We raised it from individual Deltas, all of us who lost everything we put into it, of course, but we raised it through the chapters.

TOR: Was the money to go specifically into the film? Or into the Arts and Letters Commission?

NOBLE: No, Arts and Letters had its own budget. It was to go to the film—and that's why we had to set up DST Telecommunications.

TOR: To channel the funds through?

NOBLE: Right, because it would have jeopardized our tax status. So we set it up and had our own board of directors. Lillian went around to black businessmen. Johnson—who makes hair products—invested $250,000, the biggest investment from a black business. The rest of it came from individuals in the chapters.

A great story that we always tell is about a soror named Sweet Trix, the president of the Tampa Alumni chapter. She got that money together and brought it up to Washington, and when she opened up her bag . . . there were nickles, dimes, pennies, and quarters that went scattering all over the table. [*Laughter*] The members treated this just like they were raising money for a church supper!

TOR: Once the funds were raised, did Delta have much to do with the actual production?

NOBLE: The contract stated that we were to see the dailies. I remember the first dailies that we saw. I turned to Lillian, and I said, "It doesn't have enough sex in it."

And Ossie's son, Guy, was sitting there, and he said, "You're talking about my mother!" So I said, "I'm sorry about that, but . . ."

And we said that to Ossie, too. We said, "We know the image that you have of us, but do what you think is authentic for this film. Don't deal on the level of whether or not the Deltas want to see any kissing or whatever . . . go for it." We didn't want him holding back.

TOR: Were you aware of some of the production problems they were having?

NOBLE: Oh, Lord! They had production problems unmercifully. They ordered equipment from France and other places, and for some reason or another . . . it sat on a dock somewhere for weeks. And we knew we had to get that film out of there before the rainy season. They were busy trying to find out where the equipment was, and so that delayed the start of the shoot. And the money was not always there. If the money didn't get there in time, those black actors wouldn't get in front of that camera!

Some of the Deltas were saying, "You should have known this! You should have known they would act like that!" Then of course, when the rainy season set in, they came home. And we raised more money and sent them back. Lillian said, "You have to finish this film."

TOR: She was adamant?

NOBLE: Yes, but there was also so much support. Everybody's wife or husband was all involved in this, trying to help us make it. And to this day, if I am introduced to somebody of that era, they'll say, "Oh, yes, the Deltas . . . you made that film." We gained far more than we lost.

TOR: How was the film received once it was completed?

NOBLE: We showed a rough cut first . . . we had a big to-do on the very day that Nixon announced he was resigning. We set up big screens to see him saying his speech; then some people had a chance to see the rough cut. They loved it. There were some who didn't think it was up to par . . . but we didn't hear anybody say it wasn't going to make it. And the artists on the commission kept saying over and over again, "You may have the most beautiful product, but if it can't be distributed . . ." Well, to say that to Lillian Benbow was just to galvanize her into figuring out a way that she could get it distributed.

TOR: What did she do?

NOBLE: We linked up with one of the most outstanding law firms in the world, Frankfurt, Garbus, Klein and Selz, here in New York. And Mike Frankfurt said to Lillian, "Begelman . . . at Columbia, he's your man."

So Lillian flew out to California and talked him into distributing it. Naturally, Begelman passed it onto someone else. And it's very fuzzy in my mind because I had a huge task to do at that point, which was to organize a way for the film to move into the black community. And maybe at that point [Columbia] was not really interested.

TOR: Why do you say that?

NOBLE: What we said to them was "This is the way we feel we can market the film. It goes into a city, we have a big premiere, on night one, and then we're going to have the local chapters working on ways to get schools, churches, and the community into the movie houses on the next day. Well, they were opening the film in cities without our knowing about it. They were supposed to open it here . . . but it would be opened somewhere else, or it didn't get opened on the night we thought it was going to open in Omaha!

TOR: They were not coordinating the releases with the Deltas?

NOBLE: No. And then I think they got disappointed when the numbers didn't turn out on night one, and surely if they didn't get there day two, they were finished with it. I don't think they liked the content of the film anyway.

TOR: Do you think the distributor might have done things the way they did to sabotage the project? Were there any indications of that possibility?

NOBLE: No. At the time we just internalized it all as our fault.

TOR: Whenever I've heard anything about *Countdown at Kusini*, it was always "the Deltas financed it . . . it was a bad film . . . nobody went to go see it . . . and the Deltas lost all their money. But if Columbia had waited and worked with the Deltas, you could have packed the house all week long. Then the headlines would have read "Delta Sigma Theta Makes a Profit!" Then other black organizations might have been motivated to go into this type of fund-raising activity.

NOBLE: That's right. And the most sinister part about it is that there had been a drought, a lack of black films for months leading up to the day our film was released. First there were the blacksploitation films, and then . . . there was nothing for months. The very week we came out, two other film distributors decided they were going to ride on the coattails of those Delta women. They put out a beautiful film called *Leadbelly*.

TOR: The Gordon Parks film with Roger E. Mosely?

NOBLE: You remember that film? It's a lovely film. It came out that week and didn't do well. It folded in less time than ours. But the film that made it was a film about a rock and roll group—four singers and their girlfriends . . . *Sparkle*.

TOR: It sounds like the distributors were following suit. That goes along with my sabotage theory. If there had been no black films for months, and they release three at the same time, one film would take away the box office dollars from the others.

NOBLE: Yes. Those three films came out the same week.

TOR: Tell me about the overall feeling of yourself, Ms. Benbow, and the people involved in the project, once you realized that it wasn't going to work and the money was gone.

NOBLE: We all took it very hard. Lillian thought this was going to wipe out the Commission on Arts and Letters.

TOR: Why didn't the Deltas bicycle the film around to the different chapters?

NOBLE: There was no way we could. The last bid that Lillian made for money to send the actors back to Africa to finish the film, she went to an organization that was set up during the civil rights era to give blacks a lot of money. They gave us another $250,000, I think, and they lost that too. But in the contract for that money, they legally got the film. Had we stayed together as DST Telecommunications, we could have untangled it. But I think everybody was just sick of it, and we just walked away from it. And probably walked away from Lillian too . . . which was unfortunate.

TOR: People snubbed her after that?

NOBLE: She couldn't stand people sniping at it, saying it was not the best film they ever saw. And the most painful thing occurred at our last convention, when we did a salute to the Arts and Letters Commission, which was twenty-five years old. I had said, "If you're going to look at the history of the commission, you have to show some of the footage from *Countdown at Kusini,* that is so much a part of our history. And they said, "No, we'll just have to do another film."

TOR: But if it had been a better film overall, do you think it would have been different for the Deltas?

NOBLE: No, I don't think it would have been different in terms of them snatching it out of those movie houses after two or three days—but the commission was a fabulous group of women. We were poised to really make a difference.

TOR: And I think Hollywood realized that too.

NOBLE: They must have.

7

Society Profile: 1980-1989
New Ebony Images

By 1980, migration to the North had caused a 50 percent drop in the black population of the southern states. But the trend had started to reverse, and significant numbers of blacks began moving back to the South for retirement and increasing economic opportunities.

Despite some educational gains, employment for many blacks still tended to be relegated to the lower-paying jobs. Census figures showed that the average income of black families had dropped to only 58 percent of that for white families, as compared with 61 percent in 1970. Spurred by an ever-increasing divorce rate, 40 percent of black women were heads of their households, while only 11 percent of white women found themselves in this situation.

In the 1980 presidential elections, Ronald Reagan beat incumbent Jimmy Carter. The new Republican administration reversed the antidiscrimination guidelines for minority hiring and government contracts, established by President Lyndon Johnson in 1964, and slashed the budget for many programs that had been developed to aid the poor. Under Reagan's presidency, educational assistance, benefits to families with dependent children, and federal food programs were all hit hard by what came to be known as "Reaganomics" and the infamous "trickle-down theory." A 1981 *Time*/CBS News poll confirmed that black Americans did not approve of the new president or his policies, and with good reason.

The country in general and black America particularly found itself in a major financial crisis. A recession caused poverty to rise to its highest level since 1967, with 2.2 million additional Americans falling into poverty during Reagan's first year in office. The United States went from being a creditor nation to a debtor nation, and homelessness spread. The income gap between blacks and whites continually grew larger, and by the end of Reagan's first term, the United Negro College Fund noted a significant drop in college enrollment among blacks. Reagan also undermined the country's earlier gains in civil rights. He replaced those members of the U.S. Civil Rights Commission who did not agree with his views on affirmative action, but lost a lawsuit filed by commissioner Mary Frances Berry, who was then reinstated. Thirty-three state agencies accused the Reagan administration of not enforcing civil rights laws properly and allowing dangerous deterioration to occur. Reagan's only positive act on behalf of civil rights was to sign the bill that made Dr. Martin Luther King Jr.'s birthday a national holiday, but only after it had been passed in the Senate by a vote of 78 to 22.

In Hollywood, it was an important crossover period for black actors. Richard Pryor, Eddie Murphy, Whoopi Goldberg, and other stars who had started out as stand-up comedians were featured in prominent roles in mainstream motion pictures. Many of these films were basically white comedies with a solo black lead or supporting character, including *Stir Crazy* (1980), *48 Hours* (1982), and *Jumpin' Jack Flash* (1986). But a new film genre came to prominence as *Beverly Hills Cop* (1984) and *Lethal Weapon* (1987) reenvisioned the "salt-and-pepper-cop" concept. Louis Gossett Jr. won an Academy Award for Best Supporting Actor for his role as Sergeant Foley in *An Officer and a Gentleman* (1982). Despite his previous success and his reputation as a fine actor, Gossett still had to persuade the producers that he could play a role that was not written for a black man. In literature, Alice Walker's novel *The Color Purple* won the 1983 American Book Award and made her the first black woman to receive the Pulitzer Prize for a work of fiction. Filmmaker Steven Spielberg would turn the book into a controversial movie in 1985.

The mid-eighties continued to be a checkered period for racial policy in America. The U.S. Supreme Court ruled that minority set-asides were unconstitutional, yet supported affirmative action planning and racial promotion quotas as a way to rectify blatant past discrimination. Meanwhile, middle- and upper-income blacks were moving into the suburbs while poor blacks were forced to remain in the inner cities, fighting drugs, black-on-black crime, and the deadly emergence of AIDS.

In 1988, civil rights leader Jesse Jackson sought the Democratic nomination for president for the second time. He won primaries in Alabama, Georgia, Louisiana, Michigan, Mississippi, and Virginia and became an important player in the Democratic political machinery.

Krush Groove

Warner Brothers (1985)

"It's a lot of screaming and noise! It's not music!"
—Rev. Walker to RUN-DMC

Krush Groove is to rap music what *Saturday Night Fever* (1977) is to disco. The film helped to bring rap music to a mass audience and introduced many acts that would become rap music's biggest hits, and a few who wouldn't. The story is loosely based on the early entrepreneurial efforts of music mogul Russell Simmons and presents a myriad of production numbers loosely connected by a thin plot.

Russell Walker is an ambitious young record producer who manages a stable of up-and-coming rap artists. He sees where this new style of music is going and wants to start his own record label, but he doesn't have the money to pay for studio time or print costs. He goes to his father for help, but the devout Baptist minister refuses to lend him the money; as an old-fashioned kind of a guy, the Reverend Walker believes it would make his son "more of a man" if he did it on his own. Desperate, determined, and against sound advice, Russell accepts a start-up loan from Gant, an unscrupulous wolf in businessman's clothing.

When Russell's music and the label become a big success, Gant wants more than his money back. He expects substantial interest on his loan, as well as a continuous piece of the action. When Russell refuses, Gant sends his goons to beat Russell up. The young entrepreneur's success also brings out the industry sharks, for a feeding

---

CREDITS: Director: Michael Shultz. Producers: Michael Shultz, Doug McHenry. Screenplay: Ralph Farquhar. Photography: Ernest Dickerson. Editors: Alan J. Koslowski, Jerry Bixman, Conrad M. Gonzalez. Production Design: Mischa Petrow. Set Design: John Lawless. 97 minutes. Musical drama. R.

CAST: Blair Underwood (*Russell*), Sheila E (*Herself*), Joseph Simmons (*Run*), Daryll McDaniels (*DMC*), Jason Mizell (*Jam Master Jay*), David Wimbley (*Fat Boy Kool Rock Ski*), Daniel Simmons (*Rev. Walker*), Richard E. Gant (*Jay B.*), Lisa Gay Hamilton (*Aisha*), The Fat Boys, Curtis Bloss, New Edition, The Beastie Boys, Donnie Simpson, L.L. Cool J.

A wannabe starlet auditions for a spot on the upstart Krush Groove record label in the hip-hop musical *Krush Groove*, a *Saturday Night Fever* for rap. (Warner Bros.)

frenzy. Galaxy Music's record executive dangles lavish contracts, limos, and beautiful women in the faces of the now-popular artists under Russell's care. These tangible rewards are much more enticing than the promises Russell can make. As his acts are stripped away from him, his fledgling musical empire begins to crumble.

The major disappointment comes when his own rapper brother, RUN of RUN-DMC, abandons him, partly because of Russell's burgeoning relationship with the vivacious Sheila E, whom RUN hoped would have eyes for him.

The musical numbers include RUN-DMC's soon-to-be-hits "King of Rock" and "It's Like That" and Sheila E's "A Love Bizarre" and "Holly Rock," which look, sound, and feel like outtakes from *Purple Rain*, Prince's 1984 film debut. Pioneer rap artist Curtis Blow, in top hat and tails, performs his now-classic "If I Ruled the World," and the then skinny and relatively unknown L.L. Cool J tries out for the Krush Groove label with his future hit "My Radio."

Also heavy in the story's musical mix are the Fat Boys, a trio of hefty rappers who skip school and clean out an all-you-can-eat buffet while looking for girls and their big break. During a nightclub talent competition, they belt out their theme song, "Fat Boys." Later, the then-teenybopper group New Edition energetically dance and spin to their "My Secret," which would also become a hit single. Other artists in the film or on the soundtrack include the Beastie Boys, Chaka Khan, Deborah Harry, UTFO, Nayobe, Force M.D.'s, and the Gap Band.

Through all the music and mayhem, more music, and some merriment here and there, Russell finds a way out of his dilemma and reconciles with RUN and most of the other acts. They all vow to work together to make Krush Groove a premier record label. This time, perhaps as a message to any aspiring rap artists in the audience, they put it in writing.

Review Summary: Most critics agreed that *Krush Groove* was mainly about music, rap music, but that the hard-edged message, weak story line, and predictable plot were sufficiently camouflaged by the vibrant and energetic performances. Robert Christgau and Carola Dibbell suggested that "complaining about Krush Groove's plot makes as much sense as complaining that [the] Sucker MC's don't have much of a melody."

Several reviewers attempted to put together their own rap review rhymes, but with little success. In *Time*, Richard Schickel wrote, "Now, rappin' is the latest form of talkin' the blues. By the bro's from the Bronx in their burgundy shoes. And now their story's on the screen at the Multiplex, Ralph Farquhar wrote the script; Michael Shultz he directs . . ."

Michael Shultz's directing brought mixed comments. Patrick Goldstein in the *Los Angeles Times* acknowledged the success of the jittery fast-motion editing to the beat of the music as the Fat Boys go on an eating spree. A review from the *Motion Picture Guide* suggested that the production numbers would no doubt please the fans, despite the fact that Shultz's direction was wholly anonymous.

Janet Maslin in the *New York Times* thought the film didn't do justice to rap's vitality: "Considering the kind of boisterous energy that goes into rap records, Krush Groove seems pretty tame," she wrote, noting that rap music is more original than such creaky devices as talent contests, feeble romance attempts, and the seen-before travails of the struggling young record company portrayed.

The Color Purple

Warner Bros. (1985)

"Nothing but death can keep me from it!"
—Nettie to Celie in regard to writing to her

In *The Color Purple* Celie is a young girl growing up poor in rural Georgia. She is sexually molested by her stepfather, who sells the two babies he's given her to a childless preacher and his wife. Celie is heartbroken over the loss of her children, both snatched from her arms shortly after she gave birth to them. The year is 1909, but just like back in slavery days wit' ol' Massa, there is nothing the poor black girl can do.

One Sunday after church, Mister, a mean widower, comes a-calling. He's looking for a new wife to do the household chores and mind his children. He's interested in Nettie, Celie's younger sister, but the stepfather offers him the older girl instead, since she is "already spoiled." Celie is taken to Mister's farm, where she is harassed by his children and appalled by the filthy condition of his home. No stranger to hard work, she soon has it all under control.

When the stepfather makes his move on Nettie, she seeks refuge with Celie and joins her sister in Mister's home. But when Nettie spurns Mister's sexual advances as well, he physically ejects her from his house, banning her from his property and from Celie's life. This is one of the most powerful scenes in the film, though the performances by Desreta Jackson and Akosua Busia went unrecognized by awards nominating committees. Celie undergoes nearly forty years of abuse, neglect, rape, and intimidation from Mister and grows into a shy and withdrawn woman. She waits for the postman every day, hoping for the letter that Nettie promised to write, but Mister sees to it that she never gets her hands on the mail.

Mister's son, Harpo, has grown into a bumbling fool who often trips over his own feet. He marries the strong-willed Sofia, who stands up for herself and refuses to take his abuse. Celie is in awe of Sofia's spunk and her spirit of self-determination, but when Sofia mouths off to the mayor's wife in town, she is beaten senseless and jailed. The mayor then sentences her to a life of servitude as the maid of the offended white woman, and Sofia is never the same.

One stormy night, Shug Avery, a drunken blues singer, stumbles through Mister's door. She takes one look at Celie and pronounces, with a big laugh, "You sho' is ugly!" Despite the insult, and the fact that Shug Avery is her husband's mistress, the two women become close friends, and Celie begins to change. The catalyst comes when Shug discovers a stash of hidden letters that Nettie has written to Celie over the years. We learn that the younger sister is now living at a mission over in Africa. She is a nanny for the preacher and his wife, and has been looking after Celie's two children. We hear Nettie's voice as Celie reads letter after letter, and we see visual enactments of her sister's written words—the continent's wild animals, the beautiful African countryside, and Celie's growing children. Mister's betrayal sparks Celie's rebellious spirit, and she leaves him to start a new life.

Cursed upon Celie's departure, Mister's life, his crops, and the farm all go into a downward spiral. To undo her hex, he contacts Nettie in Africa and evidently invites her back onto his land. She soon returns to the farm with Celie's grown African-looking, non-English-speaking children in tow. Mister observes the family reunion he has arranged from a distant field and grins, evidently a changed man.

The production was beautifully photographed in Union and Anson counties in North Carolina, with other location work shot in Africa. It grossed more than $100 million at the box office, making it the highest-grossing black film ever. While it received eleven Academy Award nominations, it failed to win any. Coproducer Quincy Jones's musical score was nominated, as was the popular song "Miss Celie's Blues (Sister)," performed by Shug in the juke-joint scene. It was written especially for the film by Jones, Rod Tem-

CREDITS: Director: Steven Spielberg. Producers: Spielberg, Kathleen Kennedy, Frank Marshall, Quincy Jones, John Peters, Peter Guber. Photography: Allen Daviau. Screenplay: Menno Meyjes. Based on the novel by Alice Walker. Music: Quincy Jones. Editor: Michael Kahn. Production Design: J. Michael Riva. Art Direction: Robert W. Welch. Set Design: Linda DeScenna. 152 minutes. Drama. PG-13.

CAST: Danny Glover (*Albert*), Whoopi Goldberg (*Celie*), Margaret Avery (*Shug Avery*), Oprah Winfrey (*Sofia*), Willard Pugh (*Harpo*), Akosua Busia (*Nettie*), Adolph Caesar (*Old Mister*), Rae Dawn Chong (*Squeak*), Desreta Jackson (*Young Celie*), Dana Ivey (*Miss Millie*), Leonard Jackson (*Pa*), Bennet Guillory (*Grady*).

Enjoying a leisurely walk, Nettie (Akosua Busia, left) and Celie (Desreta Jackson) are sisters soon to be torn apart in *The Color Purple*. (Warner Bros.)

perton, and Lionel Richie. In their debut screen performances, Whoopi Goldberg and Oprah Winfrey both received nominations. Pop diva Tina Turner is said to have turned down the role of Shug Avery, saying, "I don't want to play a part that I've already lived." The part went to established actress Margaret Avery, who received a Best Supporting Actress nomination.

The movie, which cost $15 million to produce, unleashed a wave of controversy and debate. Talk shows perpetuated the fervor while newspapers and magazines carried vastly different points of view. Many debated the authenticity of Steven Spielberg's perspective as the film's director. Did he and Dutch-born screenwriter Menno Meyjes stray too far from the novel's cultural context? Would a director and writer with an experience-based understanding of the forces that created the story and shaped the lives of its characters have made a better film? Probably so, but the truth is that without Spielberg the picture probably never would have been made.

Review Summary: There were few in-betweens when it came to reviewing *The Color Purple*; critics either loved it or slammed it. There were two major sources of concern: the extensive changes made by two white men in a book written by a black woman about black women; and Spielberg's preference for big moments rendered through his mastery at employing sweeping camera shots, brilliant colors, stereotypical situations, and emotional music.

Kathy Maio in *Feminist in the Dark* was typical of many who criticized Spielberg's creation. She suggested that this was incest dealt with in Disney fashion, which denied the depth of the damage done, made black men into stereotypical buffoons, depicted black women as catfighting in the juke joint and serving as eye-candy for patriarchal sensibilities, and diluted the power and redemption of the original female story. Richard Blake in *America* saw Spielberg's effort as "mismatched." He explained: "Walker makes her readers feel the brutality and squalor in the life of her heroine, Celie. Spielberg sanitizes her life and corrupts her story with sudden and improbable character transformations."

In the *New York Times*, Vincent Canby wrote, "Another director might have transformed *The Color Purple* into a film that functioned as a tribute to the book. Mr. Spielberg's film is a tribute to Hollywood. He's over his head here, but the film is insidiously entertaining." Sheila Benson in the *Los Angeles Times* observed, "Whatever the faults of Spielberg's artistic choices, exquisitely sunny photography for a story full of emotional darkness; a big thumping background score when simplicity was essential; an added gospel scene that reinforces the uneasy feeling that we have stumbled into *Cabin in the Sky*; he has collected an almost-perfect cast, and what they have done under his direction is undeniable."

On the more positive side, Rex Reed in the *New York Post* thought that this was Spielberg's finest film. "Out of the pain and sadness, Spielberg and Goldberg awaken Celie and her audience to renewed hope, and *The Color Purple* becomes a life-affirming experience, a rarefied film that revives faith in movies and mankind."

She's Gotta Have It

Island Pictures (1986)

"Please, baby, please, baby, please, baby, baby, baby, please!"

—Mars to Nola Darling

She's Gotta Have It kicked off what became known as the Black Film Renaissance of the 1990s. Spike Lee's gritty, independently produced sex comedy is about Nola Darling, a sensuous Brooklyn babe who juggles three men (and sidesteps one lesbian) within her hectic life as a graphic artist.

The first man, Jamie, is a sensitive down-to-earth kind of guy. He vows his loyalty and talks often of marriage, but he is stifling the independent Nola, and she's not about to let any one man dominate her. Greer is a status-conscious fashion model who aspires to expose the 'round-the-way girl to the "finer things" in life. Designer clothes and fancy restaurants are nice, but Nola doesn't like having to wait for sex while he neatly folds his underwear. Mars is a street-smart bike messenger who makes Nola laugh. Funny and fun, his sense of humor is about the only thing he has going for him.

Opal, Nola's lesbian friend, is determined to sway the heterosexual nymph over to her side of the bed. But Nola is in control of her own life. By conventional standards she's more like a man, pursuing sexual gratification as she pleases without letting preconceived notions define who she is as a woman.

Spike Lee, at twenty-nine and fresh out of film school at New York University, creatively meshed comedy with drama, coupled narrative with documentary filmmaking techniques, and somehow even found the inspiration to act in his own movie. The result is an innovative film that, while not always technically impressive, established him as a catalyst for growth, experimentation, and esthetics in black film.

Nola Darling (Tracy Camila Johns) attempts to discuss their failed relationship with former lover Jamie Overstreet (Redmond Hicks) in Spike Lee's ground-breaking *She's Gotta Have It*. (Island Pictures)

She's Gotta Have It was shot in twelve to fifteen days on super-16-mm film with a budget of $175,000. The low budget and tight shooting schedule are apparent in the visual quality of the film, but what's up on the screen often makes up for the technical glitches.

CREDITS: Writer-Producer-Director-Editor: Spike Lee. Photography: Ernest Dickerson. Music: Bill Lee. Production Designer: Wynn Thomas. Art Director: Ron Paley. Set Design: Clarence Jones. Costumes: John Michael Reefer. 84 minutes. B&W. Comedy-Drama. R.

CAST: Tracy Camila Johns (*Nola Darling*), Tommy Redmond Hicks (*Jamie Overstreet*), John Canada Terrell (*Greer Childs*), Spike Lee (*Mars Blackmon*), Raye Dowell (*Opal Gilstrap*), Joie Lee (*Clorinda Bradford*), Epatha Merkinson (*Dr. Jamison*), Bill Lee (*Sonny Darling*), Cheryl Burr (*Ava*), Aaron Dugger (*Noble*), Stephanie Covington (*Keva*), Renata Cobbs (*Shawn*), Cheryl Singleton (*Toby*).

The film earned Lee the Best New Director award at the Cannes Film Festival and grossed $5 million. Spurred by this early success, Lee's rise to stature seemed well planned and deftly orchestrated. He was the first independent filmmaker to come out and talk a lot of "smack" about the Hollywood film industry, as well as the state of black America in general. Within all the hype and the hoopla, Spike Lee spoke a lot of truth, stirred up a lot of controversy, and quickly became a household name.

Review Summary: Critics focused on Spike Lee's inexperience as a director and the sexual stereotypes concerning the conduct of the main character, Nola Darling. D. J. R. Bruckner in the *New York Times* thought the story very good even though it was "technically messy and some of the directing experiments ill-conceived." In the *Los Angeles Times* Michael Willmington wrote, "Lee is an impudent original with a great eye and flair for humor and eroticism." He added, "There's something genuinely different here, a perspective we don't see enough, the joy and liveliness of an often neglected present. The movie's breeziness is tonic, refreshing."

"The movie often strings out the three-pronged story line in sloppy ways, but it always tweaks our notions of sexual stereotyping," according to Mark Smith in the *Los Angeles Times*. "We see just how unfettered a woman can be when interpreting her erotic identity."

Hollywood Shuffle

The Samuel Goldwyn Company (1987)

"There's work at the post office."
—Grandmother to Bobby

"Tooommmyy . . . you killed'ed my brother, baaaby . . ." a high, strained, jive-ass voice proclaims in the opening scene of *Hollywood Shuffle*. Bobby Taylor is in the bathroom rehearsing lines for an audition to an upcoming film. His little brother Stevie sits off to the side holding the script, feeding him lines when necessary. We quickly see that Bobby comes from a loving and supportive family. His mother and grandmother believe in him and encourage his dreams, despite the obvious flaws and biases of the industry he's aspiring to.

At work at Winky Dinky Dog, Bobby makes up another lame excuse for missing his shift and is berated by his coworkers for wasting his time on that "acting thing." At the cattle call, he learns that the production may be boycotted by the NAACP because of the script's racist characters and stereotypes. This matters not to the throng of expectant young auditioners, who put on their best, or in this case their worst, most despicable street characterizations for the all-white casting committee. One Shakespearean interpretation of a street dude's hip dialogue is especially amusing.

In the film, shot in a total of fourteen days over a three-year period, Townsend succeeded in stitching together a series of satirical short skits with a firm thread of story line. The same cast members appear as different characters in various vignettes, which gives the film a great ensemble feel. Many of the segments are inspired by Bobby's thoughts and daydreams: *Black Acting School Commercial* depicts white instructors teaching students how to effectively play black characters; *Sneaking in the Movies* is a takeoff on the Siskel and Ebert shows where the critics review films titled *Amadeus Meets Salarius*, *Dirty Larry*, and *Attack of the Street Pimps*; late one night, Bobby dreams of playing roles as a black Superman, Rambro, and accepting his fifth Oscar.

Bobby (Robert Townsend, left), a struggling actor working at a hotdog stand, discusses his career and future with his boss, Mr. Jones (John Witherspoon, right) and coworker Donald (Keenan Ivory Wayans), in *Hollywood Shuffle*. (Samuel Goldwyn Company)

The "Sam Ace: Private Eye" segment was the first piece shot. Originally intended as a short, it's a gritty, b&w film noir detective spoof in which the black gumshoe kicks butt, solves the crime, and, in the end, gets the girl and all of her money. It was cleverly written into the film as a late-night rerun on television. "That's the kind of roles that I want to play," Bobby tells his girlfriend Lydia. She gives him a kiss and says, "You will," but we know those roles aren't available.

CREDITS: Director: Robert Townsend. Producers: Robert Townsend, Carl Craig. Screenplay: Robert Townsend, Keenan Ivory Wayans. Music: Patrice Rushen, Udi Harpaz. 82 minutes. R.

CAST: Robert Townsend (*Bobby Taylor*), Keenan Ivory Wayans (*Donald*), John Witherspoon (*Mr. Jones*), Helen Martin (*Grandmother*), Starletta Dupois (*Mother*), Anne-Marie Johnson (*Lydia*), David McKnight (*Uncle Ray*), Craigus R. Johnson (*Stevie*), Ludie Washington (*Batty Boy*), Kim Wayans (*Lounge Singer*), Sarah Coughlin (*Sitcom Girlfriend*), Paul Mooney (*NAACP President*), Angela Teek, Roy Fegan, Franklin Ajaye, Grand L. Bush, Don Reed, Brad Sanders, Damon Wayans.

Not surprisingly, Bobby is cast as the lead in the controversial film for which he auditioned, but he discovers he must compromise his own values if he's to play the part. For all of the comedic, hard-edged reality in *Hollywood Shuffle*, it still has an optimistic ending. Bobby lands a role he can be proud of, and the film's message becomes quite clear: "You don't have to sell out."

The second independent staple in the Black Film Renaissance of the 1990s, this film took us behind the scenes of a too-often racist film industry. *Hollywood Shuffle* is definitely a message film. However, in pointing out the multitude of black stereotypes that once so blatantly plagued the movies, Robert Townsend, the film's cowriter, coproducer, director, and star, reintroduced these old and degrading images to a new audience, but with a fresh and funny satirical twist.

Highly praised for his ingenious method of financing ($40,000 of the film's $100,000 budget was covered with various credit cards), Townsend was rapidly thrust into the spotlight. Although his film was semiautobiographical, he had previously landed decent film roles in *Streets of Fire* (1983), *A Soldier's Story* (1984), *American Flyers* (1985), and *Ratboy* (1986). In 1976, years before his success in Hollywood, he performed a monologue called "Sinner Man" from the play *God's Trombones* at a drama workshop in Chicago. His performance was so powerful and impressive that he received a standing ovation.

Townsend would go on to write, produce, and direct a series of comedy specials for Home Box Office called *Robert Townsend and His Partners in Crime*, which reunited many of his film's cast and collaborators. He would also direct *The Five Heartbeats* (1990), about a black singing group trying to make it in the 60s and 70s; *Meteor Man* (1993), in which a young man is given special powers when he is struck by a meteor (seemingly a spinoff from his black superhero dream in *Shuffle*), and *BAPS* (1997), about a couple of home girls who unwittingly take on a scam job to trick a wealthy dying man out of his money. He also directed the concert film *Eddie Murphy Raw* (1988), and appeared in his own Warner Bros. sitcom, *The Parent 'Hood*.

Review Summary: Many reviewers found the film well done, while others complained about its structure. Although they were generally in agreement about the picture's high comedic and entertainment value, many thought the scenes inconsistently appealing.

Most applauded Townsend for addressing the negative images of blacks in Hollywood, while others criticized him for his use of stereotypes within the film; some reviewers discussed both issues. For example, Jami Bernard in the *New York Post* accused Townsend of "passing the buck," contending that he criticized stereotypes about black people yet indulged in stereotypes for others, including women and gays. Ronald Varney in *Connoisseur* said, "Townsend fell into his varied scenes with an easy versatility that had the audience begging for more," and in the *Washington Post*, Richard Harring suggested, "With black comedy, one often laughs just to keep from crying—which shouldn't devalue either the humor or the pain, especially when it's Black black comedy."

A Dry White Season

Metro-Goldwyn-Mayer Pictures/UA (1989)

"Justice and law are often distant cousins. And here
in South Africa? They're just not on speaking terms
at all."

—Mr. McKinzie to Ben du Toit

In *A Dry White Season* the place is South Africa, the year 1976. A
young black man walks briskly into a government-owned bar in
Soweto. As the mostly older male patrons drink and socialize, he
leaps onto a table and shouts, "The beer that you drink buys the

Left to right, Stanley (Zakes Mokae), Margaret (Sophis Mgcina), Ben du Toit (Donald
Sutherland), Julius (John Kani), and Emily (Thoko Ntshinga) discuss the investigation into
the deaths of Emily's husband and young son while in police custody, in *A Dry White
Season*. (David James / Metro-Goldwyn-Mayer)

bullets that kill your children!" Sirens suddenly blare in the distance, and the bar becomes a madhouse of screaming, struggling, and desperate escapes.

Meanwhile, in Johannesburg, Ben du Toit, a mild-mannered white ex-soccer star turned history teacher, speaks with Gordon, his black gardener. The two men appear to be old friends, with a certain level of respect and distance between them. Ben is paying for Gordon's son's schooling, and the gardener assures the benefactor that his money is being put to good use.

Later, Gordon becomes furious when his son Johnathan plans to skip school the following day to participate in a student demonstration. He forbids the boy to participate, but his warning goes unheeded. During the rally, the chanting students, who range in age from eight to eighteen, reach a police roadblock. They are ordered to stop and disperse, and when they don't, teargas canisters streak through the sky. The frenzied kids become innocent ducks in a shooting gallery. Many run to get away and are shot in the back. Johnathan is captured by the police when he stops to help a friend who's mourning her baby sister, who has a bullethole through her chest. A tangled web of death and deceit begins.

The police have no record of Johnathan's arrest and his frantic parents are coldly told to search the morgue. (Fortunately, Gordon and his wife, Emily, are not yet among the dozens of parents already doomed to grieve the loss of a child.) When all Gordon's roads and inquiries about his missing son lead to nowhere, he asks for Ben's help. Aloof and disbelieving at first, and certain that Johnathan must be guilty of something if he is in the hands of the police, Ben is slowly drawn into a widening knowledge of what is really going on under the system of apartheid, both on the streets and in the courtrooms. When he sees the injustices with his own eyes, he under-

---

CREDITS: Director: Euzhan Palcy. Producer: Paula Weinstein. Writers: Colin Welland, Euzhan Palcy. Based on a novel by Andre Brink. Photography: Kelvin Pike, Pierre-William Glenn. Editors: Sam O'Steen, Glenn Cunningham. Production Design: John Fenner. Music: Dave Grusin. Art Direction: Alan Tomkins, Mike Phillips. 105 minutes. Drama. R.

CAST: Donald Sutherland (*Ben du Toit*), Zakes Mokae (*Stanley*), Janet Suzman (*Susan du Toit*), Marlon Brando (*Ian McKenzie*), Susan Sarandon (*Melanie Bruwer*), Jurgen Prochnow (*Captain Stolz*), Winston Ntshona (*Gordon Ngubene*), Thoko Ntshinga (*Emily Ngubene*), Leonard Maguire (*Mr. Bruwer*), Rowan Elmes (*Johan du Toit*), Susannah Harker (*Suzette du Toit*), Bekhithemba Mpofu (*Johnathan*).

goes a crisis of conscience, and his life and loyalties are forever changed.

As Ben du Toit, Donald Sutherland displays a full and believable range of emotions as he goes through the metamorphosis of being awakened, becoming aware, and eventually being galvanized to the struggle. Zakes Mokae, the fine South African actor, is the streetwise sarcastic taxi driver who guides Ben through his eye-opening quest for the truth. Marlon Brando came out of a nine-year retirement from motion pictures to portray the role of McKenzie, a human rights attorney and a well-known defender of lost causes. He received an Academy Award nomination for his performance, and many felt that Sutherland's performance should have been acknowledged as well.

Shot in Zimbabwe, the simultaneous heaven and hell that existed in one place was well defined by director Euzhan Palcy's purposeful intercutting, contrasting the lives of South Africa's black and white populations. Whites live a comfortable life of pleasure and privilege as the recipients of the country's wealth, resources, and cheap black labor, with some actually unaware of the graveness of life on the other side. They know it's there, but pay no attention to it. One white character openly acknowledges the duality of her country's majority population. "Blacks lead double lives," she says, "one you see and one you don't."

Palcy had read André Brink's novel, *A Dry White Season*, after the tremendous success of her first film, *Sugar Cane Alley* (1984), and decided to bring it to the screen. Other films such as *Cry the Beloved Country* (1951, 1995), *Cry Freedom* (1987), and *A World Apart* (1988) also helped bring apartheid into the world's critical spotlight. Before these theatrical movies, the documentary film *Last Grave at Dimbaze* (1975) was produced illegally and smuggled out of South Africa. The film graphically depicted what it was like for blacks under apartheid, the work camps, the beatings, shootings, torture, people supposedly commiting suicide while incarcerated, and the overall impoverished way of life that the land's native people were forced to endure. Singer/songwriter Stevie Wonder became a major advocate against apartheid and brought awareness to millions through his music. Political consciousness was expanded; amidst the cries and scrutiny, the International Olympic Committee banned South Africa from the Olympic games, and many international corporations brought the pressure of their economic power to bear. If "knowledge is power," then by spreading its inherent knowledge, *A Dry White Season* helped drive the final nail into the coffin of oppression and helped give South Africans and all the people of the world the power to eliminate apartheid forever.

Review Summary: Most critics pointed to the film's admirable sense of balance. Janet Maslin in the *New York Times* wrote, "A Dry White Season divides its attention more or less evenly between the story's black and white characters." According to Barbara Cramer in *Motion Picture Guide*, the film "shows the effects of racism from both white and black standpoints, balancing points of view." It also suggested that this was "the first time in a major Hollywood studio production that blacks are given more than token representations."

The critics seemed impressed with Palcy's ability to pull together such a major work in only her second effort in the world of film-making. "Rich" observed in *Variety*, "Palcy demonstrates a firm grip on bigger budget logistics, and moves the story inexorably toward its grim conclusion." In *Magill's Cinema Annual*, Anahid Kassabian noted that "Both the editing and camera work reveal much control and polish, especially for a young director." She adds that "The film-makers appear to be recording what is happening in the most direct way, whether it is marching and singing or beating and shooting."

The negative criticism faulted the film's purposeful framing and its guarded presentations. David Denby in *New York* thought the movie came off as a procession of attitudes: "*A Dry White Season* is unbearably stiff. The slaughter of black children and the scenes of intimidation and torture are shot academically, without rage or poetry." David Edelstein, of the *New York Post* called the film propaganda, adding, "The movie feels cheap, ugly and obvious."

These viewpoints were in the minority, however. Most critics praised the film as an outstanding effort. In the *Los Angeles Times*, Kevin Thomas wrote, "It is in the melding of two worlds so deliberately separated that *A Dry White Season* becomes so stunning an accomplishment."

EUZHAN PALCY

Mayflower Hotel, Washington D.C.
April 10, 1999

Also by telephone April 12, 1999, and May 2, 1999

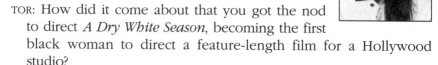

TOR: How did it come about that you got the nod
to direct *A Dry White Season*, becoming the first
black woman to direct a feature-length film for a Hollywood
studio?

PALCY: Well, since *Sugar Cane Alley* was an internationally acclaimed
movie, the studios did what they do: They wrote me five letters,
but I didn't want to go to Hollywood. Something inside me was
saying, "This is not the work for you."

In the meantime, Robert Redford invited me to go to the Sundance lab, which has nothing to do with Hollywood. In order to
be considered you had to have a project, and I had this book, *A
Dry White Season*, and I said, it's what I wanted to do.

TOR: You developed the project at Sundance?

PALCY: They flew me to Utah, and I spent a month there. Redford was very, very nice. He projected my movie *Sugar Cane
Alley* ten times during the whole Sundance lab. Many people had
seen *Sugar Cane Alley* or had heard about it, and they wanted to
see me.

Redford and I sat down at the mall and talked, you know?
And he said, "Okay, so what do you want to do about the
future?"

I said, "Well, a woman at Warner Bros. sent me a letter and
said she'd like me to come and to work with them."

So he said, "Why don't you go? Why are you closing the door?
You should go—and if you find out that you don't like it, at least
you tried." And then he said, "We'll get in touch with them and
organize a trip for you."

I went there with my book in my bag, but I didn't say anything when I met the woman at the meeting. In the beginning,
she was crying and telling me how in love she was with *Sugar
Cane Alley*. And she said, "Okay, so we have some projects that
we'd like to propose to you."

And I said, "Okay, well, all right." And she gave me all kinds
of screenplay material—and I said, "Well, no, I don't think it's
for me." I had a problem with her proposals.

TOR: What were the subjects?

PALCY: White stories. I couldn't relate to them. I just did *Sugar Cane Alley*, you know, and you propose something like that? I was hoping that she would give me a great story with at least black and white people . . . even if they didn't only have black people, but a story involving mixed characters. And then I think that she understood because she said, "Oh, oh, I know. I know exactly what I'll give you." And she opened a drawer, and you know what? She pulled out Malcolm X.

TOR: Malcolm X?

PALCY: Yes, Malcolm X on the table, bing! And she said, "What about this?"

I said "Oh, my God, Malcolm X!" And I said "You know what? I know all about this guy and his life, but I really believe . . ." And I swear to you, I remember I said that to her. I remember as if it were yesterday. I said, "You know what? I really believe that this story would be more accurate if it were told by a black American."

And she said, "Oh, that's interesting."

So finally, I said, "You know what? I have . . ."—and I opened my bag and gave her the book—*A Dry White Season.* And I started to tell her the story, the way I would do it. Because the book was about a white man, the awakening of a white man in South Africa. It's a great book—but I turned it into the story of two families, a black family and a white family, and I told her the story, and she was crying and she said, "Oh, my God . . ." They cry easily in Hollywood.

TOR: So they green-lighted the project?

PALCY: They said okay and started to work toward the screenplay. And then *Cry Freedom* came out. And then they said, "Wait a minute . . . two movies about apartheid? That's too much."

And I said, "Wait a minute! How many movies have you done about Vietnam? And you are still making them . . ." I was really upset. Finally MGM decided to pick up the whole thing. And what really makes it funny is that I had called Brando to play a part in the movie while I was with Warner Bros. I knew that he wanted to do it, but I didn't tell them that Brando already said yes, and would do it for free, because I didn't want them to say, "Oh, okay, that's different."

TOR: What was it about Marlon Brando that you considered bringing him out of retirement after nine years?

PALCY: I was very careful in my choices for all the actors to be in the movie because I was making a movie about apartheid, and I tell you . . . I checked them all out. I told the studio, "Look, I want black South African actors to be in the movie. I don't want to have any African Americans portraying African actors, simply because I'm not making a fiction here. It's a Hollywood production, but it's not a Hollywood film. I want the real people for the thing." And I said, "I want to give them a voice. I want them to speak, when they speak about being killed, their children being tortured. That will go straight to people's stomach . . . because they are the real people . . . and they are telling the truth."

TOR: And Brando already had an active sense of civil rights?

PALCY: Yes, that's right, a record, absolutely. I met him, we talked, and I gave him the screenplay. I told him, "Read the screenplay, then call me and let me know how you feel." And three days later he called me and said he wanted to do it. And I told him, "Well, I'll have to call your attention on one point. We don't have a lot of money to make this movie because it is a political film and you know?" And he said, "Are you kidding? If I'm coming after nine years . . . in a movie like that . . . it's a very important role. I'm very happy to do it. But it's a cameo, I'm certainly not doing that for the money." And I was very moved by that. And he also said, "I'm doing it because I want to leave my footprints in the South African sand." And I thought that was great, you know? He asked us to make some changes on the screenplay, and we did. And we went to do the shooting at Pinewood Studios.

TOR: In England?

PALCY: Yes, because he couldn't go to Zimbabwe. We did all the interiors of his office and the courtroom scenes over there.

TOR: Brando received an Academy Award nomination for that role—so he was the correct choice?

PALCY: Absolutely. He did a great job. At the end of the shooting he gave some people of the crew, the wardrobe people, makeup, the hair people . . . he gave people envelopes containing five hundred dollars. And then he had a speech. He was saying that he wanted to say thank you to everybody, because it was such a wonderful experience.

I offered him an African sculpture, and he gave me a photo of him that said, "Thank you for your unwavering determination to carry this story to the end . . . I'm very proud to have been a part of this adventure . . . Love, Marlon." I still have it. After that, I went back to America for postproduction, for the cutting, for the editing.

And we had one of the best editors, Sam Austin. We started to work, but at a certain moment I had a painful dilemma, but I had to make a decision as a director. We had to cut a piece of Brando's performance in one scene. It's the courtroom scene where he's supposed to insult the magistrate, and the magistrate orders the guard to drag him out of the courtroom, to expel him. It's a wonderful thing for the story, but unfortunately . . . Marlon, in his acting . . . his shirt will open . . . and his lawyer's robe will open . . . the button will go and his belly will be out, you know, exposed?

TOR: While they were dragging him out, during the struggle?

PALCY: Yes. And also, he doesn't learn his lines and he has little things in his ears, a little machine, a recorder . . . you will see that. After four takes, my producer and I, we said we will never get that. We should stop now before he has a heart attack or something. We'll see how we can manage in the cutting room.

And then we put everything together in the cutting room and it was a mess. I mean, it was hilarious. Paula, my producer, everybody was laughing because you are in the middle of such a dramatic, intense scene and you had these funny things that disturbed it.

I know that this man made the movie for free, and I know that it was important for him to do that. So we said okay, the least we can do is send him a tape of the cutting, showing him the scene with and the scene without.

We sent it and he called me. He said, "Okay, yes, I saw that . . . and I loved the scene when I'm being expelled from the courtroom."

I thought he was pulling my leg, he was just being funny. So I said, "Me, too. That's why I sent you the one without."

"No, I'm serious," he said. The guy was damned serious. He wanted that scene back.

TOR: Even with his belly hanging out, and the wires in his ears?

PALCY: He didn't care, he said, "That's good, it will be strong, and we have to leave it there."

I said, "No, we cannot have it there."

He started to argue with me and even offered to do some reshoots, but it was too late. I told him, "Look, I don't have the

final cut on this movie. Go and see with the studio. If they want
to put it back, it's no problem."

He called the head of the studio, who didn't take his call. So
Marlon sent a letter to him; he didn't respond to the letter either.
And one night he called and the head of the studio was there.
And Marlon told him, "I made this movie for free, and I want to
come to the cutting room and put my scene back." The head of
the studio did something that Hollywood had never done for a
director—they backed me up, fully. The studio refused to let him
come to the cutting room to make changes or do anything . . .
and he was infuriated.

He called me, and said to me, "Euzhan, I'm begging you. I
swear, if you put my scene back in the movie, I will do something that I never did for any director, I will go everywhere and
sell the movie with you."

TOR: He'd go on the promotional tour?

PALCY: Yes. He said, "I swear on my children's heads that I will do
that for you."

I said, "Marlon, this is a tragedy for me. For you to come back
after nine years." And he's not just any man. He is *the Man*, the
myth . . . Marlon Brando. I asked him to be there for a reason, he
came, and he was really a big supporter of the movie. I said, "I
know you are upset with me and disappointed, but I never serve
my ego. I went to South Africa, I saw these people, I heard them.
I could have been killed at any moment, and I can still be killed
with this movie that I'm doing . . . this is dangerous." And I said
to him, "I don't want to compromise the work." I told him that I
cannot do what he is asking me. God knows how I would like
to, but I can't.

And when I said that to him, Marlon became a monster. He
changed his voice, and he said to me, "Okay, you are being stub-
born, and you don't want to do what I am asking you to do,"
and he started to threaten me. My producer was there, she was
in the room, she can confirm that. He said, "I will destroy your
career, I will make you look stupid! I'll tell terrible things about
you! And you will never work again!"

I said, "You are trying to blackmail me? What are you doing?
My work will speak for me." That's why he went on that program with Connie Chung, the CBS News anchor. He called her
and said, "I want you to interview me because I have some
important things to say."

TOR: So he actually set out to sabotage the film?

PALCY: That's what he did, exactly. In his interview he said that, "The studio made a money decision because they usually don't make political films, but they cleaned it up before sending it out." Which is a dead lie. He said, "They made a lot of cuts, and they cut a very powerful scene, an important scene in the movie that would definitely nail apartheid in people's minds." But he never said what this scene was.

TOR: You watched the interview?

PALCY: Oh, yeah, absolutely. It was all over the world. He knew what he was doing. He really wanted to put down the film afterward. And then he got an Academy Award nomination for the part, and I swear to you, if I had left that in the movie . . . never . . . they would never have given him that nomination. He also got Best Actor, in the Tokyo Film Festival . . . instead of Donald Sutherland, who deserved that award. And my producer and I called Brando to let him know that he got the award, and he asked, "Did the film win? Did the film win?"

And my producer said, "No."

He said, "You see, because the film is bad."

What happened at the Tokyo Film Festival that day was a scandal . . . it was something awful. Yves Montand was the president of the jury that year, and the jury wanted to give my movie the prize, and Montand said no. I swear to you, and he is an actor that used to play in these political movies by Costa Gavras. He proposed instead to give Marlon Brando the award for Best Actor. So there was this big controversy. And the press questioned me. They asked me, "You don't find it strange that they gave Marlon Brando Best Actor when Donald Sutherland deserved this award? What do you think about that?"

I realized immediately what was going on, and I said, "Well, it's not for me to say. Ask the jury. They made the decision. It's not me." You know the press, they had already heard the buzz, so one said to me, "We heard that your movie is supposed to have the Jury Prize, but you don't have it. Why do you think that happened?"

I was still very shocked, and I said, "Why do you ask me these questions? The jury is there. Question the jury."

TOR: How did you feel about Brando's transformation?

PALCY: To be honest, I was very torn apart. I was sad. I was mad at him, but I couldn't hate him because I realized that his bitterness was equal to, or on the same level of, the love and faith that he put into the movie.

It took me almost a year to recover because I was very, very hurt. He went out and he said these terrible things which were lies! I was sad that I couldn't make him happy. I'm not an ungrateful person, and I had to remember the good things that we did together.

TOR: So you've just kept quiet about all of this until now?

PALCY: Yes, because I wanted my movie to just take off and not be overshadowed by a big controversy. The movie was more important than anything that Marlon could say. And every time I look at the movie, I am so happy that I did not accept the compromise. I would hate myself today. And the press would have been terrible. He would not have gotten the Oscar nomination and the press would say, "She's a lousy director!" The people in the profession, they know what happened; the audience does not know. And even today, people in Hollywood will say, "Oh, she's the one who said no to Brando." And I say, "No, don't say that. I cannot be proud of that because it was a painful thing for me. This man did make my movie for free; this man did come and do his job. So I can't take any credit for that. I'm not proud of what I had to do. But that's life. You learn.

TOR: Do you feel that *A Dry White Season* played a role in the dismantling of apartheid?

PALCY: Two or three months after my movie came out, Mandela was released, and I was so excited about that. Of course it had nothing to do with my movie, but at least it was shown everywhere in the world, and I'm sure that it helped people to understand what apartheid is.

TOR: Have you been back to South Africa?

PALCY: In June of 1995, *Regards*, a very important magazine in France, called me. They told me it was very important for them to have the woman who did *A Dry White Season* go over and interview Mandela. I left everything I was doing, and I went to South Africa, and I met Nelson Mandela. He told me, "You know, I saw the different movies that they did about South Africa and I've discovered that *A Dry White Season* was the one the people from the ANC (African National Congress) elected as their movie to best show the evils of apartheid." And I was very proud of that.

Lean on Me
Warner Bros. (1989)

"Go ahead, jump! You smoke crack, don't you? I say
if you want to kill yourself, don't mess around with
it! Do it expeditiously!"

—Principal Joe Clark to student Thomas Sams

Lean on Me proved that you don't have to become rich and famous
and die in order for someone to make a film reflecting your life's
work and accomplishments.

Joe Clark, a tough New Jersey schoolteacher, made national
headlines when he became the principal of the state's worst school
and with commitment, dedication, and hard-line tactics turned it
around. Eastside High in Paterson, New Jersey, was in shambles as
a result of drugs, apathy, and student violence. Clark became a galvanizing force and changed all that. With a bullhorn and a baseball
bat, he revived and energized the school's faculty and students.

In the film, Clark's first official act is to call a school-wide
assembly and expel all known troublemakers. Later he runs into
trouble himself with the city's fire ordinances, when he chains and
padlocks the school doors in an attempt to keep out the drug dealers. He was as tough on his staff as he was on the students; in one
memorable scene, Clark assembles the faculty in the gymnasium
and tells them to raise both hands high in the air. He points out the
helplessness and the hopeless feeling of being in that position and
reminds them that without their care and guidance, many of their
students will find themselves in the exact same position, only at the
other end of a policeman's gun.

Clark patrols the hallways and bathrooms, always keeping a
watchful eye. He takes a personal interest in the students and
knows most by name. To help build school pride and spirit, he
proclaims that each student must be prepared to sing the school
alma mater on demand and organizes school decoration projects
and student-to-student mentoring programs. The students appreciate

The reel and the real: Morgan Freeman, left, portrays controversial high school principal Joe Clark in the highly charged *Lean on Me*. (Warner Bros.)

CREDITS: Director: John G. Avildsen. Producer: Norman Twain. Screenplay: Michael Schiffer. Photography: Victor Hammer. Editors: John Carter, John G. Avildsen. Music: Bill Conti. Production Design: Doug Kraner. 109 minutes. Drama. PG-13.

CAST: Morgan Freeman (*Joe Clark*), Beverly Todd (*Ms. Levias*), Robert Guillaume (*Dr. Frank Napier*), Robin Bartlett (*Mrs. Elliott*), Lynne Thigpen (*Leona Barrett*), Michael Beach (*Mr. Darnell*), Ethan Phillips (*Mr. Rosenberg*), Jermaine Hopkins (*Thomas Sams*), Karen Malina White (*Kaneesha Carter*), Regina Taylor (*Mrs. Carter*).

his efforts and are there to support Mr. Clark. When he is unjustly arrested and jailed for his unorthodox tactics, the entire school rallies at the jail to demand his release.

Also prominently portrayed in the film is school board member Dr. Frank Napier, who gives Clark as much support as he can but has higher forces to answer to himself. Ms. Levias, the assistant principal, is often overlooked and underestimated by Clark, but we see that she is an intricate part of his quest for change. Thomas Sams, one of the expelled hoodlums, is given a second chance by Clark, and he struggles to make good. When Kaneesha, one of Clark's prize students, confides in him that she is pregnant, he asks for Ms. Levias's help in bringing her back together with her distraught out-of-work mother. The four work together to find common ground and a favorable solution. Leona Barrett, a concerned citizen with a not-so-hidden political agenda, has it in for the school principal and makes for a powerful antagonist in her attempts to bring an end to the reign of the man she calls "Crazy Joe Clark."

Lean on Me dramatically expresses the hardships, motivations, and triumphs of one man who is determined to improve a failed educational system. He rose to the challenge when most had given up, and made a positive difference. Veteran actor Morgan Freeman, as Joe Clark, gives a powerful performance, and every scene he appears in sizzles with energy. Yet it took another film with a vastly different role for Freeman to be considered for an Academy Award. That movie was *Driving Miss Daisy* (1989), for which he won the Oscar for Best Supporting Actor. The members of the Academy were evidently more comfortable with Freeman's proud yet subservient "Yes'em, Miz Daisy" dialogue than the "I'll crack a baseball bat over a drug dealer's head" portrayal in *Lean On Me*, a compelling film that reminds us that one person can make a difference.

Lean on Me was repeatedly compared with another film of the 1980s, *Stand and Deliver*. Both are based on true stories about educators who have come into troubled high schools in order to improve conditions by setting tough standards.

Review Summary: Most reviewers praised Morgan Freeman's performance as the controversial principal of Eastside High. Some said his performance simply helped a bad film. Only a few offered opinions that were almost entirely positive. The words of reviewer Irwin Hyman express the opinion of the majority: "The movie is moving and exciting—but also simplistic and misleading." Critics feared that

Lean on Me offered easy solutions that, by distorting the facts and oversimplifying the true story, misled its audience. Many reviewers expressed doubt over the actual success of Joe Clark. How much did he really improve the test scores of his students? Were his aggressive tactics appropriate? These questions related to the controversy surrounding the film as well as the real life situation.

Many of these reviews argued that *Lean on Me* virtually ignored the political and social roots of inner-city problems, and that the truth is blurred in Joe Clark's heroification. But the film did quite well in movie theaters, indicating, perhaps, that audiences found great appeal in a story about a strong, effective black man.

Glory

Tri-Star Pictures (1989)

"Ain't no dream . . . we runaway slaves! But we've
come back fightin' men!"

—Sergeant Rawlins to Negro kids

Glory is an eloquent Civil War epic about the 54th Massachusetts
Voluntary Infantry, the first black infantry regiment to march off into
battle for the Union army.

The film focused on its young commander, the twenty-five-year-
old Boston Brahmin abolitionist Col. Robert Gould Shaw. The script
was based on two books and on letters that Shaw had written to his
mother. "We fight for men and women whose poetry is not yet written," Shaw wrote her just before the Battle of Antietam Creek. Soon
after that bloody battle, Abraham Lincoln announced the Emancipation Proclamation, on September 22, 1862, which freed the
enslaved blacks in this country and cleared the way for many to
fight for themselves.

Motivated by a call to arms by abolitionist Frederick Douglass,
six hundred freedmen offered their services. The ensemble cast
includes: Trip, a hardened and cynical escaped field hand from Tennessee; Rawlins, an older, Union gravedigger and natural-born
leader; Sharts, a good-natured, sharpshooter from South Carolina
with a stuttering drawl; and Thomas Searles, a Boston intellectual
and freedman who had grown up as a friend of Shaw's. (This last
character may have been based on Lewis H. Douglass—son of Frederick Douglas—who was one of the 54th's first enlistees.)

Glory unfolds as a series of vignettes chronicling the 54th's
progress as the enlistees struggle for recognition and an opportunity
to prove themselves as fighting men. The narrative follows them
from their enlistment and training at Readville Camp, Massachusetts,
where they are denied uniforms, shoes, rifles, respect, and equal
pay, to a short stint in Beaufort, South Carolina, alongside a rogue
unit of black contraband soldiers led by a corrupt Union colonel,

through their first battle at James Island, South Carolina, where the 54th finally pulls together into a coherent fighting unit. From there, the story rushes forward to the afternoon of July 18, 1863, and their bloody assault on Fort Wagner at the mouth of Charleston Bay.

The fact that black men volunteered and fought in the Civil War to help maintain their own freedom had long been ignored by Hollywood. Earlier Civil War films such as D. W. Griffith's *Birth of a Nation* (1915), Buster Keaton's *The General* (1927), David O. Selznick's *Gone With the Wind* (1939), and John Huston's *Red Badge of Courage* (1951), never addressed the issue of black fighting men. Other films that dealt peripherally with the Civil War depicted blacks only as a downtrodden and displaced people, dependent for their freedom and liberty on the genteel "white boys in blue."

Glory portrays the full spectrum of the African-American men who joined the struggle. One of the most powerful scenes probably ever filmed occurs after Trip has gone AWOL in search of a pair of shoes. He is captured and brought back to camp to be flogged as a deserter. When he removes his shirt, he reveals a back that is already wealed and scarred from previous whippings. He spits on the ground, braces himself against a wagon wheel, and takes the lashes almost without flinching. While he is enduring the pain, his eyes express a strength, resistance, and vulnerability unmatched by even the bravest screen heroes. Eventually, a single tear runs down his stoic face. Denzel Washington would win an Academy Award for his portrayal.

Even though this historically important topic is enacted from the perspective of the concerned and sympathetic white commanding officer, *Glory* is a powerful film, filled with dignified black men and

---

CREDITS: Director: Edward Zwick. Producer: Freddie Fields. Screenplay: Kevin Jarre. Based on the books *Lay This Laurel* by Lincoln Kirstein, *One Galant Rush* by Peter Burchard, and the letters of Robert Gould Shaw. Music: James Horner; featuring the Boys Choir of Harlem. Photography: Freddie Francis. Editor: Steven Rosenblum. Production Design: Norman Garwood. Costumes: Francine Tanchuck. Stunt Coordinator: Bob Minor. 122 minutes. Historical drama. R.

CAST: Mathew Broderick (*Col. Robert Gould Shaw*), Denzel Washington (*Trip*), Cary Elwes (*Cabot Forbes*), Morgan Freeman (*John Rawlins*), Jihmi Kennedy (*Sharts*), Andre Braugher (*Thomas Searles*), John Finn (*Sgt. Mulcahy*), Cliff De Young (*Col. Montgomery*), Raymond St. Jacques (*Frederick Douglass*) John David Cullum (*Morse*), Alan North (*Governor Andrew*), Jane Alexander (*Shaw's Mother*), Bob Gunton (*General Harker*).

The soldiers of the 54th Regiment of the Massachusetts Volunteer Infantry parade through the streets of Boston in *Glory*. Morgan Freeman (fifth from left) portrays Rawlins, a gravedigger turned proud fighting man. (Tri-Star Pictures)

heroic performances that eloquently depict this often neglected contribution to American history.

Review Summary: While many critics mentioned the picture's sometimes over-the-top symbolism and its extreme musical accompaniments, most found *Glory* an important and powerful historical film. David Ansen of *Newsweek* wrote, "Zwick has made an engrossing, sometimes stirring, sometimes wobbly film. . . . [he] seems more concerned with 'feelings' than with history, though some of his battle scenes have a stark, intimate power." Gary Giddins in the *Village Voice* said that the battle scenes were some of the best ever filmed, but that "Glory's effectiveness is undercut by Zwick's tendency to telegraph most of the key events, as though he feared the audience wouldn't get them if the music didn't swell to signal the significance."

A number of critics noted that the film's characterizations were relatively weak. And Kevin Thomas in the *Los Angeles Times* wished that the story had been told from a black viewpoint. "For all that is commendable about *Glory*, you nevertheless wish you were experiencing it from the perspective of Trip, the man who gets put down constantly for telling the truth, but who is obliged by the script to shape up and get swept up by the film's selfless heroism, just like everyone else."

In the *New York Times*, Vincent Canby described the film as a pageant in which "the characters serve principally to illuminate a glorious moment of history, which they do with consistent conviction." He adds, "The strength of idealism that fired these men becomes apparent and dramatically urgent . . . Glory has mind as well as soul."

8

Society Profile: 1990 and Beyond

With the rapid expansion of technology and the coming of the Internet, we live more and more in a global community as computers link finances, business, the arts, people, and resources throughout the world.

Apartheid fell like the Berlin Wall in 1990 when political prisoner Nelson Mandela was released after twenty-seven years of imprisonment. When black South Africans voted for the first time in 1994, Mandela was elected the country's first black president. He moved quickly to promote unity and tolerance among all the people of South Africa, to honor those who had died in the fight for equality.

In American politics, President George Bush, who came to office in 1988, launched Operation Desert Storm against Iraq and its leader, Saddam Hussein, for invading its southern neighbor, Kuwait. In the ensuing air war, hundreds of "sorties" were flown, using the latest "smart weapons," missiles guided by lasers and on-board video cameras. Iraq finally agreed to sanctions and monitoring by the United Nations, and to destroy all its arsenals and means of producing weapons of mass destruction. Claims of its noncompliance would keep tensions high and conflict alive throughout the rest of the decade.

Racial issues still presented a major concern in America. The videotaped beating of Rodney King by four Los Angeles police officers and the subsequent riots after their acquittal in 1992 opened the eyes of all Americans to the level of injustice that was tolerated within the criminal justice system. When angered blacks and others took their disapproval of the verdict to the streets, many of the whites who lived in the hills above Los Angeles watched in shock and horror as the City of Angels burned far below.

Referred to as the "trial of the century," the O.J. Simpson case and its verdict made the different perceptions of race and justice among blacks and whites painfully clear. Simpson, a black former professional football star turned actor, was accused of murdering his white wife, Nicole Simpson, and her friend Ron Goldman. His guilt or innocence was debated across the country and the trial was covered extensively by television. The jury, composed of a majority of black Californians, found that the prosecution did not prove its case beyond the necessary "reasonable doubt," and Simpson was found not guilty. His acquittal was celebrated by most African Americans and criticized by most whites. Simpson was later found liable for the deaths in a civil trial by a majority white jury and ordered to pay millions of dollars in restitution to the deceased victims' families.

Interestingly enough, a film remake of Shakespeare's *Othello* was released around the time of the Simpson trial, starring Lawrence Fishburne as the Moor. Black men killing white women apparently was not en vogue, however, and the film made a dismal showing at the box office before rapidly disappearing into obscurity.

In the midst of this climate, a University of Michigan study reported that interracial marriages were on the rise, with 1.1 million interracial couples, and 1.9 million children born to interracial couples. Congress considered adding a "multiracial" category to the census forms but rejected the idea because of the vagueness of the term.

In 1992, Democrat William Jefferson Clinton was elected president over the incumbent Republican, George Bush. The White House's new occupant brought the country a new and optimistic outlook on race relations as compared with that of the twelve-year Reagan and Bush administrations. Clinton appointed a multiracial cabinet that looked more like America and proposed an increase in trade and investment with African countries. The Republicans controlled the House and Senate, however, and Clinton's reign became plagued with opposition, scandal, and constant accusations of misdeeds and wrongdoing.

As the country found itself in the middle of a retreat from affirmative action, a report card by the NAACP gave the majority Republican Congress an F on civil rights issues. The voters in California passed Proposition 209, ending affirmative action in hiring and admission policies. As if to add salt to the wound, the law took effect on the thirty-fourth anniversary of the 1963 Civil Rights March on Washington. Several colleges and universities quickly responded to the new policy, and minority admissions at the University of California Law School dropped drastically. In response, the Association of American Universities, representing sixty-two of the country's top research institutions, adopted a resolution defending the right to use affirmative action in admissions policies.

Meanwhile, more black people began to openly assert their faith in God. A popular spiritual counselor, Iyanla Vanzant, explained that black people have always believed in God, but they have become more comfortable expressing their faith outside of the church. Her book *Acts of Faith* remains a best-seller to this day.

In 1994, faith was tested as powerful earthquakes rocked northern and southern California. Bridges collapsed, gas mains broke, and multiple fires were sparked by downed power lines. Many people died and many others were injured or trapped in their cars or their homes. Damages were estimated in the hundreds of millions of dollars.

Two key events for African Americans during this period were the Million Man and the Million Woman marches. Unity was the rallying cry for black men in Washington, D.C., on October 16, 1995. Despite a barrage of biased and misleading press from the major media, the one-day rally, organized by Nation of Islam leader Louis Farrakhan, helped build spiritual and social commitments among black men. This momentous occasion was followed by the Million Woman March in Philadelphia two years later. In spite of rain and cool temperatures, women came together from across the country to hear Congresswoman Maxine Waters, African civil rights leader Winnie Mandela, actress Jada Pinkett-Smith, and other voices for unity.

The U.S. Department of Justice under Attorney General Janet Reno initiated a civil rights investigation when seventeen primarily southern black churches were burned in 1996. The same year, an FBI report year showed that a majority of hate crimes were motivated by race. Almost 62 percent of such crimes in 1995 were against African Americans; religious bias was found to be the second highest motivation. In response, President Clinton named a seven-person panel on race relations to study the significant issues and recommend solutions.

It had been projected that black buying power would surpass $455 billion by the end of the decade, according to the Selig Center for Economic Growth at the University of Georgia. The total personal income of African Americans had increased by 54 percent since 1990 and was expected to continue to grow at a similar rate. At the same time, the National Center for Children in Poverty at Columbia University reported that white children accounted for 6 percent of all children in poverty as compared with 30 percent for black children. In the midst of these disparities, nationally syndicated talk show host Oprah Winfry made history in 1995 as the first black woman to appear on the *Forbes* list of richest Americans.

In sports, twenty-one-year-old Tiger Woods won the 1997 Masters Golf Tournament in Augusta, Georgia. Michael Jordon came out of retirement to lead the Chicago Bulls to their fourth NBA Championship in 1996; the Bulls went on to win their fifth championship in 1997, and in 1998, they defeated the Utah Jazz for the "repeat three-peat." The following season, the league and the NBA players union found it difficult to come to terms on a new collective bargaining agreement, and the season was stalled in a lockout until early 1999. Once acceptable terms on both sides were reached, the league began with a shorter, blistering fifty-game schedule in early February. Michael Jordon had again chosen to retire, however.

Seventy-eight-year-old Eddie Robinson ended his fifty-six-year coaching career at Grambling State University as the winningest coach in college football history. His 408 wins, seventeen Southwestern Athletic Conference championships, and eight Black College National championships are legendary. In baseball, history was made, then broken again and again as Sammy Sosa of the Chicago Cubs and Mark McGuire of the St. Louis Cardinals battled for Roger Maris's 1961 home-run record. For a moment, Sosa took the lead with sixty-six, but McGuire took it back, completing the season with a total of seventy home runs in a single season. The seventieth home-run ball was later auctioned for $3 million.

Black music also had a significant impact on American culture in the 1990s. Gospel music hit the *Billboard* pop charts for the first time in history when Kirk Franklin and God's Property reached the number three spot with "Stomp." Rap music and the hip-hop culture raised concerns over violent and negative images of black men and women, as gangsta' and gang-banger music videos filled the screens. In 1996, those images spilled into real life when rapper Tupac Shakur was killed in a drive-by shooting. A few months later, another popular rap star, Biggie Smalls, was killed the same way as bulletproof street-fashions were all the rage among the hip-hop collective.

There continued to be progress and problems in education. Despite years of affirmative action efforts, the Southern Education

Foundation in Atlanta reported that higher education in the South was still segregated. The rates of black and white high school graduates were found to be almost equal, however, with 87 percent of white and 86 percent of black high school students graduating. A major debate took place in 1997 concerning "black English" when the Oakland California school board voted to recognize Ebonics as a second language. Both black and white leaders spoke out against the decision, saying that it would lower educational standards.

One sobering reality during this period was that more money was spent on building prison facilities than building college facilities, and that one out of three young black men were in prison, on probation, or on parole. According to the Justice Policy Institute in Washington, D.C., state spending decreased for education by more than $925 million in 1997 and increased for prison systems by the same amount. This despite the fact that studies showed it costs more taxpayer dollars to support a man or woman in prison for one year ($25,000–$30,000) than to provide four years of college education.

In January 1999, the 106th Congress convened with thirty-nine black members in the House of Representatives and no black members in the Senate. Despite President Clinton's having orchestrated the strongest economy and lowest unemployment rate in forty years, articles of impeachment were introduced by the Republican-controlled House of Representatives against him for lying under oath and obstruction of justice in regard to his relationship with a former White House intern.

The Census Bureau predicted that by 2050 the African American population would increase to 13.6 percent, and that the Hispanic population will become the largest minority group in America.

Daughters of the Dust
Kino International (1991)

"We are two people in one body . . . the last of the
old . . . and the first of the new."
—Nana Peazant to her family

Daughters of the Dust is an emotion-laden tale of family relationships, change, and tradition. The year is 1902 and the place is Ibo
Landing, one of the Sea Islands off the coast of Georgia. Members of
the Peazant family are gathering one last time to say good-bye, but
this is not your typical turn-of-the-twentieth-century black family.
The Peazants are Gullah, direct decendents of enslaved Africans who
had escaped captivity and fled to the islands in search of their freedom. This offshore isolation has allowed them to retain their dis-
tinctive African-based culture and traditions. Their dialect is a broken
blend of West African, Creole, and English languages that have been
merged into an odd but lyrical array of familiar sounds and syllables.
For one day only, three generations of Peazant women are reunited,
to determine the fate and the destination of their family's future.

Returning to their island home are born-again Christian Viola
and her worldly, outcast cousin Yellow Mary. But they are not
alone. Mary has brought along Trula, her controversial close friend
and soul mate. Viola has commissioned a photographer, Mr. Snead,
to document the reunion as a historic event. They arrive to find
that most of the family is split between remaining on the island and
migrating to the mainland. Nana, the eighty-eight-year-old matriarch,
is determined to stay. She will not be separated from the souls of
their ancestors. Grandson Eli, one of the few men in the film with
any say, tries to explain to her that leaving means progress and a
future for the family. But Nana is more concerned about the future
of her family's culture and values. Will they be maintained in a relo-
cation to the mainland, or lost forever?

Middle-aged Haagar agrees with Eli. She yearns for a new life
filled with new sights, new sounds, and new opportunities. On the

Three generations of women, left to right, Eula Peazant (Alva Rodgers), Yellow Mary (Barbara O), and Nana Peazant (Cora Lee Day), must plan for their family's future in Julie Dash's beautifully photographed independent film *Daughters of the Dust.* (Kino International Corp.)

CREDITS: Writer-Director: Julie Dash. Producers: Julie Dash, Arthur Jafa. Photography: Arthur Jafa. Editors: Amy Carey, Joseph Burton. Music: John Barnes. Production Design: Kerry Marshall. Costumes: Arline Burks. Art Director: Michael Kelly Williams. 113 minutes. Historical drama. NR.

CAST: Adisa Anderson (*Eli Peazant*), Barbara O (*Yellow Mary*), Cheryl Lynn Bruce (*Viola*), Cora Lee Day (*Nana Peazant*), Geraldine Dunston (*Viola's Mother*), Tommy Hicks (*Mr. Snead*), Kaycee Moore (*Haagar*), Alva Rogers (*Eula Peazant*), Cornell "Kofi" Royal (*Daddy Mac*), Bahni Turpin (*Iona Peazant*), Kai Lynn Warren (*The Unknown Child*), Umar Ubdurrahman (*Bilal*), Vertamae Grovesnor (*Hair Braider*), Trula Hoosier (*Trula*), Eartha D. Robinson (*Myown*), M. Cochise Anderson (*St. Julen Lastchild*), Sherry Jackson (*Older Cousin*), Ervin Green (*Baptist Minister*), Marcus Humphrey (*Boatman*).

other hand, her teenage daughter Iona is in love with her full-blooded Cherokee Indian boyfriend St. Julen Lastchild, and does not want to leave him behind. Eula, Eli's wife, worries about whether the baby she's carrying is her husband's or the remnant of a vicious rape. She's torn between the two camps, but despite her inner turmoil she becomes the voice of reason that makes everyone see and accept the needs on both sides.

"I focus on and depict experiences that have never been shown on the screen before," the film's writer and director Julie Dash said in an interview with Zeinabu Irene Davis in *Black Film Review.*

One of the unique aspects of Dash's film is that it shuns traditional narrative and becomes a beautiful poem set to images. Much like a free-styling jazz musician, Dash manipulates the conventions of form and structure to create her own cinematic language. The result is a slow, moody, spiritual film filled with myth, folklore, and loads of cultural history.

The title is derived from a passage in the Bible, in Ezekiel: "O ye sons of the dust." Dash changed the phrase to "daughters." "Dust also implies the past and something that's grown old, and crumbling," she explained in the interview. "The whole film is about memories and the scraps of memories that these women carry around in tin cans and little private boxes." The "scraps of memories" theme was inspired by a paper written by W. E. B. Du Bois, in which he discussed the fact that most African Americans don't have a solid lineage that they can trace; all they have are "scraps of memories" remaining from the past. "I wanted memory to be a central focus of the story," Dash added.

Dash was motivated to do the story after she heard her father called a "Geechee." When she learned that it referred to his Gullah culture, she began to write the story as a short film in 1976 while she was at the American Film Institute. Her initial thirty-page script was funded by the National Endowment for the Arts, and in 1981 she received a Guggenheim Foundation Research Grant to expand the project into a feature. Dash went to the Sea Islands for two weeks in 1987 to shoot a trailer for the film, which she presented at a PBS weekend at Sundance. Producer Lynn Holst was so impressed with it that she asked for the screenplay and persuaded American Playhouse to fund the film. Additional funds came from the Corporation for Public Broadcasting.

Daughters of the Dust was shot October 16 through November 19, 1989, on a final budget of $800,000. Coproducer and cinematographer Arthur Jafa was awarded the Best Cinematography prize at the 1991 Sundance Film Festival. As a graduate of the UCLA film school and the American Film Institute, Dash is credited with being the first African-American female filmmaker to achieve a U.S. theatrical release for a feature-length film.

Review Summary: The confusing nature of the film is almost undeniable. Many reviewers said that *Daughters of the Dust* was indeed innovative and beautiful to watch, but often quite difficult to follow. Some contended that as a result of the dialect, the story is often unclear, as well as the relationships of the characters.

Despite these problems, many reviewers credited Dash for her originality and artful skill. Some speculated about her intentions in an effort to address reactions to the confusion; for example, Malcolm Johnson of the *Hartford Courant* explained that Dash did not wish to present a linear film, but to capture a tradition. Those reviews that discuss such stylistic intentions tended to praise Dash for the authentic nature of *Daughters of the Dust* and to urge that the film be seen. For many reviewers, the stunning cinematography made up for any lack of clarity, and the poetic images of the enchanting landscape were sufficient. Others noted that despite its intelligence and beauty, the picture was too long and underdeveloped.

Boyz 'N the Hood
Columbia Pictures (1991)

"Any fool with a dick can make a baby . . . but only a real man can raise his children."

—Furious Styles to his son, Tre

Boyz 'N the Hood has been described as a hard, intensive, profanity-driven *Cooley High* of the nineties . . . with a violent streak. This was an understatement. With this powerful vision of daily life in south central Los Angeles, John Singleton, the film's twenty-three-year-old writer-director, became the West Coast's answer to Spike Lee.

The year is 1984, and Tre Styles is a ten-year-old boy being raised by his mother, Reva. She does the best she can, but when her son begins to have discipline problems at school, she knows that it's time for his father to step in. Furious Styles believes that only a man can teach a male child how to be a man. So Tre is packed up and moves in with him.

On his first day with his strict, disciplinarian father, Tre wants to play with Doughboy and Ricky, two very different brothers who live across the street with their single mom. Instead, he is ordered to rake the yard; it's a chore that takes him all day.

As time goes by, Tre experiences life in the hood: fights, burglars, a dead body in an alley, and threatening gang members are a constant everyday presence. Through it all, he receives knowledge and moral guidance from his father, but Doughboy and Ricky are not so lucky. Each has a different father, and their mother, Mrs. Baker, treats them differently as well, pampering and encouraging Ricky, while emphasizing all of Doughboy's faults. As a result, while Ricky plays with the football that his father gave him, the rebellious Doughboy is arrested for a juvenile crime and sent away for seven years.

The year jumps to 1991. Tre and Ricky are in their last year of high school and Doughboy is finally out of the joint. Ricky has a baby by his live-in girlfriend and hopes to attend college on a foot-

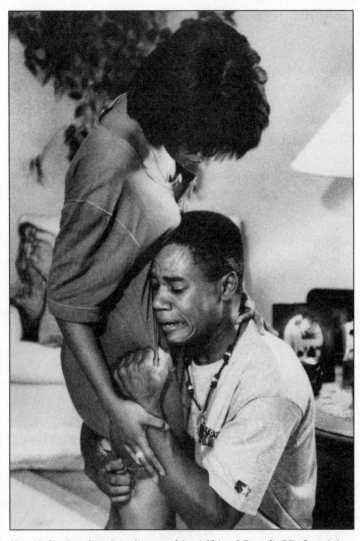

Tre (Cuba Gooding Jr.) clings to his girlfriend Brandi (Nia Long) in despair over the seemingly endless violence in south central Los Angeles, in *Boyz 'N the Hood*. (Columbia Pictures)

ball scholarship. Tre has grown into an upstanding young man. He and Brandi, his girlfriend, have grown up as neighbors over the years and plan to get married after college. The only problem is that Brandi wants to be a virgin bride, and Tre doesn't want to wait that long. Doughboy has no real plans for the future except to stay out of jail and hang with his main boyz, Dooky and Chris.

When a gang rift erupts, it leads to senseless death and violence for both camps, and Tre is caught up in the middle of it, torn between being a man of revenge and a man of reason. Brandi is there for him in his time of need, and so are the years of his father's sound advice, but then again, so is his father's gun. Weapon in hand, Tre sets off to discover which man he really is.

Despite the film's message of "Increase the Peace," which features the death statistics of young black males in the opening titles, incidents of gang violence erupted in several theaters where the film was shown. In response, many theaters refused to book the film.

However accurate it was, first-time director Singleton captured what felt like an authentic depiction of life in the hood. We don't hesitate to believe that this violent world of sporadic gunplay, sirens, searchlights, and hovering police helicopters really does exist, and the film makes us experience that world.

Review Summary: Director and writer John Singleton received much praise from critics for his powerful film. Typical was the *Atlanta Journal and Constitution*, where Eleanor Ringel wrote, "Vibrant and visceral, it packs an emotional punch that renders questions of subtlety and didacticism irrelevant. Mr. Singleton has an astonishing ability to take us inside an urban black community. He shows us how it breathes and bleeds."

A *Chicago Tribune* review by Dave Kehr suggested that the film's cry for racial justice was all but drowned out by its violent misogyny, and that sends the message that black women are too weak to raise black children. Kehr writes, "It's a sentiment that flies so firmly in the face of reality that it gives *Boyz 'N the Hood* a distinctly neurotic cast: The more the film proclaims itself as pure,

---

CREDITS: Writer-Director: John Singleton. Producer: Steve Nicolaides. Photography: Charles Mills. Editor: Bruce Cannon. Music: Stanley Clarke. 107 minutes. R.

CAST: Cuba Gooding, Jr. (*Tre Styles*), Ice Cube (*Doughboy*), Morris Chestnut (*Ricky Baker*), Larry Fishburne (*Furious Styles*), Angela Bassett (*Reva Styles*), Nia Long (*Brandi*), Tyra Ferrell (*Mrs. Baker*), Desi Arnez Hines II (*Tre, age 10*), Baha Jackson (*Doughboy, age 10*), Regina King (*Shalika*), Valentino Henderson (*Young Ricky*), Dedrick D. Gobert (*Dooky*), Redge Green (*Chris*), Ceal (*Sheryl*), Tammy Hanson (*Rosa*), Whitman Mayo (*The Old Man*).

unadulterated social reality, the more it seems purely subjective fantasy, a public dramatization of private demons."

Singleton's use of lighting, sound effects, and realistic characters is noted by many critics. Malcolm Johnson in the *Hartford Courant* wrote about what he called "a brilliant cinematic touch. Through the sound and light cast over the hood by police helicopters, a loud beating of steel wings and shafts of piercing, blue-tinged light, Singleton fills his audiences with a sense of what it is like to live in a police state, a crime-filled, always perilous environment where Big Brother is always watching you." According to Jay Carr in the *Boston Globe*, "He makes the characters count because he convinces us he cares enough to allow them to peel away layers and reveal themselves. These characters aren't just ambulatory attitudes. And they're more than just fleshed out. They've got shared humanity and Singleton makes us share his conviction that it's precious."

To Sleep With Anger
The Samuel Goldwyn Company (1991)

"I have always been wild, you know that. When
you're made to feel half-a-man, what do you think
the other half is?"

—Harry to Suzie

To Sleep With Anger takes its title from the old saying "Never go to
bed angry." It explores the turmoil that family ties can often bring,
especially when corrupted by myth and superstition.

Gideon and Suzie are transplants from the Deep South living
and making a way in the heart of Los Angeles. He's retired and
raises chickens in the backyard, and she's a midwife, helping expectant young couples prepare for the rigors of natural childbirth. Both
have long since adapted to city ways, yet have preserved their personal connections to their rural past. They've passed on what they
could to Junior and Babe Brother, their two very different sons, but
how much of their teachings and guidance have they been able to
retain? Both are grown men with wives and families of their own,
and each has a different outlook on how their lives should be lived.
Junior, older and more responsible, feels that his younger brother
takes advantage of their parents' kindness, support, and goodwill.

One day, a childhood friend from thirty years before, Harry
Mention, knocks on the door. Harry, who remained in the South, is
a charming, manipulating trickster with spellbinding stories of
down-home ways and folklore. As southern custom would dictate,
he is cordially invited to stay for as long as he wants to. Despite his
disarming manners, he quickly sizes up and exploits the preexisting
household strains for his own benefit. He further divides and sub-
verts each of the troubled family members into his deceitful web of
angst and confusion. Some are dragged back to their southern ori-
gins, while others are lured far away from their modern world.
Harry takes Gideon on a long and tiring walk along the railroad
tracks, and that night Gideon takes a trip of his own, into the deep

Junior (Carl Lumbly, center) fights with Babe Brother (Richard Brooks), as his wife, Pat (Vonetta McGee, left), Mother Suzie (Mary Alice, second from right), and sister-in-law Linda (Sheryl Lee Ralph, right) struggle to pull them apart in Charles Burnett's *To Sleep With Anger*. (Samuel Goldwyn Company)

coma of a stroke. Harry then coaxes the impressionable Babe Brother out for a walk along a stream, and he continues to float away, further from his wife, his family, and his confused life.

Harry uses the tensions, illness, and strife that he has created as psychological weapons and nearly takes over the household. But Suzie recognizes his wicked intentions and graciously asks him to leave. In the end, the consequences of Harry's visit force the family members to take a good look at themselves. They emerge from their ordeal as a closer, stronger family unit.

To Sleep With Anger presents an often forgotten segment of the black population that is in some ways tied together by inherited

---

CREDITS: Writer-Director: Charles Burnett. Producers: Caldecot Chubb, Thomas S. Byrnes, Darin Scott. Photography: Walt Lloyd. Editor: Nancy Richardson. Music: Stephen James Taylor. Production Design: Penny Barrett. Art Design: Troy Myers. Costume: Gaye Shannon-Burnett. 105 minutes. Drama. PG.

CAST: Danny Glover (*Harry Mention*), Mary Alice (*Suzie*), Paul Butler (*Gideon*), Richard Brooks (*Babe Brother*), Carl Lumbly (*Junior*), Sheryl Lee Ralph (*Linda*), Vonetta McGee (*Pat*), Wonderful Smith (*Preacher*), Ethel Ayler (*Hattie*).

beliefs and a shared common history. Our own various backgrounds and experiences do not have to match theirs for us to be enlightened and informed by this family's unique flavor. The film's poetic style of speech and surreal visualizations reinforce its stark, folkloric content. Nearly everything we see and hear seems to have a deeper meaning: a neighbor boy practicing his trumpet, pigeons flying, chickens running in the backyard, gardens dying, and a rabbit's foot attached to a huge pocketknife are all images that are rich with metaphor.

Writer-director Charles Burnett had long been in the trenches of guerrilla filmmaking and mastered a fictional-documentary style of production that often feels like real life unfolding on the screen. *To Sleep With Anger* was his third feature film, the first time he worked with color film stock, a decent budget, major distribution, and a fully professional cast.

In an interview with Al Young in *American Visions*, Burnett stated: "To me, telling a story isn't so much about 'one' issue as it is the focus. I can only tell my story, my vision. And it's about time black people began to determine what images we want." With *To Sleep With Anger*, Charles Burnett has boldly shown the types of images he wants to portray.

Review Summary: In his moving away from the era's image of south central Los Angeles as a place of riots and drive-by shootings, critics agreed that Charles Burnett created a community where middle-class blacks are comfortable and reasonably happy. Most reviewers loved *To Sleep with Anger* and found it a unique look at family life, including class struggles, sibling rivalry, and strained friendships, reflecting the clash of traditional southern roots with contemporary northern lives.

Critics seemed intrigued by the film's vague innuendoes of myth, voodoo, and superstition. They appreciated Burnett's use of metaphors to tackle the tension and turmoil between morality and family values. Some noted that the movie's structure seemed to build from a family saga to a suspenseful melodrama to finally become a black comedy farce.

Danny Glover's performance as Harry was singled out by many critics as perhaps his best role to date. Jack Garner for the *Gannett News Service* described Harry as "part charmer, part shaman, part shyster and all trouble." *New York Times* critic Vincent Canby wrote that Harry was "simultaneously charming and rude." Critics also commended the talent of director Charles Burnett: in the *Los Angeles Times*, Sheila Benson praised his "story-teller's flair, poet's ear, and mystical vision." In the *Nation*, Stuart Klawans found Burnett to be an artist of "immense talent," and *To Sleep With Anger* "a thick slice of African-American life."

CHARLES BURNETT

**At his home in Los Angeles
May 26, 1998**

TOR: What were some of the desires and politics that motivated you on making *To Sleep With Anger*?

BURNETT: I had a lot of problems trying to do this project. It started with trying to get some money from the Corporation for Public Broadcasting. I wanted to do a film on this girl who was killed. She happened to see a murder take place and she knew the person and everything. When she came forward and told the truth about what she'd seen, the police were supposed to protect her, but they didn't give her any protection at all. Her name was in the newspaper and all this ridiculous stuff. Anyway, she was on her way to school one morning and a hit man, some idiot, shot her on the way to the bus . . . killed her with a shotgun. And that bothered me so much . . . the shame and the cruelty of it. I wanted to do a film about that, and talk about [how] the community and the police, everyone . . . you know . . . failed.

I presented that story to the CPB, and they wanted to start changing things. I said, "No, this is a true story. You can't be making all these changes and taking license." They didn't want to hear it. And so I said, "Why don't we do something different, something that's not real." So I started writing *To Sleep With Anger*.

TOR: Why *To Sleep With Anger*?

BURNETT: I wanted to talk about folklore and how those anecdotal stories have an effect on you years later. In an unconscious way, they're always there if you're exposed to them early enough, and they come back over the years and stretch or shape your life. I wanted to write a story that had relevance today and impose the folkloric element on it.

TOR: Did the CPB accept that?

BURNETT: No . . . well . . . they did until we started working on it. Once they got their accounting in order, they called me and said, "Okay, we need the script, like, tomorrow."

I said, "What?" I am not the best typist in the world, so I ended up typing the script and sending it off without proofreading it. I told Jennifer [Lawson, head of programming] that it hadn't been proofread and that it was meant for her eyes only. She showed it to everybody! And then I got it back, and words are gone, sentences are crossed out, and everything like that, because the spelling was screwed up, you know?

They were more interested in the middle-class family—and they wanted to cut out the folklore and stuff.

And I said, "That's what this movie is about! There's this mixture . . ."

They didn't like it, so we parted company.

TOR: How did the film eventually get made?

BURNETT: It's strange, because I got this awful letter from [CPB] saying that I wasn't a writer.

They said I had "no competency as a writer." So I get a call— I swear to you, it's how things work out. That same day, Cotty Chub, gives me a call. Michael Tolkin, who is a writer-director, told him he should talk to me. Michael and I had talked a long time before about doing a project or a script. And Cotty calls me out of the blue and says, "I understand you do filmmaking. I am a producer, and if you have anything, I'd be interested in reading it."

I said, "I've got this script that no one wants, and I just got this letter saying it's an awful piece of work. But if you want to read it, fine." And I dropped it off.

David Putnam had this thing at Columbia. He was running the studio then. He had Neema Barnette and some other people involved in a young-producers development program over there. And this guy called me from that group who was also interested in reading the script. He said he could read it and get back to me within a week. So I took it down there as well.

Cotty calls me the next day and says, "I want to do it." Then this guy calls me from David Putnam and says, "I want to do it," you know? [*Laughter*] The funny part was that Putnam is this big company so they would definitely have the means to do it. But Cotty asked first: I had to do what was right.

Once Cotty was involved, we started looking for money. The casting agent Gail Levin got involved with it, and we went around trying to get actors involved. That was a difficult thing. Then Cotty moved over with Ed Pressman. He had worked with him before. And through John Rier, I met Harris Tolchin and Tom Burns. They had done business with Sony Video. I told Cotty he should talk to them. So they talked and made a connection with Sony SDS Video Classics. When Danny Glover got involved, all of a sudden everybody thought it was a movie.

TOR: A bankable star?

BURNETT: It took that for people to realize it was real. And that's how it happened. But I didn't get any kind of real distribution. It had a limited release. Goldwyn didn't put any money into it at the time.

TOR: They wanted to keep the overhead down and make their money back?

BURNETT: Sony SDS had the video rights. Goldwyn bought the theatrical rights to the film. Generally it would cost about $10 million to release a film properly with adequate prints and advertising . . . minimum. They had less than $700,000, and that money was gone the first day. The film has gotten around slowly, but when it first came out, a lot of people didn't even know that it existed.

TOR: What about the people who did see it?

BURNETT: I've gotten favorable reactions.

TOR: The directors' cut was about twenty minutes longer: What happened with that?

BURNETT: Well, when you get a distributor who wants the film cut down to a certain time . . . arbitrarily . . . it's just too long—they wanted it down to 102 minutes. So we went back in and cut off ends and things like that. The other thing was that there were some images in the film, some folkloric scenes, that the people just didn't get. They'd turn to me and say, "What is that about?" And for a distributor that takes the audience out of the movie.

TOR: What were the differences between dealing with the Hollywood production system and making the independent films *Killer of Sheep* and *My Brother's Wedding*, which were totally your visions?

BURNETT: There's always some obstacle to realizing your vision. I don't think there's true independence even if you have your own money and can distribute the film yourself. It's still hard and it takes its toll. Even if you have everything you need, you have to deal with actors, you have to deal with people who interpret things differently. So there's always compromise on some level in the making of a film.

Hollywood is just more structured and concrete. It's made up of people who are from many different sources, and their concerns can be way out there. There's an art to trying to make sense out of it and to sort of make them feel that you're doing what they want you to do, even when you're not somehow. Rather than directing, you spend 99 percent of your time trying to keep the thing on course. And then you may have a producer who don't know **** from Shinola, I won't say the word, but have you heard that expression?

TOR: Yeah, the word's shit. [*Laughter*]

BURNETT: Right, and they create so many problems. A lot of times it's this power thing where they want to isolate you to keep control. So you begin to feel like you're on this island by yourself—particularly if you came up through the independent ranks. Then they're even more afraid of you, because here's this oddball, who's going to go off and they don't know what he's going to do.

TOR: Why do you think black films are important to the black community, and what influence do they have?

BURNETT: It's like this writer once said. He was talking about how culture was just as important as the biological system you live in, like breathing air and all of that. And it's true.

For example, you ask yourself, "Why do they keep historical figures, heroic figures, who have made huge contributions to this country out of textbooks? Why do they want to keep you ignorant in a way? Why aren't you supposed to know about homelessness, unfair labor practices, job discrimination, you name it? And you might ask, "How do films relate to that?"

The many bad films made about the black experience helped to destroy our confidence and encouraged us to accept the image of blacks as buffoons. In cinema, we're the only ones whose language is considered realistic when it's demeaning. And if you don't have a script with a lot of profanity in it, or one where we end up on drugs or killing each other, then to them it isn't real . . . it isn't commercial.

Then we have this audience that supports that. This younger audience will go out and see these films and support them, and that's how they judge us. You can't get white actors to say too many things that are self-degrading or that will challenge their image. You can't get Jews to say stuff like that about themselves, or anybody. But, hey, we jump right on up there like it's something to be proud of! I mean, count the number of times some people use the word *nigga* in a film. We're the only ones who call ourselves such things. Some say, "It's a movie, and people are more mature." Uh-uh! It still has an effect—an impact. That's why there are correlations between violence on the screen and violence in the community. It's the same people who put those images up on the screen who make darn sure you don't have the proper images in textbooks, and that you can't get them anyplace else.

Our films should help to create self-respect, decency, higher personal expectations. But most of these films don't do that. The schools don't challenge you, and the films don't challenge you. Two years from now, where are you going to be in the new millennium? And how are you going to get there? Black films don't want to deal with these kinds of things, and our kids are being short-changed.

Bebe's Kids

Paramount Pictures (1992)

"I am pissed off to the highest level of pissivity!"
—Robin to Jamika in reference to Bebe's kids

The late comedian Robin Harris probably had no idea that he would inspire history when he first uttered the phrase, "They don't die, they multiply!" Harris was referring to Bebe's Kids, a group of characters he created for his nightclub comedy routine in the late 1980s. Filmmakers Reginald and Warrington Hudlin, who had worked with the comedian on their first hit comedy, *House Party* (1990), were in development on a live-action version of *Bebe's Kids* when Harris

Robin's first date with Jamika is ruined when they must baby-sit with her neighbor's unruly horde in *Bebe's Kids,* the first black animated feature. (Paramount Pictures)

unexpectedly died of a heart attack. To pay tribute, they turned to animation and produced the first black feature-length cartoon.

In the story, Robin, who considers himself a playa', is about to go on his first date with the lovely Jamika. He plans to take her and son Leon to Funworld Amusement Park, but he arrives to find a few surprises. His would-be ladylove is baby-sitting LaShawn, Kahlil, and Pee Wee, her good friend Bebe's troublesome and unruly kids. Robin is pissed. Not only will they impose upon his quality time with Jamika, but his out-of-pocket expenses have just tripled.

Bebe's kids, with a reluctant Leon who's along for the ride, wreak havoc on the theme park as they run amuck, dodge security, sing a few rap songs, and leave the place a shambles. Robin promptly returns the kids to their home, but when he realizes that they are alone, neglected, and have nothing to eat, he decides to care for them just a little longer. The message makes a strong social statement about addressing our personal responsibilities. It implies that all of the neglected Bebe's Kids of the world just need love, guidance, and nurturing care and suggests that perhaps with a little more time and attention they might not be so bad.

Faison Love stepped in to do an excellent impersonation of Robin Harris's voice, but you can't help imagining how hysterical an on-screen Harris would have been in a live role. Actress Vanessa Bell Calloway lends her sweet, sultry voice to Jamika, and the deep, gravelly vocals of the smelly, diaper-clad baby Pee Wee is that of rapper Tone Loc.

Another animated feature, the second ever produced by a black, could prove to be an influential educational milestone. *The Final Two*, by Willie Moore, explores what constitutes a bully and how we might better deal with bullies in our society, where violence in schools seems always to increase. When the main character is harassed by a bully in school, he enters a fantasy world in which he can better cope. While on another planet (in his mind), he finds a library containing the history and knowledge of the ancestors. He

---

CREDITS: Director: Bruce Smith. Screenplay: Reginald Hudlin. Producers: Willard Carroll, Thomas L. Wilhite. Executive Producers: Reginald and Warrington Hudlin. Editor: Lynne Southerland. Music: John Barnes. Production Designer: Fred Cline. 74 minutes. Animation. PG-13.

VOICES: Faizon Love (*Robin*), Vanessa Bell Calloway (*Jamika*), Wayne Collins (*Leon*), Jonell Green (*Lashawn*), Marques Houston (*Kahlil*), Tone Loc (*Pee Wee*), Nell Carter (*Vivian*), Myra J (*Dorothea*).

discovers and receives the three basic psychological traits needed to transform his situation and then returns to his real-life world where he can deal with the bully. *The Final Two*, a fully animated production, is scheduled for release in 2001.

Review Summary: The critics were mixed in their response to the first black animated feature. Kevin Thomas of the *Los Angeles Times* and Joseph McBride of *Variety* found it "a pleasure, a sleeper, a charmer and a winner" and "an imaginative delight and a fitting memorial to Harris." On the other hand, Ralph Novak of *People Weekly* and Gary Arnod of the *Washington Times*, degraded the effort, saying it was "a half-baked animated farce," "a mishmash of plodding adventure and flimsy jokes," and "ugly, chaotic and bordering on being both anti-black and anti-white."

The negative reviews criticized the film for a simplistic mode of animation and stereotypical images of the characters. But most critics applauded Reginald and Warrington Hudlin's effort to honor the late Robin Harris with this filmatic tribute to his stand-up comedy routine. Kevin Thomas in the *Los Angeles Times* suggested that there was charm in the film's stylized vision of south central L.A., yet it did not allow itself to skirt poverty and neglect. Overall, *Bebe's Kid's* was seen as an entertaining film that offered important social commentary concerning absent fathers and neglected kids.

Malcolm X

Warner Brothers (1992)

"We've never seen democracy! All we've seen is
hypocrisy! We don't see any American dream! We've
only experienced the American nightmare!"

—Malcolm X, in the opening speech

If ever a person's life was destined to be made into a film, Malcolm's was. Practically from the day of his untimely death, producers, writers, and directors jockeyed for the seat behind the camera
and the proper lens so that one of black America's most influential
figures could be brought to the silver screen.

Malcolm X (1992) (better known as just *X*), chronicles the many
different lives of the man who was born Malcolm Little. He begins
life as a murdered father's child who becomes a sinner on the
streets of Harlem, finds redemption in prison through the Nation of
Islam, and becomes a high-ranking Muslim minister, a husband and
father, and one of America's most influential political leaders. Then
he is assassinated and martyred at age thirty-nine, apparently by
members of the organization that once redeemed his lost soul.

The film begins in Harlem of the 1940s. Malcolm sports a zoot
suit and chemically treated hair as he jitterbugs to big-band music
with his Goody Two-shoes girl Laura. After the dance he takes
Laura home so he can rendezvous with Sophia, a luscious white
vamp who is eager to do much more than dance. Taking on his
hustling name of Detroit Red, Malcolm begins to run numbers for
West Indian Archie, a mathematical genius who keeps all his numbers in his head. Archie turns Red onto cocaine and his first gun,
but when a big misunderstanding calls Archie's reputation into
question, Red runs for his life.

With the help of Sophia, Red's longtime friend Shorty transports
him to Boston, where they set up a burglary ring. Things are going
well until they are busted and sentenced to time in prison. In the

slammer, Red is approached by Baines, a prison recruiter for the Nation of Islam. With the help of his newfound Muslim influences, Red turns his life around and begins to seek knowledge and the truth. When he is released from prison, the Honorable Elijah Muhammad himself welcomes him into the fold as Malcolm X, and he begins his life anew as a Muslim minister. He falls in love and marries Betty Shabazz, but his hard work for the cause and his busy travel schedule eventually create friction between them. His effectiveness has his fellow ministers, including Baines, concerned that he is getting too ambitious, and the seeds of contempt and deceit are sown. A shocking secret about the man he once idolized, and his transformative pilgrimage to Mecca, cause Malcolm X to split from the Nation of Islam and start his own movement. In the end, armed with a new name, a new concept of what he wants to achieve, and a new strategy on how to achieve it, El-Hajj Malik El-Shabazz is brutally shot to death in front of his wife and children as he prepares to address a meeting at the Audubon Ballroom in Harlem.

In 1967, jazz promoter Marvin Worth bought the rights to Alex Haley's *Autobiography of Malcolm X*, and for twenty-six years guided the project through various stages of production. He initially teamed with Pulitzer Prize–winning author James Baldwin to fashion a script, but creative differences over whose vision it would be forced Baldwin to back away. Arnold Perl, the man who was brought in to tweak Baldwin's completed screenplay and make it more "Hollywood," joined Worth to make the documentary film *Malcolm X* (1972), narrated by James Earl Jones.

CREDITS: Director: Spike Lee. Producers: Marvin Worth, Spike Lee. Screenplay: Arnold Perl, Spike Lee. Based on the book *The Autobiography of Malcolm X* as told to Alex Haley. Photography: Ernest Dickerson. Editor: Barry Alexander Brown. Music: Terence Blanchard. Choreographer: Otis Sallid. Production Design: Wynn Thomas. Art Direction: Tom Warren. Set Decorator: Ted Glass. Costumes: Ruth E. Carter. 201 minutes. Historical drama. PG-13.

CAST: Denzel Washington (*Malcolm X*), Angela Bassett (*Betty Shabazz*), Albert Hall (*Baines*), Al Freeman Jr. (*Elijah Muhammad*), Delroy Lindo (*West Indian Archie*), Spike Lee (*Shorty*), Theresa Randle (*Laura*), Kate Vernon (*Sophia*), Lonette McKee (*Louise Little*), Tommy Hollis (*Earl Little*), James McDaniel (*Brother Earl*), Ernest Thomas (*Sidney*), Jean LaMarre (*Benjamin 2X*), O. L. Duke (*Pete*), Larry McCoy (*Sammy*), Joe Seneca (*Toomer*), Phyllis Yvonne Stickney (*Honey*), Giancarlo Esposito (*Thomas Hayer*), Leonard Thomas (*Leon Davis*), Roger Guenveur Smith (*Rudy*), Wendell Pierce (*Ben Thomas*), Gerica Cox (*Eva Marie*), Kristan Segure (*Saudi*), Lauren Padick (*Lisha*), Zakee Howze (*Young Malcolm*).

Nation of Islam minister Malcolm X (Denzel Washington) prepares to address a crowd of Harlem residents outside the legendary Apollo Theater, in *Malcolm X*. (David Lee / Warner Bros.)

Writers David Mamet, David Bradley, and Charles Fuller also penned drafts of scripts and various revisions. Directors Sydney Lumet (*The Wiz*, 1976) and Norman Jewison (*A Soldier's Story*, 1984), had each been set to helm the production, but once word got out that Hollywood was dusting off the *Malcolm X* theatrical script for production, filmmaker Spike Lee expressed very strongly through the press and media that an African American should tell that particular story. In the end, he got the job. Lee created a controversial three-hour-and-twenty-one-minute biopic that ignited much debate. It starred Denzel Washington, who received an Academy Award nomination for his portrayal of Malcolm X. A dynamic performance was also given by veteran actor Al Freeman Jr. as the Honorable Elijah Muhammad.

An old saying holds that legends become legends because the truth is obscured. Regardless of how much truth, fantasy, or fiction is in Spike Lee's cinematic vision of "*X*," he directed and cowrote a powerful and memorable film about an effective and influential man.

Review Summary: The success of Spike Lee's film seemed to surprise many critics. Because of the tremendous controversy in the African-American community surrounding the making of the picture, and the usual controversy surrounding Spike Lee's unique filmmaking style, critics apparently expected a disaster.

Despite the more than three-hour running time, the $30 million budget, and Lee's continued inability to develop female characters as more than accessories to their male counterparts, most critics were ultimately supportive of the epic tapestry that portrayed Malcolm X's spiritual evolution. Some applauded Lee's effort to stay faithful to Alex Haley's book, his use of traditional, straightforward cinematic style, and the balanced story line, which depicted Malcolm's flaws as well as his strengths. But for other critics the interpretation of the historical facts remained a key issue.

Many reviewers noted the film's potent beginning. An American flag burns down to the letter X, while video of the Rodney King beating plays over a Malcolm X speech charging that the white man is the greatest kidnapper and murderer on earth. Steve Murray in the *Atlanta Journal and Constitution* suggested that the film moved beyond one man's life and tapped into the realm of the legend.

According to many critics, Denzel Washington's portrayal of the popular black Muslim leader was considered Oscar-worthy, and the cinematography by Ernest Dickerson, featuring varying textures and moods within the film's three-act format, was beautiful. Perhaps Zaron Burnett in the *Atlanta Journal and Constitution* said it best: "Spike Lee has made a film as loyal to Malcolm's legend as he is capable."

Waiting to Exhale

20th Century-Fox (1995)

"I asked God to send me a decent man. I got Robert,
Cedric, Darrell, and Kenneth . . . God's got some
serious explaining to do."

—Savannah, opening voice-over

Waiting to Exhale is based on Terry McMillan's best-selling mega-publicized novel about a quartet of thirty-something female friends living in Phoenix, Arizona. From one New Year's Eve to the next, they are sustained, inspired, and supported by one another as they live out their lives in search of love, honesty, career fulfillment, and the perfect man.

Savannah is a television news producer returning to Phoenix to start a new job and, she hopes, find a new love that will finally allow her to exhale. She does meet a guy at a New Year's Eve party. During a slow dance, she does exhale, only to realize she should have held her breath a little longer. Kenneth turns out to be an insensitive, self-absorbed beast, especially in bed. Other than good looks, the two have nothing in common, and the relationship is short-lived.

Bernadine is married to John, a wealthy businessman, and her long hours in his company's office during the early years helped him to get established. Just before leaving for a New Year's Eve party, he informs her that he plans to spend the evening with a white woman. Despite his eleven years of marriage and his two children with Bernadine, he adds that he plans to move in with his new ladylove. After torching his designer suits in the backseat of his late-model Mercedes Benz, Bernadine grants him a divorce. To show his appreciation, John tries to screw her on the divorce settlement.

Robin is a beautiful, upper-level marketing executive with no self-esteem. Her desperate need for a man to give her some sort of identity bounces her from an abusive drug addict to a married sleaze of an ex-flame to an overweight coworker who promises her the

Four close friends, Savannah (Whitney Houston) and Bernadine (Angela Bassett), front row, left to right, and Gloria (Loretta Devine) and Robin (Lela Rochon) head out for an evening on the town in *Waiting to Exhale*. (© 1995 20th Century–Fox Film Corporation. All rights reserved.)

moon just to get her in bed, then afterward berates and disrespects her on the job. Robin needs to find herself, for herself, and she eventually does.

Gloria is a full-figured beautician, with a seventeen-year-old son and a gay ex-husband. Her hopes for romantic fulfillment lift when Marvin, a widowed military man, moves in across the street. One of the few positive male characters in the film, he likes full-figured women and does not shy away from being a role model and mentor to her adolescent son.

CREDITS: Director: Forest Whitaker. Producers: Ezra Swerdlow, Deborah Schindler. Screenplay: Terry McMillan, Ronald Bass. Based on the novel by McMillan. Editor: Richard Chew. Photography: Toyomichi Kurita. Music: Kenneth "Babyface" Edmonds. Production Design: David Gropman. Art Direction: Marc Fisichella. 121 minutes. Drama. R.

CAST: Angela Bassett (*Bernadine*), Whitney Houston (*Savannah*), Loretta Divine (*Gloria*), Lela Rochon (*Robin*), Gregory Hines (*Marvin*), Dennis Haysbert (*Kenneth*), Mykelti Williamson (*Troy*), Michael Beach (*John, Sr.*), Leon (*Russell*), Wendell Pierce (*Michael*), Donald Faison (*Tarik*), Jeffrey D. Sams (*Lionel*), Starletta DuPois (*Savanna's Mother*), Jazz Raycole (*Onika*).

The film struck a chord with women of all colors and ages, and the phrase "You go, girl!" was often heard being yelled back at the screen. This was a new type of film for a new generation of women. Unlike *The Color Purple* (1985) and television's *The Women of Brewster Place* (1989), *Waiting to Exhale* is the first Hollywood film to show contemporary, successful black women in control of their own lives and moving forward in their careers.

The novel *Waiting to Exhale* sold 700,000 hardcover copies and more than 2 million in paperback. The film was also highly successful at the box office, earning $75 million in its initial release. Author McMillan cowrote the film script with Ronald Bass, who had previously adapted the screenplay from Amy Tan's popular novel *The Joy Luck Club* (1993). The two would take McMillan's next novel to the big screen as well, and *How Stella Got Her Groove Back* (1998) gave them another successful film adaptation.

Waiting to Exhale's director, Forest Whitaker, stepped out from in front of the camera for the second time to helm a feature. He previously directed the urban drama *Strapped* (1993) for HBO, as well as stage plays and several music videos for Propaganda Films. As an actor, he is perhaps best known for his portrayals of Charlie Parker in Clint Eastwood's production of *Bird* (1988), and as the captured IRA soldier in Neil Jordan's *Crying Game* (1992).

The film also had an extremely successful sound track, written and produced by Kenneth "Babyface" Edmonds. The sound track consisted of all-female acts, including Whitney Houston, Chaka Khan, Toni Braxton, and Aretha Franklin, and became a best-seller.

Review Summary: While the many reviews of *Waiting to Exhale* take several perspectives concerning the content, most focus on the characters as they struggle with their personal plights and on the competence of the film's director, Forest Whitaker.

Reviews were split when it came to Whitaker's Hollywood directing debut. In the *Hartford Courant*, Malcolm Johnson criticized him for "failing to pull together the episodic and essentially plotless screenplay by McMillan." Adina Hoffman in the *Jerusalem Post* said Whitaker did a good job, noting that he had "both a fluid visual sense and a musician's ear for speech rhythms. These let him weave the plot's loose pieces together into a sexy, coherent whole. And his own acting persona is apparent here . . ."

The cast received mostly favorable reviews. Many critics suggested that Angela Bassett deserved an Oscar for her role as Bernadine, and that Whitney Houston, the least experienced actress, as Savannah, held her own. In *Daily Variety* Godfrey Cheshire wrote about the power of the friendship that held the individual tales together, "with Rochon's spunky charm and Devine's earthy aplomb rounding out the quartet of well-matched personalities."

Cathy Hainer summed it up well in *USA Today*. "Every once in a while, a movie comes along that perfectly captures the zeitgeist of a particular segment of society. What *The Big Chill* did for boomer midlife crisis in the eighties, *Waiting to Exhale* is doing for black women today."

LORETTA DEVINE

By phone from her home in Los Angeles
May 27, 1999

TOR: Had you read the novel *Waiting to Exhale* before the film was cast?

DEVINE: It's so funny, because I had bought the book for my best girlfriend, Vicki Lynn Reynolds, who was pregnant at the time. I also bought a copy for myself, and I read it. It never occurred to me that I would get a chance to do the movie, because I knew that all of the major parts were already cast, and I thought I wasn't the right size for Gloria, because at that time, I was like wearing a size 14. When I finally got a call for an audition for the role, I just put on one of my outfits that was a size 12, and went in and got lucky.

I think Forest Whitaker went with more . . . voluptuous than fat. And it was a wonderful experience. I could eat! I ate the whole time we shot, which was three months, and it has been hell trying to get back to where I was.

TOR: Did you find yourself going back to the character in the book, or did you pretty much stick to the script?

DEVINE: For character development I read the book over and over and over, but the script was so different from the book—and I should say to my advantage, because Gloria was a lot looser in the book. When Gloria first appears in the book, she's naked at the top of the stairs, hollering down to her son. I was glad they didn't have anything like that in the movie!

But we did a couple of things that didn't actually make it into the movie that were really . . . erotic . . . and very interesting. And I begged Forest to at least give me the film clips of those parts, but I never did get them. There was a swimming scene, and I worked all summer to get my swimming up, because she had a heart attack in the pool—which was one of the pivotal points in the book.

TOR: That got cut too?

DEVINE: They could only do so much in the amount of time they were given for the film. Lela's entire family got cut out. Bill Cobbs and Hattie Winston played her parents, and they were cut. There were a lot of things in the book that weren't in the movie.

TOR: Was *Waiting to Exhale* the first time you'd worked with Gregory Hines?

DEVINE: I was in a Broadway musical with him before. He is a wonderful lead man. And I think we have a good chemistry. He sent me roses for my first day of shoot. All the girls were jealous.

And the young man that played my gay husband, Giancarlo Esposito, I had worked with him before as well. Of all the characters, I think Gloria's character was developed in a way that people had the most empathy for. Her character was very full and very strongly defined. So many women say, "You did my life. That's my life . . ."

TOR: I understand Terri McMillan was on the set quite a bit. Was she helpful at all in molding your portrayal of Gloria?

DEVINE: She kept telling me, "You better eat some more! You better eat!" And you know how Terry cocks her head to the side? Yes.

TOR: The film really got slammed for its male characters. How did you feel about that?

DEVINE: Well, to me it was a sound bite. It was just a way of selling the movie. They didn't do that with *First Wives Club*, which was a similar movie. It even went further. In it the women took revenge on their husbands and plotted and planned ways of destroying their ex-husband's new marriages and careers. But no one called that male bashing. And I think some of it had to do with race. I think the men in our film were all kinds of men. My son, Gregory's character, my husband—who portrayed a man that was coming into his new sexuality. There was Angela's husband—who was a very successful black man, well dressed, very well mannered. There was never any battering, or any of that kind of thing.

TOR: Right . . . just the infidelity.

DEVINE: Well, just infidelity . . . but that's what the book was about. The book was about problems that women are having. Problems in relationships, and the reasons they're having the problems, and it was about the women themselves. And so I couldn't figure out why that was the sound bite that they used to sell the movie, but it worked because everybody bought it. When you really look at the movie, that scene where they talk about how hard it is to find men . . . I think a lot of that is true. The things that they say, "A great number of black men are in prison. A greater number are on drugs. Black men have always had a hard time economically in this country because of the way they're treated." It was not like we were making it up.

And I look at the way black men are treated in a lot of other movies. Like in *New Jack City*, where they had a black man walking down the street with no clothes on, and a gun to his head . . . and you go, "Why would they pick this movie to say that that's what's happening?" A lot of black men praise, glorify, and adore their women. When you tell those stories, people don't believe it.

TOR: I'm sure those stories are much more difficult to get put on the screen as well.

DEVINE: Exactly.

TOR: How would you compare *Waiting to Exhale* in its depiction of black women, with its predecessor *The Color Purple*?

DEVINE: *Waiting to Exhale* wasn't a period piece. It's about women in their thirties. This movie hit so hard, which was like a starting point for movies like *Love Jones* and all that. They were expecting a lot of similar things to come out, but so far I don't know that it's had an effect on the way things have been portrayed since.

But it was wonderful that it was the first movie about today's women, how they felt, how they looked at things, and what their needs were.

The Nutty Professor

Universal Pictures (1996)

"Life is not about being happy with how much you
weigh, but just being happy with yourself."
—Sherman Klump

Before *The Nutty Professor* never had such modern technology gone
into a black film. Special-effects makeup used in conjunction with
state-of-the-art computer morphing and graphics programs helped to
transform Eddie Murphy into Professor Sherman Klump, a brilliant
but lonely four-hundred-pound blimp of a research scientist. Murphy
makes the transformation flawlessly and embues his huge character
with gentleness, compassion, and very low self-esteem.

A genius in the lab, he's conducting experiments in molecular
research, using plump hamsters to develop a miracle weight-loss
formula. Larry Miller, his boss, is ready to cut the project's funding
if the research doesn't show progress soon. When Carla Purty, a beautiful graduate student, takes an interest in Klump and his work, the
Nutty Professor becomes desperate to succeed.

Klump invites Carla home for dinner, but as a result of his
family's brash comments, embarrassingly direct questions, and a
hysterical round of flatulence at the table, the evening and the date
is a disaster. Back in the lab, Klump finally finds success; his formula has worked on one of his fat rodent test subjects, but will it
work on humans? Believing he can never win Ms. Purdy's heart as
the obese Professor Klump, he swallows a vial of his own test
potion, gags, and falls to the floor, gasping for air. Moments later, he
is remade into his slim, trim, supersuave alter ego, Buddy Love.
Buddy is the sharp-witted, mean-tempered, testosterone-driven exact
opposite of the portly professor, with more than enough raw nerve
and self-esteem for the both of them.

The cocky Buddy Love eventually gains strength and begins to
take over Klump's psyche. Despite his lab assistant's protests, Buddy
increases his potion routine in an attempt to rid himself of the

Klump persona forever. At a lavish departmental fund-raiser, his boss and everyone present get an eyewitness demonstration of Professor Klump's research. Ashamed and embarrassed by his alter ego's display, Klump berates himself, but the main funder is impressed enough to back his continued research.

Though the weight-related humor is often rude and offensive, the final message is "It's not what you look like, but who you are."

It was nothing less than phenomenal how Eddie Murphy portrayed the entire Klump family, including the bubbly mother and his crass, brutally frank grandmother. With the special effects and the genius of makeup wizard Rick Baker, Murphy pulled off flawless transformations, actually becoming the characters and interacting with himself. He gave each character their own believable traits, and it's hard to believe that they were all being played by the same person. This was nothing new for Murphy, however. He first portrayed multiple characters in the barbershop scene in *Coming to America* (1988) and repeated the feat with no fanfare in *Vampire in Brooklyn* (1995). Everyone should agree that Eddie Murphy is one of the most influential actors of our time, yet, unlike funnyman Robin Williams, who is constantly allowed a broad spectrum of roles, Murphy has been strictly relegated to comedies. Whether it's the Hollywood studios, his agent, or his own ego that's been limiting the range of his creative output, we believe that if Eddie Murphy were ever allowed to play a role with some emotional depth or dramatic substance, there would emerge from him an even greater talent, which he has yet to release.

Review Summary: For the most part, the reviews approved of the success of *The Nutty Professor* in its attempt to improve on the original 1963 version by Jerry Lewis. Many critics raved about the technological wit that computer-generated imagery accomplished as Eddie Murphy's character, Sherman Klump, gained pounds and then lost them in a matter of minutes. Duane Byrge in the *Hollywood Reporter* gave the special effects an A+.

CREDITS: Director: Tom Shadyac. Screenplay: David Sheffield, Barry W. Blaustein, Steve Oedekerk, Tom Shadyac. Photography: Julio Macat. Music: David Newman. 96 minutes. Comedy. PG-13.

CAST: Eddie Murphy (*Sherman Klump/ Buddy Love + 4*), Jada Pinkett (*Carla Purty*), Dave Chappelle (*Reggie Warrington*), James Coburn (*Harlan Hartley*), Larry Miller (*Dean Richmond*), John Ales (*Jason*).

Sherman Klump (Eddie Murphy) is a brilliant but lonely chemistry professor in search of the cure for obesity who finds Buddy Love, his own wilder and thinner alter ego, in *The Nutty Professor*. (Bruce McBroom/Universal Pictures)

A majority of reviewers commented on Murphy's ability to make Sherman Klump seem real. Richard Schickel in *Time* wrote, "He is able to invest his Professor Klump with an endearing dignity." Janet Maslin observed in the *New York Times* that "It's an amazing transformation, and Mr. Murphy handles it with real skill."

The makeup wizardry employed in Murphy playing seven characters is also admired. In *Entertainment Weekly* Owen Glieberman wrote, "Though I'm not quite sure how he brought it off, the effect is so convincing that Murphy effectively disappears inside that mountain of fake flesh." Glieberman goes on to describe Klump's alter ego, Buddy Love, as "a hyperbolic act of self-mockery," and suggest that through Murphy's portrayal of Klump's family around the dinner table he is "rediscovering his joy as a performer." Several critics, including Doug Hamilton in the *Atlanta Journal and Constitution*, raised an important issue concerning the film's effort to walk a fine line between sympathizing with Klump and making fun of him. "We're intended to laugh at his girth during an early exercise scene, then feel sorry for him when he's ridiculed by a nightclub comic, then laugh at him again as he's gorging the pain away."

Many critics framed their reviews of *The Nutty Professor* by labeling it a comeback effort and talking about several of Murphy's earlier films, which were not box office flops, but not the exceptional moneymakers the studios had come to expect. Murphy himself addressed this issue in a *Jet* article, saying, "The reality is there is no last chance for me. If a medium dries up, I'll go and do something else. I've never made a movie that didn't make money. They've made two billion dollars off my movies."

Get On the Bus
15 Black Men/Columbia Pictures (1996)

"A miracle at the mall! That's what I'm looking for
and that's what I'm gonna get!"

—Jeremiah Washington to Jamal

Fifteen black men invested a total of $2.4 million to make
up the production budget for Spike Lee's *Get On the Bus*. Still
low-budget by Hollywood standards, the film was shot in three
weeks on a guerrilla-style production schedule, and the investors
all recouped their money, with profit and interest, before the film
was even released.

The film tells the story of a group of men from Los Angeles
who take a bus ride to Washington, D.C., for the Million Man
March. The characters represent a microcosm of the black male
community, each with his own past, lifestyle, and reason for attending the march.

We first meet the D.C.-bound brothers in the parking lot of the
New AME Church in south central Los Angeles as they prepare to
board the bus. The trip's organizer, George, is upbeat and inspired.
Among his passengers are Jeremiah, who is the oldest of the group,
wise and anxious, with a deep regret for not making the trip thirty
years earlier to march with Dr. Martin Luther King Jr. Gary is a dedicated but embittered cop; his father, who was also a police officer,
was killed years before by a young black man who is still at large.
Someday, Gary intends to close the case. Xavier is a film student
whose video camcorder documents much of the goings-on, and he
gets tagged as "a Spike Lee–wannabe." Jamal is a former hard-core
gang member who has recently converted to Islam and turned his
life around. Two of the more interesting passengers are Kyle and
Randall, a not-so-in-the-closet gay couple trying to redefine their
on-the-outs relationship. The former lovers are constantly hassled
by Flip, an egotistical self-proclaimed actor with an obvious homo-
phobic side. Another duo on board with an interesting back-story is

The men who get on the bus: front row, left to right, Andre Braugher, Hill Harper, Hosea Brown III, DeAundre Bonds, Charles Dutton, Steve White; back row, Gabriel Casseus, Thomas Jefferson Byrd, Ossie Davis, Isaiah Washington, Roger Guenveur Smith, Harry Lennix, and Bernie Mac. They board a bus headed for the historic Million Man March as strangers but emerge three days and two thousand miles later as brothers, in *Get On the Bus*. (Columbia Pictures)

Evan Thomas Sr., and Junior, his teenage son. "Smooth," as Junior calls himself, has recently been in trouble with the law, and the strongest bonds between father and son are the steel shackles that bind them together, the result of a seventy-two-hour court order from the judge because Smooth is considered a flight risk. The remaining men on the bus serve primarily as seat-fillers, but by their dress, manner, and occasional interactions, it is clear that they too have stories to tell, only not in this film.

As the miles roll by, their discussions, arguments, singing, and bongo-beating help get the passengers from state to state. We even get a brief look at the female view of the march when Gary and Flip meet a couple of girls at a rest stop. When the "Spotted Owl" breaks down in the middle of nowhere, a replacement bus is dispatched along with a new, white driver. Some of the more militant passengers are appalled, and they hassle him. Several miles down the road, while gassing up at a honky-tonk truck stop, Rick, who is Jewish, cannot reconcile driving a group of disrespectful black men all the way across the country to support a march organized by Louis Farrakhan, a man whom he believes to be anti-Semitic. So with little concern for them, or for any repercussions about his job, he grabs his belongings and is gone. Faced with a bus full of passengers and no one to drive it, George and Evan take on the responsibility.

Meanwhile the group has picked up an additional passenger. Wendell is the owner of a successful car dealership in the small town where they'd stopped. He shows little respect for his companions' opinions, for the march, or for anything else as he chomps on a cigar, flaunting his greedy, conservative Republican-based views. But when he continuously utters the N-word and brazenly admits that he has no interest in the Million Man March other than to try and sell cars, he is literally ejected from the bus.

More serious moments develop when the bus is pulled over and boarded late one night by a white southern sheriff with a drug-sniffing guard dog. The next day, a candid confession about an unsolved murder puts Gary on edge, and that night, a fight erupts between Flip and Kyle. During the ruckus, Junior seizes his opportunity to escape, but he is finally found and the journey continues.

A life-and-death emergency interferes with the rest of the trip, and a few of the travelers don't make it to D.C. The march itself is covered by a montage of reenacted six o'clock news–style footage, but later that night, at the foot of the Lincoln Memorial, the ensemble all hold hands in a prayer. When the bus leaves for L.A., the shackles that once bound father and son are left behind.

CREDITS: Executive Producers: Larkin Arnold, Jheryl Busby, Reggie Blythewood, Reuben Cannon, Johnny L. Cochran Jr., Lemuel Daniels, Danny Glover, Calvin Grigsby, Robert Guillaume, Robert Johnson, Olden Lee, Spike Lee, Charles D. Smith, Will Smith, and Wesley Snipes. Director: Spike Lee. Producers: Reuben Cannon, Bill Borden, Barry Rosenbush. Writer: Reggie Blythewood. Photography: Elliot Davis. Editor: Leander T. Sales. Music: Terence Blanchard. Production Design: Ina Mayhew. Design: Sandra Hernandez. Sound: Oliver Moss. 120 minutes. Drama. R.

CAST: Richard Belzer (*Rick*), DeAundre Bonds (*Junior*), Andre Braugher (*Flip*), Thomas Jefferson Byrd (*Evan*), Gabriel Casseus (*Jamal*), Ossie Davis (*Jeremiah*), Charles S. Dutton (*George*), Albert Hall (*Craig*), Hill Harper (*Xavier*), Harry Lennix (*Randall*), Bernie Mac (*Jay*), Wendell Pierce (*Wendell*), Roger Guenveur Smith (*Gary*), Isaiah Washington (*Kyle*), Steve White (*Mike*).

Get On the Bus was a tribute to one of the most important and influential historical events to take place in this country since the 1963 civil rights march on Washington. It's basically a "road-trip flick": a group of black men begin a vast journey as strangers and discover not only themselves, but the various combinations of the good, the bad, and the ugly rolled up in each one of them. If we watch carefully, we become part of that discovery as well.

With *Get On the Bus*, Spike Lee was ten for ten; he had directed ten feature-length films in ten years.

Review Summary: It is difficult to avoid admiring the fact that this film was entirely financed by African-American men and shot in only three weeks. It is also difficult to separate the entertainment factor of the film from its political and social implications in relation to the Million Man March and the African-American community.

Overall, the reviews can be divided into three categories: those that willingly accepted and praised the film; the vast majority of reviewers who accepted the film, but only after acknowledging and forgiving its faults; and a few reviews that explicitly criticized the movie.

All the reviews applaud the talented cast. Leslie Felperin in *Sight & Sound* seems to capture the sentiment of those who applauded the film by naming three elements that make it a success: the realism of the dialogue, the direction, and the actors. The positive reviews admire Lee's filmmaking skills as well, and celebrate the film's attempt to reflect a diverse group of African-American perspectives as well as the spirit of the march.

The reviews that do not accept the film quite so readily agree and disagree on several levels. On the positive side, several reviewers discuss Spike Lee's talent and applaud the diverse themes addressed in the movie. On the other hand, these reviewers often argue that the movie is too "speechy" or "preachy." Moreover, many of these reviewers state that the perspective of the film is too narrow and that it is filled with contrivances.

Generally speaking, the negative reviews criticize the film for surrendering itself to conveniences, meaning that it employs stereotypes, contrivances, and rhetoric. An article by Stuart Kawans in the *Nation* is particularly harsh; Kawans accuses *Get On the Bus* of using great actors badly, poor writing, desperate directing, and implying that there is no alternative to Nation of Islam leader Louis Farrakhan.

The film generated a fair amount of discussion and debate and proved that African Americans as a people have the means to finance their own successful films. The question now becomes: when will it happen again?

REUBEN CANNON

At his offices in Los Angeles
March 30, 1999

TOR: How did you become involved in *Get On the Bus*?

CANNON: Shortly after the Million Man March I received a call from Bill Borden, a producer I've worked with in the past, saying that he and his partner Barry Rosenbush had an idea for a film they would like me to *direct.*

I don't have any ambitions in that area, but they didn't know that. They said, "What if we did a movie about a group of men taking a trip from Los Angeles to Washington, D.C., for the Million Man March?" And that's all they had. What appealed to me about the idea was that it would provide an opportunity to show diversity in black men in a way that we rarely see. I liked the idea, but they were talking very low budget. About $700,000, real guerrilla-style filmmaking.

TOR: Did they plan to shoot it on VHS? [*Laughter*]

CANNON: Just about. Almost with a camcorder on a bus, but the idea was a good one. I said, "Why don't I see if I can elevate it to another level." So I called Spike Lee. And the great thing about Spike is that he'll return almost anyone's call, especially if it's someone who's in the business. And I told him the story.

Spike said, "Well, what are they going to do? Just make the words up?"

I said, "No, we're going to get a writer."

He said, "There may be something there." He called back fifteen minutes later and said, "The more I think about this, I really like it. But if we do it . . . we should do it in the spirit of the march, and the money should come from black men."

So I said, "I'll take responsibility for that."

And he said, "Reuben, between you and me, if we can't raise $2.5 million, then both of us should be shot." [*Laughter*] So Bill Borden, Rosenbush, and I flew to New York and discussed the idea with Spike in more detail. The idea was to make the film and release it on the anniversary of the Million Man March. . . . which you realize is an incredible schedule.

TOR: How long after the march was this?

CANNON: We're having this conversation the first of November. We're going to get a script written, cast, produced, get distribution, and have it on the screen eleven months later. We had decided on the budget of $2.5 million, and that's what I was supposed to raise. Spike and I drew up a list of people that we could go to, and the idea was men. Spike's list was top-heavy in athletes, the Knicks, and basketball players. Mine was more reflective of Hollywood personalities.

TOR: The best of both worlds?

CANNON: The best of both worlds, sports and entertainers. However, many of your star athletes, as well as actors and entertainers, do not manage their own money. I understand that we hire professional people to advise us, and protect our money, but there was one conversation in particular. Spike called and told me that he had spoken to this star athlete, and he said he was down. Then I spoke to him myself, and he told me he wanted to do it.

He said, "Let me just talk to my wife." He called me back and said, "Count on it. You're going to get a call tomorrow from so-and-so." So I get a call from a guy with a heavy southern accent. The guy sounded like Bull Connor on the telephone.

And he said, "Mista' Cannon, ma client says he wonts ta in-vest in ya' movie."

I said, "That's correct. I'll send you a document."

He said, "I'm gonna tell 'im not ta do it."

I said, "Well, excuse me. Don't you work for him?"

"Yeah, I work fo'im, but I'm gonna tell 'im not ta do it."

So I said, "Well, maybe he'd like to do it because there's a cultural connection that you can't understand?"

He said, "I don't care 'bout his culture! I care 'bout his po'tfolio!" That's a direct quote.

TOR: How much were you asking for?

CANNON: The investments were $200,000.

TOR: What would that amount have done to his portfolio?

CANNON: I'm talking about a four- or five-million-dollar-a-year athlete. We were identifying high-net-worth individuals. We had to. So I called my friend Lem Daniels, who is a broker and who also became an investor, and I said, "Lem, I'm not having a lot of success with these entertainers and athletes. I want to expand the makeup of the investment pool. I'd like to have some business people involved.

TOR: Who are in control of their own money?

CANNON: Exactly. So two weeks before Christmas he gave me the name and address of Olden Lee, a VP at Taco Bell/PepsiCo. I sent a document to his office. The day after Christmas, I get a call at home. "Hi, this is Olden Lee, Reuben. I've read the business plan. I've read your prospectus. I like what I hear about you. I like the idea and the concept. Where do I send my check?"

Now this is a person I've never met before, and he's a businessman.

TOR: And writes his own checks.

CANNON: Exactly. And that's why when you look at the ultimate makeup of the investors, there are only four actors and one athlete. The rest are businessmen.

TOR: After the first check came in, did things go smoother?

CANNON: No, because we couldn't touch any of the money until all of it was in. And we had a drop-dead date of February 1. As of Christmas, we had one check. We had verbal commitments, but it wasn't in the bank. I was frantically calling and discussing the terms with people. But we were moving forward.

We were supposed to start filming April 1. So we continued. By February 9, we had maybe $1.5 million dollars . . . we were still a million short. So we sent out a letter requesting extensions, which everyone signed.

TOR: Investors had the right to take their money back by a certain date if it didn't work out?

CANNON: Exactly. But no one asked for their money back. By April 1, we were there.

TOR: Who was the writer?

CANNON: Reggie Blythwood, who had worked with Spike before and was a writer-producer on *New York Undercover* at the time. He had actually taken the bus from New York to Washington, D.C., for the march. Hearing his stories about what he had experienced emotionally and spiritually as a result of being there . . . he became the choice.

He took a Greyhound from L.A. to Washington, D.C., over the Christmas holidays and he did the outline for the script. He turned in a first draft in February. We made some changes and then commenced casting and rehearsals.

One week before we were going to start principal photography, Columbia Pictures called and met with us. At that point, we were all cast and in rehearsals. The VP of marketing at the time said, "We should take a look at how we make movies here. These guys have come up with an idea, cast their movie, and are in rehearsal. If this project was brought to us, we'd still be in development."

And that was the beauty of it. And that's why it's the highlight of my career . . . in terms of creative experience and creative freedom. You realize what's possible when you're not dealing with the bureaucracy of a studio.

TOR: So Columbia bought the film?

CANNON: Outright . . . at a profit.

TOR: So it was profitable before you even went into production?

CANNON: Right. But the dilemma was, Do we take this money that's on the table? Or do we make the movie without any distribution and put it up for bid once we've completed it? And there was two reasons why we took the offer. One was that I wanted to protect my investors.

The second was that in order to have the movie in the theaters by October, we needed to have a publicity campaign right away. And we didn't even have eight months' lead time. It was a negative pickup deal. Upon delivery of the negative to the studio, we would receive a check. That's why when we had our premiere in New York, we had all of the investors there. I called up CNN and some other media entities to make a statement that here is the first time in the history of Hollywood that a black man was distributing checks to other black men who had invested, before the film was ever released.

When the credits rolled, and it said, "This film was completely funded by fifteen African American Men," and their names came up on the screen at the premiere. That got the biggest ovation of all. If I had to do it over again, I'd put that credit in the front, because a lot of people leave, and the idea was to inspire others.

TOR: As the producer, were you ever on the bus?

CANNON: Every day, from day one. We shot the movie in eighteen days, in three different states. We all flew coach together, and there were no frills on this movie. Everyone was there in the spirit of the march, and the spirit of the march was very evident in the making of this movie.

TOR: In researching this book, I've discovered that too often we are either one-hit wonders or one-flop failures. Fifteen black men financed *Get On the Bus* and made a profit before the film was even released. Why haven't you tried it again?

CANNON: The evolution of that fifteen black men is the new company I am creating. It's based on the idea that there are roughly 200 screens in the United States that have been frequented by black people. Take *How Stella Got Her Groove Back*. It was released on 1,300 screens. Of those, 400 didn't make enough money to pay for their print costs, which is what, $1,500? So those exhibitors are pissed; they're not selling any popcorn. Of the remaining 900 theaters, 80 percent of the business was conducted on 300 screens. And where are they? They're in the twenty-five urban markets where 80 percent of us live.

TOR: So a more focused distribution campaign for a longer period of time should do it?

CANNON: Exactly. We'll go to 200 screens, and we'll also hire a black ad agency. See, the bureaucracy of the big studios don't understand the "street-teen" marketing concept. They're used to throwing money at things. Buy three spots on *Oprah*; buy three spots on *ER*. So when you say to them, "No, you have to go out and put up posters in the community, in every barbecue shop and beauty parlor, the big studios can't relate to that; they don't understand it. So we needed a marketing firm and marketing techniques that understood our market.

Star Rise is a company that will make movies that cost from one to three million dollars and release them on screens in the twenty-five urban markets. I know there are black folks in Nebraska, but I'm sorry, the films won't be running there. [*Laughter*]

TOR: They'll have to get on the bus, huh? [*More laughter*]

CANNON: That's right, and go to the nearest urban market. But that's the concept behind Star Rise. We will not be pursuing Oscars; we will not be pursuing the Cannes Film Festival. We will simply be pursuing our core audience's loyalty to these films. The goal is very clear, not compromising quality. It's putting the "business" before the "show."

Amistad

Dream Works SKG (1997)

"I meant my ancestors. I will reach back and draw
them into me . . . and they must come. For at this
moment . . . I am the whole reason they have
existed at all."

—Cinque to John Quincy Adams

Amistad opens with a torrid lightning storm at sea. Bloodied fin-
gertips scrape and claw at the tip of a large nail embedded in the
floor. Illuminated solely by intermittent flashes of lightning, the nail
is slowly pried out to become a makeshift key to the shackles that
bind Cinque Sengbe. Free at last, he releases his forty-two shackled

Captured, enslaved, escaped, enslaved again, and finally freed, Cinque (Djimon
Hounsou) is a proud African who leads a slave ship rebellion in *Amistad*.
(© 1997 DreamWorks LLC. All rights reserved.)

comrades on the Spanish slave ship *La Amistad*, and leads them on a murderous rampage against the ship's crew.

Two of the crew members are spared, and through his native tongue and some crude sign language, Cinque demands that they turn the ship around. In the daytime they do, but they pull a fast one and sail the ship in the wrong direction under cover of night. Eventually the ship arrives at the northeastern coast of the United States, where the black passengers are accosted by a U.S. Navy ship, and thrown back into chains. Now everyone wants to take possession of the human cargo: the two spared slave traders, the U.S. naval officers, who want to claim them under salvage rights, and even Queen Isabella (with toy doll in hand), who wants them returned as the rightful property of Spain. Their plight becomes a major cause for the abolitionist movement, and President Martin Van Buren is being pressured to act: "There are what? Three . . . four million Negroes in this country? Why on earth should I concern myself with these forty-three?" the president comments while on the campaign trail. The abolitionists win court trial after court trial in the name of freedom and justice, only to have their victories overturned by higher legal authority.

The abolitionists are disheartened; they have done everything right and are still thwarted at every turn. At a low point, Lewis Tappan, the main abolitionist fighting on behalf of the reenslaved cargo of the *Amistad*, considers giving up until Theodore Joadsen, a freedman involved in the struggle, tells him, "There are those who think that slavery is stronger than anything, except for the slave himself," and we know that giving up is not the thing to do. The case is sent all the way to the U.S. Supreme Court, and Roger Baldwin, the trial attorney who specializes in property disputes, knows he's out of his league. They persuade former president John Quincy

CREDITS: Director: Steven Spielberg. Producers: Steven Spielberg, Debbie Allen, Colin Wilson. Screenplay: David Franzoni, Steven Zaillian. Photography: Janusz Kaminski. Editor: Michael Kahn. Music: John Williams. 152 minutes. Historical drama. R.

CAST: Djimon Hounsou (*Cinque Sengbe*), Morgan Freeman (*Theodore Joadson*), Anthony Hopkins (*John Quincy Adams*), Matthew McConaughey (*Roger Baldwin*), Stellan Skarsgard (*Lewis Tappan*), Razaaq Adoti (*Yamba*), Abu Bakaar Fofanah (*Fala*), Nigel Hawthorne (*Martin Van Buren*), David Paymer (*Forsyth*), Pete Postlehwaite (*Holabird*), Thomas Milian (*Calderon*).

Adams to argue the case before the court. He successfully defends the stolen Africans' right to freedom and wins their passage home.

Dancer-entertainer Debbie Allen worked for years to bring the story of Cinque Sengbe to the big screen. After a century of learning in school about the failures of Nat Turner, Denmark Vesey, and John Brown, audiences have the opportunity, with the release of *Amistad*, to learn about a slave rebellion that succeeded.

Review Summary: For the most part, critics thought *Amistad* was an important and positive historical drama. Much of the criticism formed around the sensibility of the movie's director, Steven Spielberg. Adina Hoffman in the *Jerusalem Post* suggests that Spielberg perhaps sees himself as the savior of poor historical events that need him, including *Schindler's List* and *The Color Purple*, films that seem to focus on the redemption of a basically faceless group of downtrodden souls by a sympathetic and powerful outsider. Malcolm Johnson in the *Hartford Courant* observed that *Amistad* is a complex story that "reverberates with Steven Spielberg's genius as a filmmaker." The powerful presence of the main character, Cinque, played by Benin native Djimon Hounsou, is noted in all the reviews.

Other reviewers agreed about the fact that *Amistad* was another black story being told from the perspective of a white savior, and criticized the weak role of Morgan Freeman's abolitionist character, the clichéd musical score by John Williams, and the film's slow-going courtroom structure. Jay Carr in the *Boston Globe* admired the film. "It's permeated by a thrilling level of conviction and commitment; big in its passions, big in its generosity, and big in its humanity." But the critic for *USA Today*, Susan Wloszczyna, summed it up by saying "*Amistad* is no masterpiece, but no disaster either."

Eve's Bayou
Trimark Pictures (1997)

"Memory is a collection of images . . . the tapestry
tells a story . . . and the story is our past."
—Narrator

Eve's Bayou revisits a tragic summer in the life of a Creole family in
Louisiana. Sensuous in look and feel, the film explores a nostalgic
past as seen through the eyes of a bright but highly emotional girl.

The film's title and location refer to an enslaved African woman
who saved the life of a white settler, Jean-Paul Batiste. In return, she
was given a piece of land and sixteen children by the appreciative
white settler. Her name was Eve, and the Batiste family are her
twentieth-century descendants. The story takes place in the early
1960s and boldly addresses the consequences of making a rash
decision and taking action on it. An opening voice-over establishes
that the film will be told as a remembrance.

"The summer I killed my father I was ten years old," the soft voice
of an adult woman confesses, pulling us in with an unquenchable
interest to find out how and why she did it.

The family Batiste is now headed by the wealthy and charming
Dr. Louis Batiste, who is admired and coveted by most of the
women in the town. His beautiful wife tries to turn a blind eye to
his philandering, but she often breaks down and expresses her concern through tears and rage. His youngest daughter, whose name
also happens to be Eve, adores her father, and does battle for his
attention against the many other women in his life. When she accidentally witnesses one of his many indiscretions, however, her
image of him begins to change. Eve has a tense relationship with
her older sister, Cisely, and when another terrible revelation about
their father's actions comes to light, Eve sets out to seek revenge.

She solicits the help of the local voodoo woman to put a fatal
curse on her father. Eve later changes her mind, but she has already
set a series of wheels in tragic motion. Her aunt Moselle is a psy-

Doctor, husband, father, and womanizer Louis Batiste (Samuel L. Jackson) relaxes at a local bar in Kasi Lemmon's directorial debut film *Eve's Bayou*. (Chris Helcermanas-Benge / Trimark Pictures)

CREDITS: Writer-Director: Kasi Lemmons. Producers: Caldecot Chubb, Samuel L. Jackson. Photography: Amy Vincent. Editor: Terilyn A. Shropshire. Music: Terence Blanchard. Production Design: Jeff Howard. Art Director: Adele Plauche. Costumes: Karyn Wagner. 109 minutes. Drama. R.

CAST: Jurnee Smollett (*Eve Batiste*), Samuel L. Jackson (*Louis Batiste*), Lynn Whitfield (*Roz Batiste*), Meagan Good (*Cisely Batiste*), Debbie Morgan (*Mozelle*), Jake Smollett (*Poe*), Ethel Ayler (*Gran Mere*), Diahann Carroll (*Elzora*), Vondi Curtis Hall (*Julian Grayraven*), Roger Guenveur Smith (*Lenny Mereaux*), Lisa Nicole Carson (*Matty Mereaux*), Branford Marsalis (*Harry*), Afonda Colbert (*Henrietta*), Tamara Tunie (*Narrator*).

chic advisor with the gift of second sight who often sees what's going to happen before it does. Moselle knows that Eve, who is beginning to develop a second sight of her own, is up to something, but she is powerless to read it. One night, outside of a bar, the deadly mix of destiny and fate that Eve has conjured finally catches up to her father. She tries to stop what she has begun, but it's too late.

The scenes in the film, as well as the characters, are layered in a way that allow the rivalries and relationships to unfold intriguingly among the moss-covered visions of the swampy bayou. First-time director Kasi Lemmons had peddled her script to the Hollywood studios for years with no success. She even directed a short film to convey her talents behind the camera, but it wasn't until Samuel L. Jackson signed on to star and coproduce the film that the project received a green light. Lemmons herself was previously an actress, with minor roles in *Silence of the Lambs* (1991) and *Candyman* (1992). As the highest-grossing independent film of 1997, *Eve's Bayou* proved again that top Hollywood executives often ignore talent and a good script. *Eve's Bayou* can be considered a sensual sleeper that worked magic, on the screen and at the box office.

Review Summary: In her directing debut, Kasi Lemmons was praised by critics who found the film a wonderfully mystic story woven within a tight, compelling script and featuring outstanding performances.

The cinematography of Amy Vincent is praised by several critics. Jay Carr in the *Boston Globe* wrote that the picture was "lush, powerful, beautifully crafted . . . a languid, velvety dream of a film that stakes out patches of physical and metaphysical turf and inhabits them hauntingly." Many critics were so impressed with Lemmons's film that they mentioned that it was unfairly overlooked at the Academy Awards.

The single concern that seemed to echo among critics was the vagueness of the story's conclusion. In the *Houston Chronicle*, Louis Parks said that the film's mystery rested in the "believe-whom-you-choose tradition of Rashomon." Judy Gerstel in the *Toronto Star* wrote that "this film accords a rare humanity and dignity to its characters who, like all of us, struggle to be good and decent, and usually fall short of the goal."

The Best Man

Universal (1999)

"Go on and be a dog . . . dog."

—Lance to Harper about Jordan

"Finally!" This was a word used by many black moviegoers about writer-director Malcolm Lee's directorial debut film, *The Best Man*. At last, on screen is a group of strong, positive, and definitely out-of-the-'hood black men who are well on their way to achieving higher aims and obtaining permanent upward mobility.

Harper is a writer living in Chicago. His first novel, *Unfinished Business*, is about to "blow up" and take his career right along with it. On the verge of this success, he's not ready to settle down with Robin, his caterer girlfriend of two years, who seems to be turning up the heat and the pressure on the direction of their relationship. Lance is an NFL running back who has just signed a new multimillion-dollar contract. Despite the throng of female fans who continually grasp for his autograph, his wild oats are sown, and he plans to live a subdued and God-fearing life with his college sweetheart and bride-to-be Mia.

Merch is a teacher and guidance counselor who works with troubled inner-city youth. We learn that he is resisting accepting a six-figure salary with a major law firm just so that he can continue his work with kids. His long-term, high-stress, high-maintenance girlfriend Shelby wants him to take the job, and is totally befuddled when her usually henpecked man doesn't do as she says. Quentin has yet to determine his career path. The creative type, he has much talent, lots of options, and a father who owns a ritzy New York hotel. He considers himself a player with the ladies, and although the others see him as a wild card, his blatantly honest comments and observations keep them all in check.

A New York City wedding brings this diverse group of college friends back together after seven years for one crazy weekend. It might have been a quiet, bland, and uneventful reunion, but Jordan,

Harper (Taye Diggs, left), Jordan (Nia Long, center), and Murch (Harold Perrineau, right) are reunited college chums in Malcolm Lee's out-of-the-hood wedding flick *The Best Man*. (David Lee/Universal Pictures)

who is now an ambitious television producer and the "best girlfriend that Harper never had," has passed around an advance copy of his upcoming novel, which happens to be about all of them. "Embellishment sells books," Harper says, but many of his written words are read as fact.

Throughout the intermingling, gift-buying, reacquaintance talks, and wedding preparations, the tension builds as an old secret hidden deep within the pages of Harper's book is slowly revealed. It all comes to a head at the wild and near-disastrous bachelor party, and once-close and undeniable friendships become tested and strained.

CREDITS: Writer-Director: Malcolm Lee. Producers: Spike Lee, Sam Kitt, Bill Carraro. Photography: Frank Prinzi. Editor: Cara Silverman. Casting: Robi Reed-Humes. Original Music: Stanley Clarke. Costume Designer: Danielle Hollowell. Music Supervisors: Bonnie Greenberg, Lisa Brown. Production Designer: Kalina Ivanov. 118 minutes. Comedy. R.

CAST: Taye Diggs (*Harper*), Nia Long (*Jordan*), Morris Chestnut (*Lance*), Harold Perrineau (*Merch*), Terrence Howard (*Quentin*), Sanaa Lathan (*Robin*), Monica Calhoun (*Mia*), Melissa DeSousa (*Shelby*), Victoria Dillard (*Anita*), Regina Hall (*Candy*).

The ensemble cast of relatively new and extremely talented performers each brought their characters to life with all the fresh and enlightening differences that make up such a diverse group of individuals. We believe that they *were* actually old college friends, returning to reestablish endearing friendships that would be shaken and forged more strongly by their ordeal.

The Best Man created a young, progressive black world established on a higher echelon than anything seen on screen before. Recent films such as *Boomerang* (1992), *Waiting to Exhale* (1995), *Soul Food* (1997), and *Love Jones* (1997) all touched on characters trying to stay in or get to the upper class while still tied to the levels below, but this film made it a complete world unto itself, not false or exclusionary, but positive, real, and very obtainable.

Review Summary: Despite the audience acceptance and box office success of *The Best Man*, the critics either loved it or hated it, with very few in between. Many were quick to comment on the talents of Malcolm Lee, the film's first-time writer-director. Jan Stuart in *Newsday* suggested that he showed "a flair for the sort of tart, grown-up repartee once favored by Cary Grant and Audrey Hepburn, reinvigorated with a knowing '90s New York edge."

Two of the main areas of complaint were also major areas of praise. The first involved the film's well-worn focus on wedding antics, which was called "overdone," "cheating," and even "predictable" in some reviews, yet described as "witty," "insightful," and "appealing" in others. The second surrounded the film's mainstream context, which was often described as a buppie-middle-class romantic comedy. Amy Taubin in the *Village Voice* suggested that the film was "escapist entertainment, plain and simple."

Most reviewers seemed to agree that much like *Soul Food, Waiting to Exhale,* and *Love Jones, The Best Man* is another welcome story that moves away from the "boys in the hood" theme to portray affluent young black characters in professional careers as NFL superstars, novelists, lawyers, and television producers.

9

Influential Independent Efforts

Hellbound Train

James and Eloyce Gist (1930)

"The Hellbound Train is always on duty . . . and the
Devil is engineer."
—Opening Title Card

For years several film canisters containing the lost and forgotten
remnants of an early black independent film collaboration sat
packed away in a dark vault at the Library of Congress. In the early
1970s, film historian Thomas Cripps submitted a letter to the director of the archives, encouraging that something be done with this
footage, but nothing happened. In the early 1990s, Eloyce Gist's
granddaughter-in-law contacted film scholar Gloria Gibson and
informed her of the existing footage. Gibson had been researching
a paper on Gist's historic films and wasted no time in contacting the
archives for a look at the footage.

Shot in Washington, D.C., *Hellbound Train* (1930) had been
shown mostly in churches. James Gist, a self-proclaimed Christian
evangelist, had already shot much of the film when he married
Eloyce King Patrick. Both agreed on basic Christian principles and
wanted to share their spiritual beliefs with their community. Realizing the power that film had on society's actions and attitudes, they
wanted their film to condemn sinful living and promote a moral
lifestyle. The first thing the new bride did was to rewrite the script
and the title cards to her husband's film. It is also believed that she
assisted in adding or reshooting several of its segments.

Eloyce had studied music at Howard University, and before the film's church screenings she would play the piano and sing hymns with the congregation. After the film was shown, James would give a sermonette. Tickets were sold in advance or a collection was taken up, and the Gists would split the offerings with the church. At one time, Roy Wilkins of the NAACP offered to cosponsor additional screenings to a broader audience. There is no evidence, however, of that ever happening, and *Hellbound Train* faded from the scene.

Unlike the Hollywood religion-based films of the time such as *Hallelujah* (1929) and *Green Pastures* (1936), *Hellbound Train* shunned a narrative story line for a series of short, loosely related morality plays. As a silent film, the scenes are shot as stand-alone segments that are strung together by a central theme, and many of the now-unknown cast members reappear in scene after scene as different characters.

According to *Hellbound Train*, hell is where practically everybody is going. Liars, cheats, drunks, sporting women, smokers, gamblers, disobedient children, and people who mistreat animals need to repent. At the end of several of the sequences that end in a sinner's death, a man in a satanic-looking suit dances a happy jig while the next title card reads: "How the devil rejoices!"

One living-room location serves as a juke joint, a brothel, a gambling den, and as many of the characters' homes. Several local business establishments were used as location backdrops, and there are dozens of different shots of trains coming and going, static shots, wide shots, close-ups, and several odd tracking shots from a moving car. Throughout the film, various scenarios of sin, corruption, wickedness, and lurid temptation are acted out. A man comes home from work to find his wife with another man, and he shoots them both. A gambler loses his shirt (and his pants too) in a crooked crap game. A cheating card dealer receives a bullet in his chest for his dishonest efforts. Despite their mothers' warnings, several kids play ball in a busy street until one gets run over. For anyone who's involved in destructive behavior, *Hellbound Train* has a free one-way ticket. But it's not too late to save your soul by

---

60 minutes (recut version). B&W. Silent. NR.

repenting and giving your life to the Lord, your only salvation (according to another title card).

The footage appears to have been shot with a handheld camera over a long period of time. Segments were shot on location, both interior and exterior, and the weather reflects all seasons. The scenes are covered mostly in long-take master shots using in-camera editing (set up the first shot, shoot it, set up the next shot, shoot it, etc.). Occasionally, the camera operator would tilt or pan to reveal more information, or get a close-up, but there are no second takes. It seems that if there was a mistake made, the camera would just stop, reposition, and keep filming from that point on. Most of the scenes contain flash frames and jump cuts caused by the camera's starting and stopping. Several shots show the actors looking directly into the camera, or talking to an off-screen director. None of these mistakes were edited out, so it seems that there was not a lot of editing done on the film, and the only splice marks are at the places where the title cards had been cut in. Another possibility for why the title cards are the only visible splices is that they were all replaced when Eloyce became involved.

The film concludes as a flaming toy train crashes into the pits of hell. The fires of damnation rage as tortured souls are helplessly tormented, beaten, and burned by the devil. This certainly doesn't look like fun, and it would be interesting to know how many sinners were saved after seeing this film. It would also be interesting to find out how the 1930s audience reacted to the message, the music, the sermonette, and the overall Gist service program. Unfortunately, all of the documentation, press write-ups, and legal paperwork were lost years ago when the Gist family home was destroyed by fire.

Hellbound Train is probably the first truly independent film effort to involve a husband-and-wife team working together, especially an African-American husband-and-wife team.

Eloyce Gist's directorial debut is thought to be a film titled *Verdict Not Guilty* (begun in the thirties but never completed). The film was ahead of its time as it addresses the issue of abortion. The story centers on a woman who acts boldly to keep from becoming an unwed mother, nearly dies in the process, and has to plead her case before the Lord. Unfortunately, there's not enough footage to cut the film into a complete story, but some of the sets and costumes are extensive and quite interesting.

The White Girl

Tony Brown Productions (1988)

"I don't see colors . . . only people."
—Kim to classmates

The "white girl" of the film's title is a slang term used for cocaine. It is also symbolic of the main character's attempt to assimilate into white society.

Kim Barnes is a black middle-class high school student with everything going for her. She lives in a nice upscale neighborhood, her grades are excellent, and she receives all the love and support that her parents can give. Having a color-blind mind-set, Kim does not distinguish between the races, and hardly acknowledges her own. She leaves home for college with plans to study law, but her world and her grades begin to change once she becomes addicted to cocaine.

Kim is now on academic probation. A campus counselor tries to intercede, but Kim does not heed her advice and slips deeper into the drug's deadly grip. Despite an initial resistance to the idea, she joins the Black Student Union, and there she meets Bob, a premed student who helps her get back on track. As her first black boyfriend, he is very supportive and caring, and is the first to get her to recognize that she has a drug problem. He helps her to kick the habit, until Vanessa, her new, power-hungry, cocaine-driven roommate, coaxes her back over to the white side.

Vanessa is determined to be a TV news anchor and has no problem with sleeping her way into the limelight. She even promises an influential television executive sexual favors from Kim in order to advance her own career. Eventually, Vanessa's involvement with a sleazy drug-dealing pimp has tragic consequences for her and her unwitting roommate. Luckily for Kim, Bob is there to pick up the pieces, and she gives up drugs again, this time for love and a new life with her man . . . her black man.

In *The White Girl* Kim (Troy Beyer) is a confused college coed in search of true love, self-identity, and her next high; Bob Mann (Taimak) is the devoted friend who tries to help get her on the right path. (Courtesy of the Museum of Modern Art)

CREDITS: Writer-Director: Tony Brown. Executive Producer: Sheryl Cannady. Producer: James Cannady. Photography: Joseph M. Wilcots, Tony Vigna. Music: George Porter Martin, Jimmy Lee Brown. Production Design: Brent Owens. Set Design: Bill Webb. Costumes: Paul Simmons. 94 minutes. Drama. PG-13.

CAST: Troy Beyer (*Kim*), Taimak (*Bob*), Teresa Yvon Farley (*Vanessa*), Dianne B. Shaw (*Debbie*), O.L. Duke (*Nicky*), Petronia Paley (*Dr. McCullough*), Donald Craig (*Mr. W*), Don Hannah (*Karl*), Michael Duerloo (*Charles*), Sherry Williams (*Mrs. Barns*), Twila Wolfe (*Tracy*), Kevin Campbell (*Roger*).

Written, produced, and directed by TV journalist Tony Brown, the picture's warning is clear and its messages obvious: Drugs and people involved with drugs are dangerous; self-pride, self-respect, and a sense of ethnic heritage are a necessity for positive growth; and true love can conquer all.

(*A personal note by Tor Berry:* It was at a Saturday matinee at the Cheltenham theater in Philadelphia that I saw the film. On a small stand, just outside theater 3, a flyer read: "This is the first 'BUY FREEDOM' motion picture!" It stated that the profits from *The White Girl* were going to help build an independent and self-sustaining black-owned-and-operated film industry outside the existing and often exclusionary Hollywood system. "It's about time!" I thought.

(Buy Freedom, as conceived by Brown, was all about black people supporting black people and combining our economic leverage to raise ourselves up to a position of power and control. Years before, while I was in film school at UCLA, my fellow film students of color and I often sat in the hallway outside our editing rooms and discussed this topic, the need for a black system of film financing, production, distribution, and exhibition. We talked strategy, form, structure, and how this nurturing monolithic system would be controlled and maintained. We debated on whether or not it would even be supported by people of color and by others interested in a true black film esthetic. We also discussed why Bill [Cosby], Eddie [Murphy], Michael [Jackson], and some of the other big-name, big-buck black entertainment types had not already put a plan into action. This was between 1981 and 1984, pre-Spike, pre-Townsend, and pre-Singleton, so the outlook for us within the Hollywood system seemed very bleak at the time. Now, years later, someone was finally doing it! They weren't just talking yip-yap and trying to make themselves sound good, either; there was a plan of action in play, and the initial step had already been taken. And by someone with enough clout to possibly pull it off!

(I had arrived at the theater early, so I slipped down a couple of screening rooms to where the Hudlin Brother's *House Party* [1990] was showing. The theater was about two-thirds full and the mostly black teenage audience was laughing and enjoying the sophomoric antics on the screen. I had already seen the film, so after standing in the back for about five minutes and laughing myself at times, I returned to my designated screening room, to find only five people in the audience.

(I was appalled. Why was this Buy Freedom motion picture, a film that would do so much for the organization of a black film industry, receiving so little support? To top it off, four out of the five people in those seats were white! I wanted to take a handful of the flyers down to the *House Party* screening and yell out, "My people, my people! What are you doing?" I wanted to say, "Wake up! You're watching a fine film that is worthy of your support, but do you realize what you're neglecting down the hall?" Instead, I took one of the many empty seats and anxiously waited for the film to begin. The lights dimmed, and less than a half hour into the film, a feeling in the pit of my stomach told me we would have to wait a bit longer for a black film industry to materialize. We're still waiting.

(The first Buy Freedom motion picture was influential in its progressive concept. If only the creative elements of the film had been as well planned out and clearly defined as the underlying purpose! It seemed to be a well-conceived blueprint to do what has been talked about for years, which is to do it ourselves. I can't help but imagine the black motion picture industry that might exist today if Tony Brown's *White Girl* had brought in the box office profits of, say, *House Party*. Unfortunately, no one has picked up the Buy Freedom blueprint and tried again.)

Sankofa

Mypheduh Films, Inc. (1994)

"Stop! Don't you know me? I'm Mona! I'm not
African! I'm an American!"

—Mona to slavers

Mona is an African-American model on a fashion shoot on the
grounds of Ghana's Cape Coast Castle. The site is a dungeon where
Africans were imprisoned until slave ships arrived to haul them off
across the Atlantic Ocean.

The photographer is snapping away when suddenly Sankofa,
the guardian of hundreds of thousands of enslaved African spirits,
interrupts the shoot. "Back to your past! Return to your source!" he
commands in the Akan language, pointing his huge staff at Mona.
She giggles, finding the old man to be funny, as she hides behind
her bemused white picture taker. Her hair is a bright orange to
match her wild "Tarzan-esque" bathing suit. Mona is obviously out
of touch with her African history and heritage and totally unaware
that she is disrespecting hallowed and sacred ground.

Later that day, she follows a group of white tourists into the
bowels of the dungeons where the captives were once held.
Remaining outside of the cell door, she overhears the guide explaining how the Africans were captured and stored there, sometimes
for months, often wallowing in their own feces. When the tourists
move on, the cell goes dark. Mona is startled by the sudden blackness, but when she leans forward to peer into the cell, a campfire
erupts in the middle of the room, and an African chant begins. The
flames illuminate a group of solemn, silent, manacled men locked
together by chains and the dark color of their skin. Mona screams
and runs away. She comes upon another cell, filled with somber,
ebony-skinned African women, all chained together as well. Again
she screams, and runs for the exit, but the huge double doors are
closed and locked. She beats on them until they open into a dark
and threatening nineteenth-century world. The petrified model is

Mona (Oyafunmike Oguniano) is an African-American fashion
model about to be enslaved in the dungeons of Ghana's Cape
Coast Castle and transported back in time to experience a past
life of bondage in Haile Gerima's *Sankofa*. (Mypheduh Films)

CREDITS: Writer-Director-Editor: Haile
Gerima. Producers: Haile Gerima, Shiri-
kiana Aina. Line Producer: Ada Babino.
Photography: Augustin Cubano. Produc-
tion Design: Kerry Marshall. Costume:
Tracey White. Music: David J. White.
Makeup: Henry Brown. 124 minutes. His-
torical drama. NR.

CAST: Oyafunmike Oguniano (*Mona/
Shola*), Mutabaruka (*Shango*), Alexandra
Duah (*Nunu*), Kofi Ghanaba (*Sankofa-
Drummer*), Afemo Omilani (*Noble Ali*),
Nick Medley (*Joe*), Mzuri (*Lucy*), Jimmy
Lee Savage (*Mussa*), Maxwell Parris
(*Baby Ngozi*), Hasinatu Camara (*Jumma*),
Jim Faircloth (*James*), Reginald Carter
(*Father Raphael*), Louise Reid (*Esther*),
Stanley Michelson (*Mr. Lafayette*), Alditz
McKenzie (*Kuta*), John A. Mason (*Big
Boy*), Roger Doctor (*Nathan*), Chrispan
Rigby (*Photographer*).

immediately accosted by slave traders, dragged back into the dungeon, stripped of her clothes, and scarred forever with a red-hot branding iron.

Mona's soul flies over the ocean, across the middle passage to the Lafayette sugar plantation where she is Shola, a house slave with no recollection of her previous life as an American model. What follows is a realistic depiction of what life was like as an enslaved human being, as Shola is subjected to rape, cruelty, and constant abuse not only by the white master and his overseers, but by the black head-slaves as well. As Shola the slave, Mona experiences the pain and degradation of plantation life, but it is not until she rejects that fate, fights back, and joins the larger revolution that her spirit is carried back to her modern persona, a changed woman.

Hollywood distributors rejected the movie, but Haile Gerima, the Ethiopian-born filmmaker who spent twenty years researching, writing, funding, and getting this powerful slave epic to the screen, was able to independently four-wall the film around the country. It played to packed theaters, and the lines stretched around the block. In some cities, two and three screenings were sold out in advance.

Originally titled *Nunu* after one of the film's other characters, it was renamed *Sankofa*, a word in the Akan language which means "return to your roots, regain what you've lost, so you can move forward."

The basic cinematic structure of *Sankofa* is unique. Gerima rejected the straight-narrative story line in favor of a character "relay" structure. Instead of following one main character throughout the film from point A through point Z, *Sankofa* is an ensemble cast film with the story line "stair-stepping," or being passed like a baton from one character to the next. Mona took the story to Shola, and it went from Shola to Shango, to Nunu, to Joe, Lucy, and back to Shola again, etc. This confused a lot of people, but when its unique filmic structure is seen in perspective, it's clearly how this story needed to be told.

Initially, all the different voices and dialects that the film's characters speak are confusing. Hollywood films and television shows almost always depict a generic "Yesa, dissa, dassa, Massa" type of dialect that is spoken by everyone. In *Sankofa*, with the possible exception of Joe and Noble Ali, both of whom were born into slavery, few of the characters talk like this. They all have different dialects, sounds, and rhythms to their words, and we struggle with this oddity until we hear a much broader truth speaking from the screen. The diverse enslaved Africans would naturally speak in different dialects, depending on what language they originally spoke and on how long they had been in captivity. There would not have been the one-voice-fits-all slave vernacular that was used in the landmark television miniseries *Roots* (1976), in which, fresh off the boat, Kunta Kinte spoke with the same southern broken-English dialect as Chicken George, who was born generations later.

The historical accuracy of *Sankofa* shifts our understanding of what the truth was. If we realize that films are often viewed as the truth, we should realize that images in films are often misleading. *Sankofa* corrects many of the distorted images of the past, and in the process creates a fresh new Afrocentric film style, structure, and cinematic language to do it with.

Truly an international production, *Sankofa* was shot in Ghana and Jamaica on a budget of $1 million. It was edited in Washington, D.C., and Virginia with a sound mix done in Toronto. Working off of inexpensive word-of-mouth advertising, the film is probably the most successful independently produced, self-distributed black film effort to take place since the early days of Oscar Micheaux.

HAILE GERIMA

**In his office, RTVF Department, Howard University
May 21, 1998**

TOR: How did *Sankofa* come about?
GERIMA: Initially with this whole notion of my personal journey, a journey that brought me from Africa to the United States—and to African descendants whom I found here. There was this notion of trying to know and understand African Americans. It could be because of my own initial introduction to them and the way films depicted black people. It was the kind of introduction that made African diasporans distant from Africa, so you have this notion of a people who had no origin, a no-beginning, no-end kind of thing.
TOR: Were you surprised to find that black people were different here?
GERIMA: When I came to America from Ethiopia, I found people that looked like me, people who embraced me even when I was not embracing them, because of my orientation to African Americans as told to me by whoever was informing me.
TOR: And who was doing that?

GERIMA: It could be through the United States Information Service, the American embassy, the Peace Corps . . . or the biggest diplomatic pouch, cinema. Also, the mass media, newspapers, and the deceptive way the racial conflict is transported into other people's countries. If you looked at these transported images of black people from far away, you would think they are real.

So I would say to you that *Sankofa* is a synthesis of my wanting to come to grips with and know further where these folks came from.

TOR: Did the film allow you to synthesize your thoughts and confusion?

GERIMA: It synthesized itself. It was almost a twenty-year endeavor, especially from the research stage. I wanted to know the road black people took and to locate them for myself . . . or to relocate African descendants to Africa. To know that they too had come from Africa a long time ago . . . and in a special journey. Of course, when I tell you this, I'm not telling you about my value judgment and the fact that I felt black people looked bizarre, crazy, irredeemable.

TOR: Because of the way you saw blacks portrayed in films before you came here?

GERIMA: Oh, yeah, as I said, films are my background. I'm not well armed, information-wise; I'm miseducated. I didn't know anything about slavery, so the presentation of black people or the representation of African descendants in this country in films made me believe they were something crazy.

And you begin to believe it when you have no historical context or information about how racism operates. Whites continue to disfigure black people to make them look irredeemable. They do not tell you the true story of the conflict between these two groups. If you look at black people who are angry at white people, and if your background is that white people are all nice, good people, people who even helped black people to be free from slavery, then black people look crazy for going against them.

TOR: I take it your angelic view of white people came mostly from the cinema?

GERIMA: Of course. When we look at the fact that the Native Americans used to kill them in films—it was very sad. These nice venturing white people. Blond-haired, blue-eyed, nice white people being attacked by savages—they looked good. And you don't know about racism, about the power of the dominant ethnic group, the white society, about how black people are represented from a white-supremacist cultural point of view. And it's not only me. Most foreigners are shocked at the rudeness, loudness, angriness, and militantness of black people. But when you know from where black people have come, then you start to bite your tongue. In fact, you start to get angry because you feel lied to.

TOR: Since white people were always portrayed as nice in the films you'd seen, how did you feel when you found out they had in reality perpetrated such horrendous acts?

GERIMA: It was very hard. It was like separating from the Catholic Church, from your religion, separating from God. For me, white people became so godly when I was growing up in the time of Kennedy and Eisenhower, from the way the American culture came to me through cinema. So to separate from them was very turbulent, very chaotic. Not to hate them—though you go toward that also. You begin to hate them, but to level off from all of the contradictions, soberly, it takes a great deal, because you also begin to discover they messed you up as well.

TOR: So making *Sankofa* was your way of coming to terms with all of this?

GERIMA: I don't think I became negative, but I will not anymore appease that state of mind. Like the Bible says, I don't have no loyalties to false idols, you know?

TOR: You said that *Sankofa* was a twenty-year struggle. What was the film's final budget and how did you arrange financing?

GERIMA: I wish I could talk about financing outside of racism. When you're dealing with white supremacy and ideological thought systems, including the idea of ownership—the fact that I wanted to own my movie—automatically displaces me. Because white people, even when they let you do anything, have to be the owners of that intellectual property. And so the United States was not conducive to any type of a normal producing approach for us.

TOR: How did you get around that?

GERIMA: With the coproducer, Shirikiana—who's also my wife and partner. We had initially thought about how the different geographically located black people, from Brazil to Africa—here and in Europe—hunger for most of what we are hungry for. We felt that Africans would want to see whatever I want to see. Brazil is the same, African Americans the same.

This thought brought us the idea of giving a conference (the Fespaco International Film Festival), in Ouagadougou in 1985, where we presented a Pan-African approach to film production, training, etc. We felt if all black people from different parts of the world put together whatever they have—some have skills and talents, some have money, some have locations, equipment, etc.—then we could overcome the obstacle of finance.

TOR: How did it work out?

GERIMA: The organization that was formed was dropped by people who were not as motivated as we were. After that, I went all over for nine years trying to gain financing by doing coproductions. I went to Cuba, Martinique, Venezuela, Jamaica, and Louisiana. And in most places, bureaucratically, people who lacked the vision were the obstacles. We ended up working with Burkina Faso and Ghana. Ghana brought money in the sense that they arranged to feed the actors, the crew, and house them in that country. Burkina Faso brought equipment, lights, generator, and the camera—a beautiful new 35-mm camera. And the rest, the currency needed, we put together from outside.

TOR: Where did the cash come from?

GERIMA: Most of the time we brought the money from ourselves. We presold arrangements with Europe—German and English television. We also had money we had saved from earlier films. We put all that together.

TOR: I know you completed filming *Sankofa* with what you had, but was it enough?

GERIMA: No. We were constantly going for a loan to continue to complete the different stages of production. We finally got one print and opened it here in Washington, D.C. It did well and we were able to make more prints. It wasn't easy.

TOR: What was your experience in trying to obtain distribution through the normal channels?

GERIMA: The usual naked reality of racism and white supremacy, hidden in all forms of euphemistic justifications. We knew it would be there to some extent, but we had no idea how far white people will go when they feel threatened in areas that they control.

TOR: What were they threatened by?

GERIMA: Virtually the ownership and the shaping of the idea, from the inventing to the distribution. They are used to owning it. And here you are coming from left field with a film that a great many people are responding to. And most whites in powerful positions did not like this, and they would respond by saying stupid things. But we were sophisticated and aware of the racial texts.

TOR: When did this first become apparent?

GERIMA: When we opened in Berlin. I don't know of any movie that got the opportunity that *Sankofa* got at the Berlin Film Festival. They will tell you a lot of stories of how from *Northern Lights*, all the way to *Hoop Dreams*, a film is discovered after it played in this festival. We were propelled from a basement production to the Berlin Film Festival—an independent film—to be in final competition against mega-produced, highly financed movies.

TOR: *Sankofa* made them nervous?

GERIMA: When it came out, without even seeing the content of the movie, the *Hollywood Reporter* praised it: "What a historical landmark!" But once the members of the news media saw the movie? They all hid in their little squirrel homes, you know? And they fit into every little hole to keep from dealing with *Sankofa*.

TOR: They didn't cover it? Or they stopped covering it?

GERIMA: They just stopped covering it. They hid, they avoided us, they canceled interviews with us. The day of our showing, the night before it was sold out. The whole audience, whatever the number, these Germans got up and applauded this movie. The international press wrote about it, but the American press disappeared.

TOR: They squashed it?

GERIMA: Yeah, *Sankofa* disappeared from the festival, and they made it nonexistent in the American landscape. And this is not the establishment press like the *New York Times* . . . this is like NPR, independent film magazines, these same magazines who have celebrated every movie done by outsider groups, from gays and lesbians, what have you, outside-of-the-establishment films . . . yet they did not mention us. Even when we were in Montreal, they did not mention us. We were in Toronto, they didn't mention us. It's a sophisticated press technique. You make somebody that you don't want—you make them nonexistent by not mentioning them—and nobody knows if you are born, or if you lived or died.

TOR: Despite the lack of press, how did the distributors react?

GERIMA: A sister who worked for Sony saw the film in Ouagadougou and went berserk, okay? And she went back to Sony and made Sony look into this movie. They had a print, they saw it in a committee. I think she fought with them for two months to really take it seriously and said, "This film is really going to be hot in the black community!" And they didn't care!

TOR: They didn't want to make the money?

GERIMA: You see, a lot of black people—forget white people—I don't care about what white people say—but many black people do not know that capitalism is not colorblind. They think that if it's a good thing to sell and make money that white people will go for it . . . uh-uhn. It's not even how powerful the film is: It is the fact that they didn't make it, that they didn't sponsor it, that Kevin Costner does not play Shango's role.

TOR: Do you remember any of the specific reasons that they used for not distributing *Sankofa*?

GERIMA: One said, "It's too black!" We have it on record. He said, "It's too black and I would not show this movie in this country." Blockbuster said, "We don't have clientele for this type of movie," they said—and there are black people in every Blockbuster video store in this land. All of them are reaching for straws! You add it up and it becomes white supremacy . . . period.

TOR: You ended up distributing *Sankofa* yourself and did a helluva job. The grassroots word of mouth was phenomenal. How did you orchestrate that?

GERIMA: First, you have to know that the power of ordinary people is what put *Sankofa* into the map of the world—all the way to London. I was at the train station in London and there was a guy passing out the leaflets for *Sankofa* when it was opening there. He came to pass a leaflet to me and said that if I should die without seeing this movie it would be a tragic life on earth. He was telling everybody that. Harassing people literally with the leaflets. Saying, in his West Indian accent, "You have to see this movie!" And when he saw me at the theater and I was introduced, he was just having a heart attack. He said, "Were you just walking by yourself like that without anybody protecting you?" Because he felt white people would kill me at any minute, you know?

TOR: Why do you think people are so passionate about the film?

GERIMA: I'll tell you stories that will blow your mind . . . but I'll say this . . . it has a lot to do with the hunger. People are hungry for filmmakers who do not compromise the kinds of movies we make. They want to see movies that engender our humanity. They are tired of all these stereotyped things that were concocted to make white people feel at ease at the expense of black people.

TOR: But wasn't *Sankofa* the kind of movie it was *because* Hollywood or white people didn't get a chance to put their foot in it?

GERIMA: That's right, but since we didn't have any white people fronting us, white power got threatened. I didn't have a white wife to front me, I didn't have a white producer or a gay white lover to front me. If we did have white people fronting us, we would be distributed all over the country.

TOR: But would they sponsor a film like *Sankofa* without wanting to change certain elements?

GERIMA: They would sponsor the Black Panther Party if they are in charge of the agenda. But if they are not in charge of the agenda? Hey, my brother . . . they will make you nonexistent. They are saying that black people cannot put things together and bring it out without white people playing a role. They want to make our children mortgagees of their power.

TOR: But don't you also think it was the power of the story that threatened them and kept them from distributing *Sankofa*?

GERIMA: I don't want to make it sound like the film was so great or so militant. I've seen more militant films. And I say I'm not against white people, but black people have to own everything that they invent. Some will sell out for human reasons, but most black people should learn and show little black kids that we own too.

TOR: So you were very determined to own the film?

GERIMA: Yeah. To me, what's the use of inventing? It means you've never lived if you don't own and copyright things. Because you always have to go back to them when you don't have no property. Though you're good in singing, good in dancing, in art and culture . . . if you don't own it? It doesn't refinance. That's the cycle of a dependency.

TOR: You had experimented before with "four walling" films [taking the film by hand from theater to theater] with varying degrees of success. What enabled you to do that successfully with *Sankofa*?

GERIMA: We brought Kay Shaw in as the public relations person to implement our ideas, our vision. Kay was the key. She knew how to go into a city and pinpoint the real black community— through research or something—and began to launch a thing that we call the "*Sankofa* Family." Everywhere we went, we established a Sankofa Family. Wherever the Sankofa Family was divided, we failed; where they were united, we succeeded.

TOR: The Sankofa Families were grassroots organizations that would sponsor the film, do the PR, etc.?

GERIMA: Oh, yeah. Word of mouth was very much like a brushfire. Even when we were still in Washington, we had already been heard about all the way in South Africa. We were getting phone calls from all over. A sister even came by plane all the way from

Arkansas to see it because she felt this type of a movie would never get to her there. When I went to California to open in Oakland, several preachers had talked about the movie so much that we just had to light the match to start the fire.

TOR: You, or Shirikiana, or somebody would always talk to the audience before the film began. Why?

GERIMA: That's the most important thing we started in Washington when we first opened. We had learned that we had to build the audience. The filmmakers had to explain and bring the audience along to the history of the production: what you are trying to say and what your struggle is in film.

The idea was to build the awareness of how the movie was made and stress the responsibility the audience has to help our filmmakers emerge. We cannot afford laid-back audiences in the African community here or in Africa. We need an active partnership starting before the film is made. We told them, "If you feel this film is worthy, don't just sit back and do nothing. Go home and call at least ten people by phone and tell them about our film. Then you help us." Otherwise, telling us "You're great; we like your film" does us no good. And that, I think, was an important ideological position I took early.

TOR: Tell me about *Sankofa*'s opening in Los Angeles.

GERIMA: I left my job here at Howard and lived three months in Los Angeles to push the movie, until we were evicted from the United Artists theater.

TOR: Why did they evict you?

GERIMA: They didn't know the movie they had picked. They suddenly told us, "There is another movie coming in and you have to get out." We said, "We agreed that if the film does good we'll stay." They said, "No, no . . . you've got to get out."

TOR: That's cold.

GERIMA: The United Artists vice president said to me . . . listen to this now. "The manager has checked into a hospital," he said to me. I said, "So, what's that got to do with us?" He said, "It's from the '*Sankofa* tension.' " I said, "The *Sankofa* tension?" He said, "Yes, since this film has come, there's been a tense situation." I said, "Is there a *Die Hard* tension?"

In that theater, Torriano, not to brag, but two shows were always sold out in advance. You had to wait two shows to see *Sankofa*. Even the very last show on that Sunday was sold out.

And there were seven or eight other movies in this multiplex that were doing zero audiences, and they were there longer than us.

TOR: And they still kicked you out?

GERIMA: Oh, yeah. So to me it's like, no white person will look me straight in the face and tell me, "It didn't have box office" or "It is not a box office case." Earlier, when I told you someone said the film was "too black," there have been others that have said, "It's not commercial." Sony came back and opened *Sankofa* at the Magic Johnson Theaters in L.A., because that was the only way they could baptize their theater in the black community. They needed *Sankofa* as a libation pourer to open that theater there.

TOR: But didn't Sony reject *Sankofa* before?

GERIMA: Yes, but after we had a fight with United Artists and got evicted, the black community told Magic Johnson and his people, "Hey, you'd better bring this movie down here."

TOR: With this type of community response, how would you say that the film has influenced society and your audience?

GERIMA: I don't know that. I'm still trying to process what *Sankofa's* calling is, because I've known people from Baltimore, to New York, to Oakland, who have come out of the theater crying, and who would just hug each other.

TOR: Tell us about the Myphaduh Film Complex.

GERIMA: After *Sankofa*, we needed to take our vision a step higher. When I did *Sankofa*, all the preproduction and conception of the film was done from a basement office beneath my house. For postproduction I rented an editing room at Bono's Film Labs in Arlington.

I always thought I should have these things as a base, where I edit, produce, and distribute my own work and films that I believe in. Myphaduh was started in 1984 to distribute films. At that time, the films were warehoused in New Jersey. The coming of *Sankofa* enabled us to purchase a building here in D.C., where we have our offices and a postproduction facility. We also have some production equipment. We have our own super 16mm camera, and some minimum packages for sound and light. Our idea is to go into coproductions with other people and other countries. We feel that we also need to present black cinema the way books are presented. We have created our own bookstore, video sale and rental, and gift shop at the complex to make African and African-American-made films accessible in the area.

We also did it because video distribution companies rejected us. After Blockbuster refused to carry our video, we started business with black bookstores across the country, whereby we make them outlets. That's how Blockbuster started. The difference between them and us is that they have affinity and solidarity with bankers for loans. We have a problem getting loans, but we have a very worthwhile experiment going. Our idea is to package and distribute more black films at the wholesale places, or retail them in our store here. We want to show young people that you can begin to own your stock, and wholesale to black stores if whites refuse you. For more information, contact Myphaduh Film Complex, 2714 Georgia Ave., Washington, DC 20001, 202–234–4755.

Naked Acts

Kindred Spirits Productions (1996)

"They'll try to convince you it's a good career move
when they tell you to take your clothes off."
—Lydia to Cicely

Naked Acts is an emotionally charged drama about a young
woman's journey toward acceptance of the body she once despised.
Cicely, the film's protagonist, was sexually molested as a little girl.
Her sense of self-loathing in the years that followed caused her to
use food as a crutch. Now twenty-seven, she has shed fifty-seven
pounds and has a beautiful body, and like her mother and grandmother before her she has decided to become an actress.

Cicely and her mother have not been on speaking terms for
several years. Lydia was a successful blaxploitation queen in the
seventies and well known for showing her curvaceous body on the
screen. But she was always too busy working to give her daughter
the time, attention, and protection that she craved. Cicely shows up
at Lydia's video store after a four-year absence to discuss her new
career plans. Her mother is skeptical. She knows the business and
knows what her daughter will be put through and eventually asked
to do. But Cicely assures Lydia that unlike her, she is capable of
exuding talent, beauty, and sensuality without ever exposing her
body. A heated argument ensues and Cicely leaves, vowing never to
return.

As fate would have it, *Body of Art*, the low-budget film in which
our lead has landed a role, is about a male artist who paints nude
portraits of black women. In spite of the apparent truthfulness to
her mother's warning, the aspiring actress becomes determined to
keep both her part in the film and her clothes on her body. In the
process, she realizes that getting emotionally naked is much more of
a challenge than taking off her clothes could ever be.

Naked Acts breaks new cinematic ground in several ways. It is
the first film to explore issues of body image and nonsexualized

nudity as they relate to African-American women. It is a film that uses a film as a backdrop. And Davis is the first African-American woman to write, produce, direct, and entirely self-distribute a feature-length film in the United States.

"People have all these questions about why, why, why about black film. And why more can't happen with it," Davis stated in a personal interview. "*Naked Acts* is a classic example of why. It's because the decision often comes down to one white man, sitting in a room watching the film by himself, and the film was not made for him."

To prove that there was an audience for a black art-house film, Davis and her publicist husband Rob Fields decided to distribute the film themselves. Fields booked a one-week engagement at the Thalia theater in Manhattan and pressed forward with his strategy for an extensive mailing, flyers, e-mail, and word-of-mouth advertising campaign, and it worked. On the opening night, September 25, 1998, they had a line of more than six hundred people that wrapped around the block. People were turned away at the door, but they all came back, and the film grossed $17,031 during the first week. That number broke box office records for a single-screen "exclusive" release for a film with no-name actors and no advertising budget.

"The *Amsterdam News* did a big faux pas about the premiere, and we got media!" Davis explained, speaking of what helped to get the word out. "We got a wonderful big piece in the *Daily News* that said, like a headline, 'Naked Acts a Success!' or something like that, with a big picture of me in front of the marquee! And that

---

CREDITS: Writer-Producer-Director: Bridgett M. Davis. Executive Producer: Henri E. Norris. Associate Producers: Michele Blackwell, Rita R. Davis, Rob Fields, Jake-ann Jones. Photography: Herman Lew. Editor: Brunilda Torres. Music: Cecilia Smith. Sound: Pam Demetrius, Charles Blackwell. Art Director: Fred Holland. Set Design: Kim Howell. 87 minutes. Drama. NR.

CAST: Jake-ann Jones (*Cicely*), Patricia DeArcy (*Lydia*), John McKie (*Marcel*), Ron Cephus Jones (*Joel*), Renee Cox (*Diana*), Sandye Wilson (*Winsome*), Natalie Robinson (*Randi*), Lee Dobson (*Jesse*), Maranantha Quick (*Grandmama*), Ajene Washington (*Ronnie*), Annette Myrie (*Little Cece*), Rodney Charles (*Leading Man*), Simone Hunt (*Baby Cece*), Jairus Hunt (*Daddy*), Sabrina Lamb (*Comic*), Laura Washington (*Waitress*), Jerome Bailey (*Homeboy*), Beatrice Brazoban (*Street Artist*), Bridgett M. Davis (*Rae*), Peekoo A. Lewis (*Bathhouse Attendant*), Tara Greenway (*Woman 1*), Leslie Hoffman (*Woman 2*), Tracie Garvin (*Wardrobe Assistant*).

Now fifty-seven pounds lighter, Cicely (Jake-Ann Jones) is an aspiring actress who must learn to love and accept her new and improved body in Bridgett M. Davis's independently distributed film *Naked Acts*. (Renee Cox)

spurred even more sort of like, really mania! We were supposed to only be there one week, and we stayed for four."

Naked Acts was called "fresh, funny and original" by *Variety* and "a brilliant gem" by the *Amsterdam News*. It received the 1997 Best Feature Film award from the Black Filmmakers Hall of Fame; was a "Best of the Fest" selection at the Minneapolis International

Film Festival; and Best Film at the Berlin Black Film Festival. It has also been aired on the premium cable Sundance Channel.

"I've gotten so much satisfaction from watching it at these festivals, and women coming up to me crying, and having people e-mailing me and sending me letters. It's very gratifying," Davis said. "Your ego gets fed that way, and I felt satisfied and validated."

Davis is an associate professor of English at the City University of New York's Baruch College. She teaches film and TV writing, journalism and fiction writing. She is currently developing her next feature film project, entitled *Abbey's Road*, about an urban folksinger who tries to get her style of music recognized by a narrowly categorizing music industry.

A Note on the Availability of Films

The availability for home viewing of early films of African-American making, both those discussed in the text and those mentioned in passing, presents a mixed picture. Many have been been transferred to videocassette, although some have been entirely lost. And some are available only on 35-mm. or 16-mm. film stock. These last can sometimes be viewed by appointment, as at the Library of Congress or the Donnell Branch of the New York Public Library.

Videocassettes, of course, are widely available in video stores, but a much wanted film made before 1940 may not be found in your local store. Traveling halfway across America just to view one film may well be inconvenient, but libraries in large cities, such as Chicago, Philadelphia, and New York, and university archives, such as the UCLA Film Archives, do have major holdings of videocassettes (and films, too). On-line searches through library catalogs via the Internet make it possible to determine whether what is wanted is in fact available. Viewing a film at the Motion Picture and Television Reading Room of the Library of Congress, as to see the Johnson-Jeffries fight film or *The Birth of a Race*, must be arranged in advance. The same is true of the New York Public Library.

For determined searchers (and researchers), library catalog entries may be used to find the names of the producers of videocassettes, and only one further step is needed to locate the producers, who may then be contacted. And there are distributors. Readers who wish to obtain copies of such films as *The Scar of Shame*, *Hallelujah*, *Imitation of Life*, *The Emperor Jones*, among others, may contact Facet Video, 1517 W. Fullerton Avenue, Chicago, IL 60614, telephone 1-800-532-2387.

Bibliography

The Railroad Porter (1912)
Reid, Mark A. "Early Black Independent Filmmakers." *Black Film Review* 2 (Fall 1986): 21–22.
Richards, Larry. "The Railroad Porter." *African-American Films Through 1959: A Comprehensive Illustrated Filmography*, p. 138. Jefferson, N.C.: McFarland & Company, 1998.

The Realization of a Negro's Ambition (1916)
Klotman, Phyllis R. "The Realization of a Negro's Ambition." *Frame by Frame: A Black Filmography*, pp. 425–26. Bloomington: Indiana University Press, 1979.
Moss, Carlton. "The Birth of Los Angeles' Black Film Industry." *Los Angeles Times*, November 27, 1977, p. 60.
Reddick, Lawrence. "Educational Programs for the Improvement of Race Relations: Motion Pictures, Radio, Press and Libraries." *Journal of Negro Education* 18, 3 (Summer 1944): pp. 367–89.
Richards, Larry. "The Realization of a Negro's Ambition." *African-American Films Through 1959: A Comprehensive Illustrated Filmography*, p. 139. Jefferson, N.C.: McFarland & Company, 1998.

The Birth of a Race (1918)
"The Birth of a Race." *Variety Film Reviews 1907–1920*, 1 (December 6, 1918). New York: Garland Publishing, 1983.
Cripps, Thomas. "The Making of the Birth of a Race: The Emerging Politics of Identity in Silent Movies." In *The Birth of Whiteness: Race and the Emergence of U.S. Cinema*, edited by Daniel Bernardi, pp. 38–55. New Brunswick, N.J.: Rutgers University Press, 1996.
Richards, Larry. *African-American Films Through 1959: A Comprehensive Illustrated Filmography*, p. 17. Jefferson, N.C.: McFarland & Company, 1998.

Body and Soul (1924)
Bogle, Donald. "Body and Soul." *Blacks in American Films and Television: An Encyclopedia*, pp. 32–33. New York: Garland Publishing, 1988.
Bowser, Pearl, and Louise Spence. "Identity and Betrayal: The Symbol of the Unconquered and Oscar Micheaux's 'Biographical Legend.' " In *The Birth of Whiteness: Race and the Emergence of U.S. Cinema*, edited by Donald Bernardi, pp. 56–80. New Brunswick, N.J.: Rutgers University Press, 1996.

The Scar of Shame (1927)
Bogle, Donald. "Scar and Shame." *Blacks in American Films and Television: An Encyclopedia*, p. 184. New York: Garland Publishing, 1988.
Cripps, Thomas. " 'Race Movies' as Voices of the Black Bourgeoisie: The Scar of Shame." In *Representing Blackness: Issues in Film and Video*, edited by Valerie Smith, pp. 47–60. New Brunswick, N.J.: Rutgers University Press, 1997.
———. "The Scar of Shame." *Black Film as Genre*, pp. 65–74. Bloomington: Indiana University Press, 1978.

Gaines, Jane. "The Scar of Shame: Skin Color and Caste in Black Silent Melodrama." In *Representing Blackness: Issues in Film and Video*, edited by Valerie Smith, pp. 66–81. New Brunswick, N.J.: Rutgers University Press, 1997.

Hearts in Dixie (1929)
Benchley, Robert. "Hearts in Dixie: The First Real Talking Picture." *Opportunity Magazine*. April 1929, pp. 122–23. Also in *Black Films and Filmmakers: A Comprehensive Anthology From Stereotype to Superhero*, compiled by Lindsay Patterson, pp. 84–87. New York: Dodd, Mead, 1975.
Hall, Mordaunt. "The Screen: Way Down Yonder." *New York Times*, February 28, 1929, p. 30.
Noble, Peter. "The Coming of Sound Film." In *Anthology of the Afro-American in the Theatre: A Critical Approach*, edited by Lindsay Patterson, pp. 247–66. Comwell Heights, Pa.: Publishers Agency, 1967.
Sid. "Hearts in Dixie." *Variety Film Reviews 1926–1929*, v. 3 (March 6, 1929). New York: Garland Publishing, 1983.

Hallelujah (1929)
Allen, Cleveland G., Reverend A. Bennett Haines, and Pare Lorentz. "Primitive Emotions: A Flame in a Negro Film." *Literary Digest*, October 5, 1929, pp. 42–52.
Beaton, Welford. "Hallelujah." *Sound Magazine*. 1929, p. 229.
Carr, Jay. "Vintage Films." *Boston Globe*, Arts & Film, October 4, 1991, p. 46.
Cocchi, John. "Hallelujah." *Magill's Survey of Cinema*, v. 2, edited by Frank N. Magill, pp. 704–707. Englewood Cliffs, N.J.: Salem Press, 1980.
Howard, Jessica. "Hallelujah!: Transformation in Film." *African American Review* 30 (Fall 1996): 441–51.
Nash, Jay R., and Stanley R. Ross. "Hallelujah." *The Motion Picture Guide 1927–1983*, v. 4, p. 1143. Chicago: Cinebooks, 1986.

The Emperor Jones (1933)
Davy, Charles. "The Cinema: 'The Emperor Jones' at the Marble Arch Pavilion." *Spectator*, March 23, 1934, p. 448.
Kagan, Norman. "The Return of the Emperor Jones." *Negro History Bulletin* 34 (November 1971): 160–62.
———. "Reviving 'The Emperor Jones' (2): Across the Awareness Divide." *Village Voice*, July 1, 1971, p. 57.
———. "Reviving 'The Emperor Jones' (1): Black Experiences in the Cinema." *Village Voice*, June 24, 1971, pp. 69–71.
Karr, Kathleen. "The Emperor Jones." *Magill's Survey of Cinema*, v. 2, edited by Frank N. Magill, pp. 709–11. Englewood Cliffs, N.J.: Salem Press, 1981.
Nesteby, James R. "All-Black to Hollywood Films (The Emperor Jones)." *Black Images in American Films, 1896–1954: The Interplay Between Civil Rights and Film Culture*, p. 164. Washington, D.C.: University Press of America, 1982.

Imitation of Life (1934, 1959)
Argus. "On the Current Screen: Imitation of Life." *Literary Digest* 118 (December 8, 1934): p. 31.
Bogel, Donald. "*Imitation of Life:* Mother Knows Best." *Toms, Coons, Mulattoes, Mammies, and Bucks: An Interpretive History of Blacks in American Films*, pp. 57–59. New York: Continuum, 1994.
Johnson, Timothy. "Imitation of Life." *Magill's Survey of Cinema*, v. 3, edited by Frank N. Magill, pp. 1128–31. Englewood Cliffs, N.J.: Salem Press, 1981.
Land. "Imitation of Life." *Variety Film Reviews 1934–1937*, v. 5 (November 27, 1934). New York: Garland Publishing, 1983.

Pulleine, Tim. "Retrospective: Imitation of Life." *Monthly Film Bulletin (BFI)* 48 (November 1981): 229.
Sennwald, Andre D. "The Screen: Imitation of Life." *New York Times*, November 24, 1934, p. 19.
Walsh, Moira. "Imitation of Life." *America* 101 (May 9, 1959): 314–19.

Harlem on the Prairie (1938)
Abel. "Harlem on the Prairie." *Variety Film Reviews 1938–1942*, v. 6 (February 9, 1938). New York: Garland Publishing, 1983.
Carr, Sabin W. "Cinema: The New Pictures." *Time*, December 13, 1937, p. 24.
McCarthy, Guy. "Harlem on the Prairie." *Motion Picture Herald*, November 27, 1937, p. 54.
Nash, Jay R., and Ross, Stanley R. "Harlem on the Prairie." *The Motion Picture Guide 1927–1983*, v. 4, pp. 1162–63. Chicago: Cinebooks. 1986.
"Reviews of the New Films: Harlem on the Prairie." *Film Daily*, February 5, 1938, p. 4.

The Blood of Jesus (1941)
Cripps, Thomas. "The Blood of Jesus." *Black Film as Genre*, pp. 87–99. Bloomington: Indiana University Press, 1978.
Hyatt, Marshall. "Blood of Jesus." *The Afro-American Cinematic Experience: An Annotated Bibliography and Filmography*, p. 189. Wilmington, D.C.: Scholarly Resources. 1983.
Thomas, Kevin. "Screening Room: Swan's Rarely Seen 'Queen Kelly' to Screen." *Los Angeles Times*, Part F, June 19, 1995, p. 5.

Cabin in the Sky (1943)
Bogle, Donald. "Into the 1920s (Hallelujah)." *Toms, Coons, Mulattoes, Mammies, and Bucks: An Interpretive History of Blacks in American Films*, pp. 27–34. New York: Continuum, 1994.
Farber, Manny. "The Great White Way." *New Republic*, July 5, 1943, p. 20.
Hartung, Philip T. "The Stage and Screen: Lighter Side." *Commonweal*, June 18, 1943, pp. 225–26.
"Movies: Hollywood Cabin." *Newsweek*, April 26, 1943, p. 88.
Pryor, Thomas M. "The Screen: Cabin in the Sky." *New York Times*, May 28, 1943, p. 19.
Sterne, H. "Cabin in the Sky." *Rob Wagner's Script.* May 15, 1943, v. 29, p. 14.

Stormy Weather (1943)
Bogle, Donald. "Stormy Weather." *Blacks in American Films and Television: An Encyclopedia*, pp. 205–7. New York: Garland Publishing, 1988.
"Cinema: The New Pictures." *Time*, July 12, 1943, p. 94.
Hartung, Philip T. "The Screen: Rain! No Game!" *Commonweal*, July 23, 1943: pp. 344–45.
Nash, Jay R., and Ross, Stanley R. "Stormy Weather." *The Motion Picture Guide 1927–1983*, v. 7, p. 3142. Chicago: Cinebooks, 1986.
Pryor, Thomas M. "Stormy Weather." *New York Times*, July 22, 1943, p. 15.
"Taps and Zoot Suits." *Newsweek*, August 2, 1943, p. 78.

Home of the Brave (1948)
Brown, John M. "Seeing Things: Land of the Free." *Saturday Review of Literature* 32 (June 11, 1949): pp. 26–27.
Crowther, Bosley. "Home of the Brave." *New York Times*, May 13, 1949, p. 29.

Farber, Manny. "Films: Home of the Brave." *Nation*, May 21, 1949, pp. 590–91.
Hatch, Robert. "Movies: Good Intention." *New Republic*, May 16, 1949, pp. 22–23.
Kahn. "Home of the Brave." *Variety Film Reviews 1949–1953*, v. 8 (May 4, 1949). New York: Garland Publishing, 1983.
McCarten, John. "The Current Cinema: The Color Line, Home of the Brave." *New Yorker*, May 21, 1949, p. 68.
Voyeur. "The New Films." *Theater Arts* 33 (July 1949): p. 9.

The Jackie Robinson Story (1950)
Berkow, Ira. "So Large a Sports Hero, He Filled the Screen." *New York Times*, sec. II, April 13, 1997, p. 19.
Crowther, Bosley. "The Jackie Robinson Story." *New York Times, Film Review.* May 17, 1950, p. 2421.
Hartung, Philip. "The Screen: The Jackie Robinson Story." *Commonweal*, June 2, 1950, p. 198.
Hatch, Robert. "Movies: Jungle Tales." *New Republic* 122 (June 12, 1950): 23.
"The Jackie Robinson Story." *Christian Century*, June 21, 1950, p. 775.
"The Jackie Robinson Story." *Variety Film Reviews 1949–1953*, v. 8 (May 17, 1950). New York: Garland Publishing. 1983.

Carmen Jones (1954)
Baldwin, James. "Life Straight in the De Eye: Carmen Jones, Film Spectacular in Color." *Commentary*, January 1955, pp. 74–77.
———. "Carmen Jones: The Dark Is Light Enough." *Black Films and Filmmakers: A Comprehensive Anthology from Stereotype to Superhero*, compiled by Lindsay Patterson, pp. 88–95. New York: Dodd, Mead & Company, 1975. Originally published in *Notes of a Native Son*, by James Baldwin, 1955.
Carr, Jay. "Preminger's Carmen Is Still Lively." *Boston Globe*, Arts & Film, February 4, 1994, p. 52.
De La Roche, Catherine. "Film Reviews: Carmen Jones." *Sight and Sound* 24 (Spring 1955): 198–99.
Hartung, Philip. "The Screen: The Jones Girl and the Alan Lad." *Commonweal*, November 19, 1954, pp. 188–89.
Kap. "Carmen Jones." *Variety Film Reviews 1954–1958*, v. 9 (October 6, 1954). New York: Garland Publishing. 1983.
Walsh, Moira. "Films: Carmen Jones." *America* 96 (November 6, 1954): 165–66.

St. Louis Blues (1958)
Cripps, Thomas. "The St. Louis Blues." *Black Film as Genre*, pp. 75–85. Bloomington: Indiana University Press. 1978.
Crowther, Bosley. "St. Louis Blues." *Variety*, February 8. 1939. p. 17.
Feather, Leonard. "Jazz: A Long Way from the Gene Krupa Story." *Los Angeles Times*. June 1, 1986, cal, p. 82.
Garner, Jack. "St. Louis Blues." *Gannett News Service*, February 16, 1995.
Hartung, Philip. "The Stage and Screen: Cinders, Sarongs and Cold Cream." *Commonweal*, February 24, 1939, pp. 496–97.
Nash, Jay R., and Stanley R. Ross. "St. Louis Blues." *The Motion Picture Guide 1927–1983*. v. 7, p. 2709. Chicago: Cinebooks. 1986.

Sergeant Rutledge (1960)
Gluck, Marvin. "The Trial of Sergeant Rutledge." *Film Quarterly* 13 (Spring 1960): 60.
Hartung, Philip. "The Screen: Americana." *Commonweal*, June 17, 1960, p. 305.
Hatch, Robert. "Films." *Nation*, June 11, 1960, pp. 519–20.

Houston, Penelope. "Sergeant Rutledge and the Unforgiven." *Sight and Sound* 29 (Summer 1960): 142.

Thompson, Don K. "Sergeant Rutledge." *Magill's Survey of Cinema.* v. 5, edited by Frank N. Magill, pp. 2135–37. Englewood Cliffs, N.J.: Salem Press. 1981.

Thompson, Howard. "The Screen: In Pursuit of Success in the Big City, Sergeant Rutledge." *The New York Times Film Reviews*, May 26, 1960. p. 1.

Walsh, Moira. "Films: Sergeant Rutledge." *America* 10 (June 4, 1960): 342.

A Raisin in the Sun (1961)

"Acute Ghettoitis." *Time*, March 31, 1961, p. 64.

"A Raisin in the Sun." *Ebony*, April 1961, pp. 53–56.

Hartung, Philip. "The Screen: Angry Young Black Man." *Commonweal*, April 7, 1961, pp. 46–47.

Kauffmann, Stanley. "Movies: With Negroes in Suburbia." *New Republic*, March 20, 1961, pp. 19–20.

Knight, Arthur. "SR Goes to the Movies, Theatre Into Films." *Saturday Review*, March 25, 1961, p. 34.

Oliver, Edith. "The Current Cinema: The Sun Still Shines." *New Yorker*, April 8, 1961, pp. 164–65.

Walsh, Moira. "Films: A Raisin in the Sun." *America* 103 (April 8, 1961): 133–34.

Black Like Me (1964)

Alpert, Hollis. "Mood Ebony." *Saturday Review*, April 25, 1964, p. 25

"Black Like Me: Story of White Man Passing as Negro in South Is Tense Movie." *Ebony*, May 1964, pp. 37–38.

Clifton, James. "Black Like Me." *New York Times*, May 21, 1964, p. 1.

Crowther, Bosley. "Black Like Me." *New York Times*, May 21, 1964, p. 42.

Gill, Brendan. "The Current Cinema: Danger! Virtue at Work." *New Yorker*, May 23, 1964, pp. 151–52.

Harrison, James B. "Movies: Skin Deep." *Christian Century*, June 17, 1964, p. 807.

Kauffmann, Stanley. "The Fire This Time." *New Republic*, May 23, 1964, pp. 24–27.

Nothing but a Man (1964)

Chamberlin, Philip. "Nothing but a Man." *Film Society Review*, September 1966, pp. 23–24.

Cohen, Saul B. "Michael Roemer and Robert Young: Film Makers of 'Nothing but a Man.'" *Film Comment* 3 (Spring 1965): 8–13.

Crowther, Bosley. "Nothing but a Man." *New York Times*, September 21, 1964, p. 37.

Mapp, Edward. "Chapter 8: 1964 (*Nothing but a Man*)." *Blacks in American Films: Today and Yesterday*, pp. 98–101. Metuchen, N.J.: Scarecrow Press, 1972.

O'Doherty, Brian. "Classic of a Negro who Stopped Running." *Life*, February 19, 1965, p. 15.

Thomas, Kevin. "Movie Reviews: Nothing But a Man." *Los Angeles Times*, January 8, 1994, cal, p. 6.

Guess Who's Coming to Dinner (1967)

Birstein, Ann. "Vogue's Spotlight, Movies: Glorious Spencer Tracey." *Vogue*, January 1, 1968, p. 56.

Elliston, Maxine H. "Two Sidney Poitier Films: Guess Who's Coming to Dinner, For Love of Ivy." *Film Comment* 5 (Winter 1969): 26–33.

Lerman, Leo. "Catch Up With: Movies." *Mademoiselle*, January 1968, p. 26.

Lovell, Glenn. "The Color of Love: Interracial Romance Still Makes Hollywood a Little Nervous." *Chicago Tribune*, Arts, September 18, 1994, p. 34.

Nash, Jay R., and Stanley R. Ross. "Guess Who's Coming to Dinner." *The Motion Picture Guide 1927–1983*, v. 3, p. 1118. Chicago: Cinebooks, 1986.

Smith, Mark C. "Special Screening: Guess Who's Coming to Dinner Dishes Up Glib Fare." *Los Angeles Times*, OC Live, April 15, 1993, p. 19.

Sugy, Catherine. "Guess Who's Coming to Dinner." *Take One* 1, 9 (1968): 23–24.

The Learning Tree (1969)

"The Black Path to Hollywood: The Gordon Parks' 'Learning Tree.'" *Sepia*, April 19, 1970, pp. 50–52.

Bosworth, Patricia. "How Could I Forget Who I Am?" *New York Times*, sec. II, August 17, 1969, p. 11.

Hartung, Philip. "Black, White and Technicolor." *Commonweal*, September 5, 1969, pp. 543–45.

"NCOMP Charges Hollywood Lacks Black Sensitivity." *Christian Century*, September 10, 1969, p. 1157.

Nash, Jay R., and Stanley R. Ross. "The Learning Tree." *The Motion Picture Guide 1927–1983*, v. 5, p. 1643. Chicago: Cinebooks, 1986.

"Ten Most Important Black Films Between 1962 and 1972." *Black Creation*, Winter 1973, p. 35.

Sweet Sweetback's Baadasssss Song (1971)

Bogle, Donald. "Sweet Sweetback's Baadasssss Song." *Blacks in American Films and Television: An Encyclopedia*, pp. 210–12. New York: Garland Publishing. 1988.

Cripps, Thomas. "Sweet Sweetback's Baadasssss Song." *Black Film as Genre*, pp. 128–40. Bloomington: Indiana University Press. 1978.

Holden, Stephen. "Film View: Sweet Sweetback's World Revisited." *New York Times*, July 2, 1995, p. B9.

Parks, Louis B. "Blaxploitation Bijou." *Houston Chronicle*, June 1, 1996, p. 1.

Thomas, Kevin. "Special Screenings." *Los Angeles Times*, September 11, 1992, cal, p. 6.

Shaft (1971)

Cocks, Jay. "Summer Coolers: Shaft." *Time*, July 26, 1971, p. 51.

Leab, Daniel J. "Shaft." *From Sambo to Superspade: The Black Experience in Motion Pictures*. London: Secker and Warburg, 1975.

Milne, Tom. "Shaft." *Focus on Film* 8 (October 1971): 7.

Murf. "Shaft." *Variety Film Reviews 1971–1974*, v. 13 (June 16, 1971). New York: Garland Publishing, 1983.

Nash, Jay R., and Stanley R. Ross. "Shaft." *The Motion Picture Guide 1927–1983*, v. 7, p. 2856. Chicago: Cinebooks, 1987.

Oberbeck, S. K. "Black Eye." *Newsweek*, July 19, 1971, p. 80.

Walsh, Moira. "More Brief Takes." *America* 125 (July 24, 1971): 48.

Buck and the Preacher (1972)

Bogle, Donald. "Reviews: Buck and the Preacher." *Blacks in American Films and Television: An Encyclopedia*, pp. 40–41. New York: Garland Publishing, 1988.

Gow, Gordon. "Buck and the Preacher." *Films and Filming* 18 (June 1972): 54.

Klotman, Phyllis R. "Buck and the Preacher." *Frame by Frame: A Black Filmography*, p. 83. Bloomington: Indiana University Press, 1979.

Nash, Jay R., and Stanley R. Ross. "Buck and the Preacher." *The Motion Picture Guide, 1927–1983*, v. 1, p. 310. Chicago: Cinebooks, 1985.

Blacula (1972)

Nash, Jay R., and Stanley R. Ross. "Blacula." *The Motion Picture Guide 1927–1983*, v. 1, p. 228. Chicago: Cinebooks, 1985.

Bogle, Donald. "Blacula." *Blacks in American Films and Television: An Encyclopedia*, pp. 27–28. New York: Garland Publishing, 1988.

Klotman, Phyllis R. "Blacula." *Frame by Frame: A Black Filmography*, p. 64. Bloomington: Indiana University Press. 1979.

Weaver, Richard. "Blacula." *Films and Filming* 20 (November 1973): 49.

The Spook Who Sat by the Door (1973)

Hankins, Paula. "Film Reviews: Gordon's War, The Spook Who Sat by the Door." *Cinéaste* 6 (1974): 47–48.

Kantor, Meyer. "This Spook Has No Respect for Human Life." *New York Times*, November 11, 1973, sec. II, p. 11.

Klotman, Phyllis R. "The Spook Who Sat by the Door." *Frame by Frame: A Black Filmography*, p. 489. Bloomington: Indiana University Press, 1979.

Coffy (1973)

Bogle, Donald. "Coffy." *Blacks in American Films and Television: An Encyclopedia*, p. 58. New York: Garland Publishing, 1988.

Claessner, Verina. "Coffy." *Monthly Film Bulletin (BFI)* 44 (July 1974): 145.

McKegney, Michael. "A Pound of Nails for Coffin." *Village Voice*, August 2, 1973, p. 69.

Nash, Jay R., and Stanley R. Ross. "Coffy." *The Motion Picture Guide 1927–1983*, v. 2, p. 453. Chicago: Cinebooks, 1985.

Williams, Whit. "Coffy." *Variety Film Reviews 1971–1974*, v. 13 (May 16, 1973). New York: Garland Publishing, 1983.

Claudine (1974)

Champlin, Charles. "Movies: . . . but Human Comedy Leavens Gritty 'Claudine.' " *Los Angeles Times*, May 12, 1974, pp. 26–27.

Crist, Judith. "Available in All Colors." *New York*, April 22, 1974, pp. 90–91.

Gans, Herbert J. "Gans on Film: Black Poverty as Comedy." *Social Policy* 5 (September–October 1974): 59–60.

Murf. "Claudine." *Variety Film Reviews 1971–1974*, v. 13 (April 10, 1974). New York: Garland Publishing, 1983.

Schickel, Richard. "Fried Chicken Romance.' *Time*, May 20, 1974, pp. 66–68.

Westerbeck, Collin L., Jr. "Color Television: The Screen." *Commonweal*, October 18, 1974, pp. 65–66.

Cooley High (1975)

Jackson, Elizabeth. "Michael Schultz." *Black Film Review* 7, 1 (1975): 4–5.

Jefferson, Margo. "Black Graffiti." *Newsweek*, July 21, 1975, p. 64.

Rosenbaum, Jonathan. "Cooley High." *Monthly Film Bulletin (BFI)* 44 (February 1977): 21.

Slater, Jack. "Cooley High, More Than Just a Black 'Graffiti.' " *New York Times*, August 10, 1975, pp. 74–75.

Thomas, Kevin. "Cooley High's Universal Appeal." *Los Angeles Times*, July 13, 1975, cal, p. 36.

Van Gelder, Lawrence. "Cooley High." *New York Times*, June 26, 1975, p. 35.

Walcott, James. "Takes." *Village Voice*, July 21, 1975, p. 70.

Countdown at Kusini (1976)

Baird, Keith E. "Countdown at Kusini." *Freedomways* 16 (1976): 251–52.

Bogle, Donald. "Countdown at Kusini." *Blacks in American Films and Television: An Encyclopedia*, pp. 69–70. New York: Garland Publishing, 1988.

Nash, Jay R., and Stanley R. Ross. "Countdown at Kusini." *The Motion Picture Guide 1927–1983*, 2, p. 493. Chicago: Cinebooks, 1985.

Thomas, Kevin. "Countdown at Kusini." *Los Angeles Times*, April 28, 1976, p.17.
Walker, Alice. "Film: Black Sorority Bankrolls Action Film." *Ms. Magazine*, June 1976, p. 45.
Winsten, Archer. "Countdown at Kusini." *New York Post*, April 8, 1976, p. 24.

Krush Groove (1985)
Christgau, Robert, and Dibbell, Carola. "Film: One from the Motormouth." *Village Voice*, November 12, 1985, pp. 30–45.
DiMauro, Phil. "Schultz Lensed 'Groove' in 26 Days for $3,000,000." *Variety*, November 6, 1985, p. 7.
Goldstein, Patrick. "Krush Groove." *Los Angeles Times*, October 25, 1985, p. 12.
Kelleher, Ed. "Krush Groove." *Film Journal* 88 (November 1985): 58.
Maslin, Janet. "Film: 'Krush Groove,' by Michael Schultz." *New York Times*, October 25, 1985, sec. III, p. 8.
Nash, Jay R., and Stanley R. Ross. "Krush Groove." *The Motion Picture Guide 1986 Annual*, p. 103. Chicago: Cinebooks, 1987.
Schickel, Richard. "Rushes: Krush Groove." *Time*, November 18, 1985, p. 94.

The Color Purple (1985)
Benson, Sheila. "Movie Reviews: Two Women of Substance in Unlikely Settings." *Los Angeles Times*, December 18, 1986, cal, p. 1.
Blake, Richard A. "Films: Survivors." *America* 154 (February 1, 1986): 75.
Canby, Vincent. "Film View: From a Palette of Cliches Comes the Color Purple." *New York Times*, January 5, 1986, sec. II, p.17.
Halprin, Sara. "The Color Purple: Community of Women." *Jump Cut* 1 (March 1986): 1+.
Maio, Kathi. "The Color Purple Fading to White." *Feminist in the Dark: Reviewing the Movies*, pp. 35–44. Freedom, Cal.: Crossing Press, 1988
Norment, Lynn. "The Color Purple: The Controversial Prize-Winning Book Becomes an Equally Controversial Movie." *Ebony*, February 1986, pp. 146–57.
Reed, Rex. "The Color Purple." *New York Post*, December 18, 1985. p. 27.

She's Gotta Have It (1986)
Ansen, David. "Movies: Sex and the Single Girl, Spike Lee's Funky Hit." *Newsweek*, September 8, 1986, p. 65.
Bruckner, D. J. R. "Film: Spike Lee's She's Gotta Have It." *New York Times*, August 8, 1986, p. C14.
Fusco, Coco. "Independent Film Reviews: She's Gotta Have it." *Cinéaste* 15, 3 (1986–1987): 24.
Lee, Spike. *Spike Lee's Gotta Have It: Inside Guerrilla Filmmaking*. New York: Simon and Schuster, 1987.
Smith, Mark C. "Special Screening: She Is Priority in Gotta Have It." *Los Angeles Times*, April 13, 1995, OC Live, p. 12.
Stanton, Louise. "She's Gotta Have It." *Films in Review* 32 (November 1986): 549.
Wilmington, Michael. "Nola's Jazzy Love Life in She's Gotta Have It." *Los Angeles Times*, August 21, 1986, cal, p. 1.

Hollywood Shuffle (1987)
Als, Hilton. "Reeling on the Good Foot: Hollywood Shuffle." *Essence*, May 1987, p. 28.
Bernard, Jami. "Hollywood Shuffle." *New York Post*, March 20, 1987, p. 24.
Donoloe, Darlene. "Screen: In Hollywood Shuffle Comic Actor Robert Townsend Wields Hit Wit Against Movie Industry Racism." *People Weekly*, May 18, 1987, pp. 61–62.

Harrington, Richard. "Hollywood Shuffle." *Washington Post*, March 21, 1987, sec. II, p. 1

Pines, Jim. "A Choice of Rambo or Sambo?" *New Statesman*, April 8, 1988, pp. 29–30.

Singleton, Janet. "Interview: Robert Townsend on the Real Hollywood Shuffle." *Black Film Review* 3 (Spring 1987): 6–7.

Varney, Ronald. "A Shuffle from Hollywood Turns Up an Ace." *Connoisseur*, February 1988, p. 122.

A Dry White Season (1989)

Cramer, Barbara. "A Dry White Season." *The Motion Picture Guide 1990 Annual*, pp. 64–65. Evanston, Ill: CineBooks, 1990.

Denby, David. "Movies: Pacific Grim." *New York*, October 2, 1989, pp. 66–75.

Edelstein, David. "A Dry White Season." *New York Post*, September 20, 1989, p. 23.

Kassabian, Anahid. "A Dry White Season." *Magill's Cinema Annual 1990*, edited by Frank N. Magill, pp. 107–10. Englewood Cliffs, N.J.: Salem Press, 1990.

Maslin, Janet. "Sutherland Catches on to Apartheid Slowly." *New York Times*, September 20, 1989, sec. C, p. 19.

Rich. "A Dry White Season." *Variety's Film Reviews 1989–1990*, v. 21 (September 13,1989). New Providence, N.J.: R. R. Bowker, 1991.

Thomas, Kevin. "Movie Review: Dry Season a Potent Look at South Africa." *Los Angeles Times*, September 22, 1989, part 6, p. 1.

Lean on Me (1989)

Benson, Sheila. "Lean on Me Leans Heavily on Freeman." *Los Angeles Times*, March 3, 1989. cal, p. 4.

Epstein, Charles. "Lean on Me." *The Motion Picture Guide, 1990 Annual (The Films of 1989)*, pp. 133. Evanston, Ill.: Cinebooks, 1990.

Hyman, Irwin A. "The Make-Believe World of 'Lean on Me.' " *Education Digest*, November 1989, pp. 20–22.

Maslin, Janet. "Reading, Writing the Riot Act." *New York Times*, March 3, 1989, sec. III, p. 16.

O'Brien, Tom. "School of Hard Knocks: Avildsen's 'Lean on Me.' " *Commonweal*, April 21, 1989, p. 245.

Schickel, Richard. "Cinema: Tough Love, 'Lean on Me.' " *Time*, March 13, 1989, p. 82.

Glory (1989)

Ansen, David. "Movies: Glory." *Newsweek*, December 18, 1989, p. 73.

Canby, Vincent . "At Close Range: The Human Face of War." *New York Times*, January 21, 1990, sec. II, p. 139.

Canby, Vincent. "Review Film: Black Combat Bravery in the Civil War." *New York Times*, December 14, 1989, sec. III, p. 15.

Frechette, David. "Glory: A Tentative Step." *Black Film Review* 5 (Fall 1989): 24.

Giddins, Gary. "Why We Fight." *Village Voice*, December 19, 1989, p. 98.

McPherson, James M. "The Glory Story." *New Republic*, January 8, 1990, pp. 22–27.

Thomas, Kevin. "Movie Review: 'Glory,' An Epic of Wanting Proportions." *Los Angeles Times*, December 14, 1989, cal, p. 1.

Daughters of the Dust (1991)

Johnson, Malcolm. "Impressionistic Celebration of African Past." *Hartford Courant*, May 6, 1992, p. C6.

Jones, Jacquie. "Daughters of the Dust." *Cinéaste* 19, 2–3 (1992): 68–69.

Macinnis, Craig. "Visual Poetry Captures South Carolina's Sea Island Culture." *Toronto Star*, May 29, 1992, Metro, p. C8.

Miller-Monzon, John, ed. "Daughters of the Dust." *The Motion Picture Guide, 1993 Annual,* pp. 86–87. New York: Baseline II, 1993.

Murray, Steve. "Dash's Dust nominated for NAACP Image Award." *Atlanta Journal and Constitution,* January 1, 1993, p. 7G.

Terry, Clifford. "Gold Dust." *Chicago Tribune,* January 3, 1992, Friday, p. C.

Turan, Kenneth. "Daughters Recaptures Power of Gullah Past." *Los Angeles Times,* March 6, 1992, cal, p. 12.

Boyz 'N the Hood (1991)

Carr, Jay. "From LA Streets Straight to the Heart." *Boston Globe,* July 12, 1991, Living, p. 41.

Johnson, Malcolm. "Hood Deftly Explores Black Youth's World." *Hartford Courant,* July 12, 1991, Lifestyles, p. B3.

Kehr, Dave. "Boyz Town the Hood Is No Place for a Woman." *Chicago Tribune,* July 12, 1991, Take 2, p. C.

Ringel, Eleanor. "Movies: This Weekend." *Atlanta Journal and Constitution,* July 19, 1991, p. 7B.

Siskel, Gene. "Boyz 'N the Hood Visits L. A.'s Mean Streets." *Chicago Tribune,* Take 2, p. C.

Sterritt, David. "Boyz 'N the Hood." *Christian Science Monitor,* July 22, 1991, p. 11.

Turan, Kenneth. "Boyz 'N the Hood." *Los Angeles Times,* July 12, 1991, cal, p. 1.

To Sleep With Anger (1991)

Ansen. David. "A Visit From a Trickster." *Newsweek,* October 22, 1990, pp. 75–77.

Benson, Sheila. "Magical, Mystical Tour of South Central Los Angeles." *Los Angeles Times,* November 2, 1990, p. 8.

Brown, Georgia. "The Trouble with Harry." *Village Voice,* October 16, 1990, p. 59.

Canby, Vincent. "Black Middle Class Home. Enter Comic, Lost Demon." *New York Times,* October 5, 1990, sec. III, p. 10.

Garner, Jack. "There Should Be More Films Like This." *Gannett News Service,* December 24, 1990.

Hinckley, Tom. "To Sleep With Anger." *The Motion Picture Guide, 1991 Annual (The Films of 1990),* edited by Frank N. Magill, p.173. New York: Baseline II, 1991.

Klawans, Stuart. "Films." *Nation,* November 5, 1990, p. 537.

Young, Al. "Charles Burnette Spellbinds Viewers With His Personal Vision," *American Visions* 5 (December 1990): 36–39.

Bebe's Kids (1992)

James, Caryn. "Neglected Monsters in Fun World." *New York Times,* August 1, 1992, sec. I, p. 16.

McBride, Joseph. "Review: Bebe's Kids." *Variety,* August 3, 1992, p. 39.

Novak, Ralph. "Bebe's Kids." *People Weekly,* August 17, 1992, p.13 .

Thomas, Kevin. "A Spirited Outing With Bebe's Kids." *Los Angeles Times,* April 1, 1992, part F, p. 1.

Whitehead, Colson. "Bebe's Kids." *Village Voice,* August 25, 1992, p. 62.

Wloszczyna, Susan. "Bebe's Kids, Toon Attitude." *USA Today,* August 3, 1999, p. 6D.

Malcolm X (1992)

Brown, Georgia. "True Stories." *Village Voice,* January 26, 1993, p. 56.

Burnett, Zaron. "The World on Malcolm X." *Atlanta Journal and Constitution,* November 18, 1992, p. 4E.

Clark, Mike. " 'X' Sets a Standard for Movie Bios." *USA Today*, November 18, 1992, p. 1D.

Murray, Steve. "Lee's Impressive Visuals Bridge the Past, Present." *Atlanta Journal and Constitution*, November 20, 1992, p. 8D.

Romney, Jonathan. "A Saint Goes Marching on." *New Statesman and Society*, March 5, 1993, pp. 34–35.

Steele, Shelby. "Malcolm Little, And Big." *New Republic*, December 22, 1992, pp. 27–31.

Turan, Kenneth. "Malcolm X: Hero for Troubled Times." *Los Angeles Times*, November 18, 1992, part F, p. 1.

Waiting to Exhale (1995)

Cheshire, Godfrey. "Waiting to Exhale." *Variety*, December 18, 1995, p. 66.

Hainer, Cathy. "Film Gives Exhale a Second Wind." *USA Today*, January 4, 1996, p. 5D.

Hoffman, Adina. "Black, Proud, Still Single." *Jerusalem Post*, February 12, 1996, Arts, p. 5.

Holden, Stephen. "Four Divas Have Lots of Fun Telling off Mr. Wrong." *New York Times*, December 22, 1995, sec. III, p. 3.

Johnson, Malcolm. "Weak Screenplay; Green Director Leaves Audience Waiting to Exhale." *Hartford Courant*, December 22, 1995, Town, p. E1.

Lane, Anthony. "The Current Cinema: What Friends Are for." *New Yorker*, January 15, 1996, p. 80.

Wloszczyna, Susan. "Whitaker's Debut Runs Out of Steam." *USA Today*, December 22, 1995, p. 1D.

The Nutty Professor (1996)

Byrge, Duane. "Box Office Gets an Unexpected Boost." *Hollywood Reporter*, August 6, 1996.

"Eddie Murphy Is 400-pound Teacher in Comedy Film." *Jet*, June 17, 1996, v90, p. 54.

Gleiberman, Owen. "The Nutty Professor." *Entertainment Weekly*, June 28, 1996, n333–334, p. 82.

Hamilton, Doug. "Movies." *Atlanta Journal and Constitution*, June 28, 1996, p. 14H.

Maslin, Janet. "Film Review." *New York Times*, June 28, 1996, Sec. III, p. 5.

Millar, Jeff. "Good Grades for Murphy's Professor." *Houston Chronicle*, June 28, 1996, p. 1.

Schickel, Richard. "The Nutty Professor." *Time*, July 8, 1996, p. 66.

Get on the Bus (1996)

Felperin, Leslie. "Get on the Bus." *Sight and Sound* 7 (July 1997): 40–41.

Gilroy, Paul. "Million Man Mouthpiece." *Sight and Sound* 8 (August 1997): 6–18

Hoffman, Adina. "Spike Lee's American Dream." *Jerusalem Post*, July 27, 1998, Arts, p. 7.

Johnson, Malcom. "Spike Lee's 'Get on the Bus' A Long Ride, But Worthwhile Trip." *Hartford Courant*, October 17, 1996, p. 20.

Klawans, Stuart. "The Big Stall." *Nation*, November 18, 1996, pp. 35–36.

Maslin, Janet. "An Anniversary Tribute to the Million Man March." *New York Times*, October 16, 1996, sec. III, p. 11.

Millar, Jeff. "Film Marks Million Man March." *Houston Chronicle*, October 16, 1996, p.1.

Amistad (1997)

Arnold, Gary. "Movies." *Washington Times*, December 11, 1997, Weekend, p. M28.

Carr, Jay. "Dignity Unbound." *Boston Globe*, December 12, 1997, Arts, p. C1.

Hoffman, Adina. "An Uplifting Uprising." *Jerusalem Post*, March 9, 1998, Arts, p. 9.
Johnson, Malcolm. "Amistad, An Eloquent Epic." *Hartford Courant*, December 12, 1997, p. F1.
McCormick, Patricia S. "Taking the Children." *New York Times*, December 14, 1997, sec. II, p. 32.
Pardi, Robert. "Amistad." *The Motion Picture Guide, 1998 Annual (The Films of 1997)*, edited by Edmond Grant, pp. 13–14. New York: Cinebooks, 1998.
Wloszczyna, Susan. "Moral Compass Keeps Amistad on Sure Course." *USA Today*, December 10, 1997, p. 1D.

Eve's Bayou (1997)
Carr, Jay. "Enchanted by the Spell of Eve's Bayou." *Boston Globe*, November 7, 1997, p. D5.
Clark, Mike. "Lush Landscape of 'Eve's Bayou' Thoughtful Tale Told With Originality." *USA Today*, November 7, 1997, p. 8D.
Gerstel, J. "Gentle Family Tale Transcends Gothic Form." *Toronto Star*, January 30, 1998, p. B3.
Parks, Louis B. "Jackson Takes Detour to Bayou." *Houston Chronicle*, November 8, 1997, p. 1.
Petrakis, John. " 'Eve's Bayou' a Rich, Strange Tale of a Family's Struggles." *Chicago Tribune*, November 7, 1997, sec. 7A, p. H.
Riley, Phil. "Eve's Bayou." *The Motion Picture Guide, 1998 Annual*, edited by Edmond Grant, pp. 130–31. New York: Cinebooks, 1998.
Siskel, Gene. "Jackson a Standout in Eve's Bayou." *Chicago Tribune*, December 5, 1997, Zone CN, p. A7.

The Best Man (1999)
Harrison, Eric. "Friends of Best Man Steal the Show." *Los Angeles Times*, October 22, 1999. Home Edition, p. 12.
Kirkland, Bruce. "Lee's Best Man Could Be Better." *Toronto Sun*, October 23, 1999, p. 4.
Maslin, Janet. "The Best Man: Party, but be True to Your Sweetheart," *New York Times*, October 22, 1999. sec. E, p. 26.
Morris, Wesley. "Best Man Handsome, Innocuous," *San Francisco Examiner*, October 22, 1999, sec. C, p. 3.
Stuart, Jan. "Best Man Marries Story and Style," *Newsday*, October 22, 1999, p. B09.
Taubin, Amy. "Come on In, the Mainstream's Fine," *Village Voice*, October 26, 1999, p. 162.
Waxman, Sharon. "The Best Man Wins." *Washington Post*, October 27, 1999, sec. C, p. 1.

General Sources:
"About One Third of Black Children Live in Poverty: Study." *Jet*, December 30–January 6, 1997, p. 32.
"African Affairs: South African President Nelson Mandela Signs the Country's New Constitution." *Jet*, December 30–January 6, 1997, p. 15.
Anderson, Lindsay. *About John Ford*. London: Plexus, 1981.
Black Americans: A Statistical Source Book. Palo Alto, Calif. Editions information Publications, 1990, 1995.
"Black Cinema." *The Black Filmmakers Foundation Brochure*, 1982. p. 2.
"Black Women Gather to Promote Unity at Million Woman March." *Jet*, November 10, 1997, pp. 4–5.
Bogle, Donald. *Toms, Coons, Mulattoes, Mammies, and Bucks: An Interpretive History of Blacks in American Films*. New York: Continuum, 1991.

Christian, Charles M. *Black Saga: The African American Experience.* New York: Houghton Mifflin, 1995.

Cripps, Thomas. "The Birth of a Race Company: An Early Stride Toward a Black Cinema." *Journal of Negro History* 59, 1 (January 1974): 28–57.

Dickinson, Thomas H. "Movies Changing Life of Nation." *New York Times Encyclopedia of Film,* edited by Gene Brown. New York: New York Times Book Co., 1984.

Ford, Dan. *Pappy: The Life of John Ford.* Englewood Cliffs, N.J.: Prentice-Hall, 1979.

Gallagher, Tag. *John Ford: The Man and His Films.* Los Angeles: University of California Press, 1986.

Herring, Robert. "Black Shadows." *Close Up,* 5, 2 (1929): 100.

Kimmel, Daniel M. "Naked Acts." *Variety,* May 20, 1996, p. 41.

Moorer, Talise D. "Naked Acts: A Brilliant Movie About a Touchy Subject." *Amsterdam News,* September 24, 1998, p. 1.

"National Report: Kerner Commission's 'Separate and Unequal' Societies Exist Today: Report." *Jet,* March 23, 1998, p. 4.

"National Report: Number of Hate Groups in U. S. Up, Report Says." *Jet,* April 13, 1998, p. 6.

"Race Is Motive Behind Most Hate Crimes." *Jet,* November 25, 1996, p. 46.

Index